80 Lessons Learned
On the Road from $80,000 to $80,000,000

The information in this book is provided for information purposes and are intended to be general guidelines only. It is not legal, financial, tax, insurance or accounting advice. Such advice may only be given by licensed professional. It is just the author's (informed?) opinion.

ISBN: 978-0-9921083-0-4

Publisher: Prestigious Properties® Canada Ltd.
Copyright Canada, USA & the World 2013

First Edition: October 2013

Author: Thomas Beyer

Also available in electronic format as three ebooks as follows:
ISBN: 978-0-9921083-1-1 – 80 Lessons Learned – I - In Life
ISBN: 978-0-9921083-2-8 – 80 Lessons Learned – II - In Business
ISBN: 978-0-9921083-3-5 – 80 Lessons Learned – III- In Real Estate

Feedback & Comments: thomasbeyer808080@gmail.com

May you learn a thing or 8 ! Please feel encouraged to drop me a line on what was most insightful .. and please drop me another line if you did not learn at least 8 things (or if you actually found an error or typo) !

CONTENTS

Part 2: Business Lessons

Part 3: Real Estate Lessons

Epilogue

Afterthoughts by Greg Habstritt

80 Lessons Learned:
From $80,000 to $80,000,000

FOREWARD BY DON R. CAMPBELL

There is a hard and fast rule in life, business and personal relationships, a rule that governs my choices. This simple yet very effective rule helps me stay focused on what works and allows me to propel myself forward in all aspects of life, while at the same time keeping me away from unwanted and frankly dangerous distractions. Most importantly, it helps me choose who to listen to and whose advice to take. I call this rule "The Final 30 Feet Rule."

The Final 30 Feet Rule states: Never take advice from someone who has not already successfully accomplished what you want to be successful at. For a comedian, it means do not listen to anyone who hasn't walked that final 30 feet from behind the curtain to standing alone in front of an audience. For investors or business owners, it means the only people worth listening to are those who have created business or investing success that far surpasses yours.

WHO IS YOUR TRAIL GUIDE?

By following this rule, you quickly eliminate most of the authors, advice givers or coaches because so many of them are theorists, with limited success in business. If I am on a dangerous and unfamiliar trail, I don't want a guide who just has an idea about the trail, I want a guide who knows the trail like the back of their hand. They've been on the trail many times and they know the twists, turns and dangerous spots.

Why is this important for you to understand as you consider

this book?

Simply, the author of this book, Thomas Beyer, is on my very small list of people who fit this description.

I continually learn from him.

To name just a few of the lessons included in this book:

- Don't Confuse Getting Things Done with Doing Them Yourself
- The Phases of "Cleaning Up Your Life Messes"
- The Anatomy of Uncomfortable Change
- Asking Questions Separates You from the Crowd
- How to Choose a Partner
- Green Money vs. Red & Blue Money

When I look for insights into my business or investments I make sure that I speak with Thomas as part of my diligence. He is successful in business, in personal relationships and in real estate investing and in this book he shares 80 tips that will help propel you forward—as many of them have done along my journey.

Pick up the book, listen to someone who has already cleared the path forward with his own hard work and your journey will become much clearer.

Don R. Campbell
Investor, Bestselling Author & Philanthropist
www.DonRCampbell.com

80 Lessons Learned:
From $80,000 to $80,000,000

AUTHOR'S NOTE & ACKNOWLEDGEMENTS

Real estate has been around hundreds of years. I didn't invent apartment buildings nor their proper management nor their passive income or their leverage potential with income nor their tax deferral options nor their (usual) increase in value through time and improvements. Neither, for that matter, am I exceptionally good at investing in them. Knowing what you want is important as is careful p(l)anning, but execution is key, as is a sense of urgency, listening, reading and kaizen. Knowledge helps a lot, as does a sense of life's opportunities and the ability to take advantage of them, but also useful is awareness of life's risks and how to mitigate or manage them. Being in the market at the right time helps too. And thanking God and others is important, as is having fun while doing what some people call "work." And there are no guarantees or advice in this book, just (informed?) opinions!

Knowledge is no one's sole domain. I acknowledge shamelessly copying other people's good ideas that I picked up during conversations, telephone calls, meetings, presentations, education, courses, tapes and CDs over the years. Those people also learned and possibly also copied some of those ideas from other people's books, tapes, CDs, courses, seminars or lectures. I have used material from the people listed below, and probably dozens more. Please forgive me if I have copied your original thought and not given you credit.

Many people have influenced my life, my values, my thought processes and my business and real estate investment career.

I wish to give credits to their sometimes very small or sometimes hugely influential contributions, many of which are sprinkled throughout this book:

Don & Connie Campbell, Greg Habstritt, Ozzie Jurrock, Raymond Aaron, Wright Thurston, Robert Allan, Patrick Francey, Robert Kiyosaki, Douglas Gray, Tom Peters, Stephen Covey, Ron LeGrande, Tim Johnston, Douglas Thiessen, Dale Carnegie, Charles Givens, Harry Dent, John Murphy, Lou Gerstner, Jesus, Warren Buffett, Steve Jobs, Bill Gates, Terry Regenwetter, Janet Perna, Dave Rencz, Barry McGuire, Richard Bell, Tom Docking, Gary Allard, George Fabi, John Stobbe, George Hilton, Matthew & Stephen Johnston, Zig Ziglar, Sasha & Greg & Mike Uhryn, Jim Vincent, Dominic Mandato, Paul & Monica Prochnau, Randy Jamieson, Brian & Donna Barnett, Rick Jenkins, Christian Lendi, Ross & Teresa Gilker, Neil & Sandy Kaarsemaker, Peer Rumland, Richard Dolan, Achim & Hilde Goldbach, Thomas Heiden, Howard Weale, Val Toffoli, Debbie Bradford, Rory Sutter, David Steele, Peter Hebb, Jan Fialkowski, Chris Biasuti, Nancy Ternowski, Brian Tracey, Dennis Aitken, Don Rumpel, David Jennings, Pat Gilker, Marianne Engel, Michelle Naffin, John Kish, Doug Bittle, Rick & Sheila Bayer, Bernie Garnhum, Len & Janica Williamson, Peter Tsukahira, Jeff Coors, Paul Szkiler, John Beckett, David Davis, Scotty & Annie Grubb, Christine Kopr, Denise Odam, Keith & Linda Weaver, Charlie Bredo, Rick & Lyn Linklater, Bob Short, Adam Killam, Chad & Evie Willox, Mike & Sandy Hammerlindl, Keith McMullen, Prod & Elenor Laquian, Richard Alexander, Charles Menzies, Erica Frank, Jens & HsingChi von Bergman, my sister Barbara and her husband Steven Ongena, my brother Holger and his wife Martina Steinhauer, Abe & Elfrieda Friesen, my father Detlef, my mother Ursula, my amazing wife Lynda, and our two children, Sonja Marie & David Benjamin.

Thank you, thank you all, for encouraging me to write down my thoughts, actions and insights, for inspiring me, for teaching me and for correcting me (often repeatedly until I get the message) so that others may benefit and leave God's Kingdom in slightly better shape.

Thank you also to Zander Robertson and Nicole Langlois for helping me to write, re-write, illustrate, edit and re-edit this book and sticking with it to its 21st (or was it the 25th ?) iteration!

The book cover was created by Nick Toth, owner & founder of www.tothcreative.ca a boutique advertising, communications and webdesign firm in Toronto. Nick did most of our magazine or newspaper based ads before we switched to a primarily GoogleAds based web campaign strategy around 2010. He is the best genius I know in taking an idea and making an ad with high visual impact. Thank you, Nick.

The buildings on the book cover are buildings we either have owned or still own today.

80 Lessons Learned:
From $80,000 to $80,000,000

DEDICATION

I dedicate this book to three people, although of course many more are worthy a detailed mention.

First of all I want to dedicate this book to my mother Ursula who taught me love, kindness, gentleness, softness, tenaciousness, table manners and this little gem here: "The first million is the hardest". I did not comprehend this when I was in my teens, and she was never a woman of means, even to this old age, but she had a fairly wealthy friend in her Turnverein (gymnastics club) and that saying rubbed off on her, and onto me. Not until my 40's did I recall it, when I actually did make my first million, and a second shortly thereafter; only then did I realize how right she was. It took me about 30 years from hearing it to implementing it, proving that real estate is not a get rich quick scheme (but a "get rich for sure scheme").

Secondly I want to dedicate this book to Chris Mica, my favourite onsite manager ever. She managed three buildings for me, including two very valuable ones in StonyPlain and Edmonton with almost 200 tenants. She exhibited the two attributes any owner looks for in an onsite manager, something I call "tough love" and talk about later in the book: true customer service, kind words, dedication to her job, punctuality, friendliness, a true interest in fellow human beings and a great heart but also a toughness when it comes to evictions, late rent payments, drugs or all those nasty social habits that humans exhibit from time to time when a 100 or so of them live in a building. She passed away far too young in her late 50's in the spring of 2013 after being diagnosed with cancer in 2011. She will be missed.

Thirdly I want to dedicate this book to my (then) best friend Peer Rümland with whom I spent many a night philosophizing

& dreaming in Munich during my four years of study there, and with whom I travelled to Canada in the summer of 1986 before I was starting my MBA in Edmonton. He was meant to graduate from Computer Science, as I did just before we departed to travel, a mere six month later, and also embark on a successful computer career in the then booming computer years when Steve Jobs and Bill Gates revolutionized the computer world and PCs in the pre-internet age were exploding onto the world scene. Unfortunately he too was diagnosed with cancer (leukemia) and passed away in 1993 after we had moved back from Munich to Toronto. This early and lengthy in-your-face death process of a dear dear friend caused me to seek out more risk, to live life at a fuller realization, to develop a deeper faith in God but also humans, to trust more, to delegate more, to love more, to give more and to enjoy life more.

Chapter one of this book is especially dedicated to both Chris and Peer as they both embodied that chapter's meaning so well.

80 Lessons Learned:
From $80,000 to $80,000,000

PART 1 :
LIFE LESSONS

LESSON 1:
MAN PLANS GOD LAUGHS

"What you thought you came for is only a shell, a husk of meaning from which the purpose breaks only when it is fulfilled .. for us there is only the trying. The rest is not our business." T.S. Elliott

I've lived an incredible life. I've worked hard and had much fun along the way. I've had many successes and my fair share of setbacks. I believe in setting a strong intention, and in making prudent decisions based on a firm understanding. I believe that knowing and understanding the background or context of issues gets one closer to making the right decision. In other words, I believe in taking prudent action based on a prudent and valid thought process.

However, life has forced this lesson upon me perhaps more than any other: Man plans, and God laughs. Our perfect plans, which we often take so seriously (as though our plans were written in stone), become a bad joke when imperfect events happen in our lives.

Ask me how I know this! It's happened often enough in my life that I finally had no other choice but to accept it as true. Many choices in life will have a huge impact on your life, such as what school to attend, what girlfriend (or boyfriend) to select or drop, or whether to move to a new location. Other choices in life also have an impact, usually not as large, such as what exit to take on a highway, what car to buy, what computer to buy or what cell phone plan to select. We plan, given the context and knowledge at the time, and expect a certain outcome, sometimes realizing later that the intended consequence did not happen.

Let me give you one example of many that I could have chosen and that could fill another book.

My primary business is a company called Prestigious Properties®. We buy, upgrade, rent and hold multi-family properties in North America, primarily in Alberta. One place we've owned a multi-family building for many years is a town called Stony Plain. It's a small commuter city to the west of Edmonton, Alberta, Canada.

At one of our buildings in Stony Plain we had a married couple as onsite managers. Let's call them John and Vanessa (not their real names). John and Vanessa made a fantastic team. They had a great working system that we liked. Vanessa was excellent at keeping the building rented with top-notch tenants, she kept well-organized paperwork, and we never had a problem with her reporting. John was very handy. He could fix almost anything. He made his repairs quickly, at a favorably low cost, and he was highly productive, often working long hours without complaint.

You see, in the multi-family investing arena, a good onsite manager (or managers) is probably the most important asset to running a successful business. Each building is its own business, and without the continuous guiding hand of the onsite manager, the property simply doesn't perform as an asset, so we were ecstatic with John and Vanessa.

Recognizing that John had the ability and the desire to be productive, we quickly employed him to do repairs and renovations on our other properties in the Edmonton area. It was a win/win arrangement for all parties— John made extra income and we had a quality renovator at a reasonable price, which is why I could see no problem entering into further business arrangements with John.

John came to me one day and told me that he sometimes came across single-family properties that needed repairs. He'd always thought he could add a great deal of value to those properties, but had never been in a position to purchase them. He suggested that we partner on some of these types of properties.

The arrangement proposed was that John (and Vanessa) would do all the repairs and take care of all management of the properties during the rental period. I would put up my money and my credit for the purchase. It was very similar to what I do every day in my business. I am a strong enabler, so I often partner with people who have skills that I don't possess. I work to get those partners whatever they need to do their job well. More often than not, these partnerships work well.

Even within Prestigious Properties®, my top lieutenants and I have a very similar relationship. Scotty is wonderful at sales. He raises capital for our investments. Mike, our acquisitions manager, is excellent at analyzing every aspect of a deal, from the physical details such as boilers, roofs and the interior condition to the mortgage and the region's growth potential. Mike filters out the bad properties, and green lights the good ones.

I'm decent at both of those things, but what I'm really good at is enabling those two (and the rest of the team) to excel at their job.

I had planned to do the same thing with John—enable him to do his job and for the most part get out of his way. For the first three years of the partnership, everything went as planned. As you'll see below, things didn't end so well, but in the end John's mother replaced him. She is truly awesome as a property manager and has an additional building under her management too.

We started to buy—first purchasing a small two-bedroom bungalow in Stony Plain. John fixed it up, and he and Vanessa lived there. Our agreement stated that all repairs would be John's responsibility and that John and Vanessa would pay the mortgage payments. In turn, I put up the down payment money and I qualified for a mortgage, which we put in both of our names.

Eventually, John and Vanessa wanted to move out of that house and onto an acreage outside of Stony Plain. Vanessa, who had a strong understanding of the Stony Plain rental market, told me that the first house could be rented for about $1,500 per month, which was enough to cover all our expenses. The plan was that John and Vanessa would move to the acreage, and the original house would be rented. Vanessa would manage the property and John would continue to do repairs if any would be necessary.

Eventually we purchased an acreage for them as the price dropped from well over $600,000 to $430,000. Again, I provided the down payment money. John and Vanessa did repairs and paid the mortgage payments as planned.

Everything was going well until the summer of 2011 (three years after the first deal) when I received a call from the bank. They said "Hello, Mr. Beyer, why are you three months behind on your mortgage payments?" I was stunned!

Until that point, I had had no indication that anything was awry. After the initial purchase period, I had checked in with John once or twice a year. When I'd visit Stony Plain, John and I always went around and looked at the properties. Usually when a routine is established and certain people act a certain way for three years in a row, one can expect the same behavior to continue. Up until then, I had every reason to trust John and think our relationship was working.

But when I received that first call I couldn't help but think that there might be a problem with the second property too (the acreage). I called the second bank, and sure enough, the second property was three months behind as well!

I had made my decision to enter into partnership with John based on the information I had at the time, and it made perfect sense.

John and Vanessa had a great track record working for Prestigious Properties®. John had skills and abilities that I didn't have. He had access to the deal, and he had the willingness to work hard to achieve the goals. Vanessa was excellent at the management and detailed recordkeeping. The biggest component here is that I had a reasonable background of proof that these were two trustworthy people. Based on my knowledge of taking prudent action (which has worked several times in the past), entering this partnership was reasonable. So what went wrong?

I knew John on a professional level, but he didn't tell me all the details of his life, and I didn't pry. As it turned out, he had already been divorced twice and he had one child with each of his ex-wives. He was paying child support for both of those children, which by itself wasn't such a bad thing. Child support is costly but John managed to maintain his child support commitments for a portion of our working relationship in addition to maintaining all the financial commitments related to our jointly owned properties. At a certain point before I received the phone call from the bank, John stopped paying his child support.

As I learned later, what pushed John over the edge (from being financially responsible to irresponsible) was the fact that his third marriage (to Vanessa) was on the rocks. When things went downhill between the two of them, John started drinking, acting erratically, and I suspect he was taking drugs too.

He had hit rock bottom and was experiencing depression. Of course my heart went out to him, but as a businessman I had a mess to clean up. When John's personal life went downhill, our business partnership did as well.

He had left me with two properties behind on mortgage payments, and one (the acreage) that had mold issues. In addition, there were liens on both properties (from Child and Family Services) for overdue child support payments!

As I write this, it's more than one year later, and I have fully renovated the acreage. The final price tag was close to $120,000 for the renovation. The liens have been removed since I was forced, in lieu of a court action, to buy John out of the property, so there is no need for the lien to be attached to the property. The acreage has been sold as a rent-to-own deal for $535,000 to free up most of the invested cash, and for a valuable lesson learned. I have decided to keep the smaller property as a rental with a very capable property manager specializing in single family houses and perhaps to a rent-to-own exit here also in the future.

There's no doubt that I've had my share of successful partnerships. With John and Vanessa, I applied my normal rules for partnering, and I even had a successful track record with them. But in spite of the track record, and in spite of my (and their) best-laid plans, the partnership ended as a costly mess!

I could analyze where I went wrong over and over again (in fact, I have done that already). I have learned from the experience and will be more diligent in choosing partners in the future, but do I regret the partnership? Actually, I don't! One must make decisions in life and business. You can never know exactly how it will end up, but to move forward, you still have to act. This will be the topic of a later lesson called "Ready, Fire, Aim."

I urge you to go ahead and make your plans. Do your due diligence and project the final result. Plan for success and growth, write down your plans, share them with your key life partners such as your spouse or kids, and give it your best shot, but always remember that man plans and God laughs. If your best-laid plans go awry, don't let that stop you from taking a chance again, and again, and again.

LESSON 2:
CLEAN UP YOUR MESSES (PART 1)

When I say "Clean up your messes," you may think I'm speaking only about the big messes. While I do believe you should clean up your big messes, I actually believe that messes are an inevitable part of life, and cleaning them up is a minute-by-minute, hour-by-hour, and day-by-day process.

When you wake up in the morning, how do you look? If you're like most people, you're a mess!

Nobody is saying you're broken, that you're no good, or that you're never going to be a success because you're messy in the morning. However, it's commonly expected that you would clean yourself up in the morning.

Personally, my desk is the point of convergence for much paper, many envelopes, newsletters, slips, phone messages e-mails, faxes, sticky notes and reminders. A lot of stuff comes across my desk in an enterprise with more than a dozen employees, 20+ corporations and 600+ investors. I like to read newspapers, I like books, and I have various electronic devices that may sit on my desk on any given day. My desk can become a mess, but that's only if I don't clean up my mess. But nobody would say that I'm a bad person, that I'm hopeless, or that I'll never amount to anything because my desk, like many others', can get messy if I don't clean it.

But I do clean my desk regularly (although my wife would argue it could be a lot better, and she is usually right). The reason for that is simple: I like a relatively clean desk. I like a clean and tidy work environment, house, condo, car… (insert your favorite place here). I like to clean up my messes.

We must regularly use some of our energy to clean up our messes. I'm not saying we should spend a significant part of our time cleaning up messes, or that we should be obsessive about it. At various times, though, cleaning up messes might be the only activity you're able or willing to do. At times like these, you might have to drop every other endeavor and only focus on cleaning up your messes.

Imagine that your doctor says to you, "Hey, you're going to die within one year unless you stop smoking, stop drinking, stop eating cinnamon buns for breakfast, lunch and dinner, and replace your bad diet with a healthy balanced diet, and start exercising five days per week."

This is one of those situations where you will likely have to stop everything else in your life and clean up the mess that you've made of your health.

Generally, our messes aren't fatal, which means you won't likely have to focus all of your energy on cleaning them up. Every morning you shower (although as a former European I have the habit of doing it less regularly than that), shave, comb your hair, put on deodorant, brush your teeth, etc. This doesn't mean you drop everything else in your life.

Most messes are like that. You must do a little bit of cleanup every day in order to keep your messes from overtaking your life.

What stops people from cleaning up their messes is the belief that they don't have time for it. They think, "I'm too busy doing important stuff, so I don't want to waste time and energy on that old problem."

But the reality is that by avoiding messes, you're actually letting them take up more energy and time. Money is an infinite commodity, whereas your time and energy are not. Use them wisely.

Every day has only 24 hours. Don't waste your precious energy and time on worrying and wondering about the result of messes around you. You must clean them up, starting with the big ones. Failing to address messes regularly is one of the surest roads to catastrophe. A relatively small mess can lead to a huge headache, and the longer you let it sit, the worse it gets.

For example, think back to the mess I spoke about in the previous lesson. Relatively speaking, those two houses in Stony Plain represent a small percentage of my holdings. Most of my real estate is wrapped up in Prestigious Properties®. As a company, we own close to 1,000 rental units. Total rental units owned from the Stony Plain properties is two, which means they are less than 0.2 percent of total holdings. The ratio is only slightly higher in terms of value, maybe 0.5 percent.

Does this mean that the mess was unproblematic? Relatively speaking, it was a small mess, but it took up more than 50 percent of the mental energy and maybe 25 percent of the time that I set aside for real estate that year.

With those two houses, I was able to quite easily track my effort. How often do we continue on while messes drag our mental energy down without us even knowing it?

Recognize that cleaning up messes is not a waste of time, nor is it a backward step, nor is it anything bad at all. There's growth in going back, taking whatever steps you must take, and getting those messes cleaned up

LESSON 3: CLEAN UP YOUR MESSES (PART 2) – RELATIONSHIPS

R Relationship messes are big messes. They're never easy to untangle. And you really never know what will happen when you get deep into a relationship.
I believe (and my actions have proven correct) that partnerships can move life and business forward. It's been proven true in

my business, marriage, Prestigious Properties® (my main vehicle for wealth), and my days as a software consultant. These are all instances of partnerships that have served both partners well.

However, I've also formed partnerships that didn't work out quite as well. The biggest example is the relationship I had with my former partner at Prestigious Properties®. Let's call him Dave.

Dave is a bold man, and I took him into the company in the belief that his boldness would help push PP to a new level. Dave did possess some great qualities. As mentioned, he was bold, and indeed we did grow from $20 million in assets to almost $70 million in assets during his tenure at PP.

However, Dave was the kind of guy who left a mess in his wake wherever he went. It wasn't long before I became the guy who went around behind Dave, cleaning up his messes, and the stress of cleaning up his messes deeply affected me. At one point, I even considered splitting up Prestigious Properties' assets and selling everything. I love my business, but at that point, the stress of it was greater than the benefits.

I remember sitting with Dave at the beginning of our partnership and saying, "Well, perhaps we can buy one building per quarter." He freaked out! He didn't think I was just a little bit too conservative, he thought I was nuts. "We need to buy a lot more properties than that," he said.

Dave convinced me that my slow and steady growth wasn't good enough, in spite of the fact that it had always served our investors, our company and me very well in the past. I liked being an expert in a very focused geographical space. I knew the Edmonton market very well, and had most of my real estate holdings there. Growing at the pace Dave envisioned meant rapidly expanding beyond Edmonton. Eventually—in spite of my conflicted emotions—Dave convinced me and PP was set on a path to much faster growth.

Don't get the impression that I was somehow coerced or fooled into going along with the plan. I liked the idea of fast growth also, but it would have been impossible to undergo the kind of growth envisioned while staying in our Edmonton comfort zone.

We had to be open to new markets.

This alone was not a problem, but we opened up too many markets too quickly, and we weren't knowledgeable enough or connected enough in some of the markets that we entered.

During that period of rapid growth, we bought buildings in Powell River, Fox Creek, Dallas, Camrose, Yorkton, Wetaskiwin, and, most incredibly, Detroit.

The Detroit story is a book chapter in its own right, but for now let's say that it's not a good thing when you can't make a building cash flow even when there's no mortgage on the property.

In theory, we were doing the same as we always had. We were taking buildings that needed a little bit of TLC, buying them for great prices, enhancing the property through sensible improvements and raising the management quality of them along with the value of the buildings. We were holding onto them, and we were letting time and the markets force mortgage pay-down and appreciation.

At the end of the Dave experiment, it was our commitment to the fundamentals that saved us. In spite of some of our initial blunders, it was our fundamental approach that eventually made these buildings profitable, some wildly so in the Tiger Woods years of 2005 to 2007. However, the returns on some of them weren't as impressive as we'd become accustomed to with our earlier investments.

Profitability aside, we created a huge mess when acquiring all those buildings in several cities across North America. Two years after the Dave experiment began, I sat down and examined our company's position. It suddenly dawned on me that we were invested in a hodge-podge of locations. I remember at the time thinking, "Wow, that was stupid."

The truth stared me in the face. Our portfolio wasn't as strong as it once was, even though it was much larger.

Around the same time— independent of my own realizations—I had six separate investors approach me to express their concern about Dave. These respected investors used terms like "crazy," "dangerous," and "nut case" to describe him. The fact that none of them knew each other, and that they each approached me separately, was a big eye-opener for me. I knew Dave was bold, that I didn't share his too-fast growth strategy, and that he liked to push hard, but finally I was starting to see that his presence in the company was a danger to our survival.

I had nobody to blame but myself, and I knew it was time for me to start cleaning up the mess. The problem buildings in problem cities were draining PP financially, but more importantly (for me and my family) I was personally suffering from extreme stress, which was having negative effects upon my health and happiness.

At that point in my life, my relationship with Dave was a lot like a marriage gone wrong, and in our case, there were multiple children (apartment buildings) involved—each of which would require a separate child support payment. For perhaps the first time in my life, I was ready to throw in the towel, sell all the assets and split them with Dave.

Ultimately, I didn't throw in the towel. I decided to stay in the company, but I knew it was time to cut the connecting link between Dave, myself and PP. We started the process. I had to clean up my mess for the future strength of PP and also for my own sanity. Thus, the divorce began. It took a large legal bill and eventually quite a few years to settle all the messes that Dave's involvement had created (and some are still with us, since a building usually takes on its own life after acquisition).

In the end I had to settle with Dave out of court (as he threatened to go there), sell buildings, fix management issues and continue to amalgamate and clean up mess after mess until we got the company back under control.

LESSON 4:
CLEAN UP YOUR MESSES (PART 3) – THE BIGGER THE MESS, THE MORE TIME IT TAKES TO CLEAN

We don't always see it, believe it, or understand it, but the decisions we make affect us for years. You can look at that in a very negative way if you choose, but you can't escape the fact that the decisions we make do affect our lives for many years, decades even.

As I'll discuss later in this book, I firmly believe that there is growth in discomfort. I also believe in small incremental growth, but at a certain point we must make a big change to grow faster. One such fundamental change that I made—which caused discomfort at the time—was when I left my first "real" job in Munich, Germany, with Siemens, a large multinational firm. When I left, I went to Canada to pursue an MBA at the University of Alberta in Edmonton.

I actually avoided a big mess by leaving Munich, as I had a girlfriend there who wanted to marry me. I'm certain it would not have worked out well. Instead I came to Canada and met the woman who is now my wife, Lynda. The results of our union have been stunning.

Who knows how many years it would have taken me to clean up after that mess. I was lucky or had foresight—either way I lived with the positive effects of my decision not to marry this woman from Munich.

However, I don't want to pretend that every decision I've ever made has worked out perfectly. I don't believe avoiding bad decisions is even possible. Even Steve Jobs came up with the terrible computer named "Lisa," which was a flop. Man plans and God laughs.

Compared to some of my other messes, the messy relationship with Dave was massive. Our breakup began five years ago, and I'm still dealing with the fallout. The mess of the Stony Plain houses took more than a year. The mess of waking up after a night's sleep takes only a few minutes to clean up. The bigger the mess, the more time it takes to clean up, and this can make it all the more daunting to tackle such messes. But the power of cleaning up messes is enormous. Although it has taken a long time to clean up the messes caused during my partnership with Dave, the result of the cleanup has made the mess worthwhile—and then some.

I'm proud to say that as of today many of the hodge-podge buildings have been sold, and wherever selling was not possible, our buildings were made to cash flow through impeccable property management. In spite of spending $250,000 to reach a settlement with Dave, we're now in better shape because of the cleaning up of the mess.

It takes time to clean up messes, and the bigger the mess, the more time it will take. When you delve into a complex cleanup, be prepared to invest the time necessary. It will not likely be easy, but you will become a better person for undergoing the process, and the end result of a cleaned up mess is always success.

LESSON 5:
CLEAN UP YOUR MESSES (PART 4) – PHASES OF A MESS

How well you tackle messes and execute the cleanup is important. Anything worth doing is worth doing well. To do something well, it's necessary to understand the process so as to repeat the process and even improve upon it the next time it's employed.

To understand the process, one must understand the pattern. The lifecycle of a mess is no different. To improve upon the remediation of messes, one must first understand the pattern so as to take action on the cleanup. Below is a basic outline of what a mess looks like, along with the process for cleaning it up.

1. MAKE THE DECISION.

I'm speaking here about the decision that gets you into the mess! In my relationship with Dave, it was the day that I decided to enter the partnership. For better or worse, I chose to bring Dave into Prestigious Properties® and partner with him. While I could not have known exactly what would happen (man plans, and God laughs), the fact remains it was this decision that brought about the eventual mess.

2. TIME FOR THE MESS TO MANIFEST.

I'd like to say that I immediately knew that Dave was causing a mess, but the reality is that I didn't. While the big vision to expand rapidly went against my intuition of caution, I also got caught up in it. I thought, "Maybe he's right. Maybe I'm just too conservative." We raised money and bought buildings at a faster and more aggressive pace than before. I was comfortable with this initially, but the mess didn't show up immediately either. It wasn't until the economy slowed down that we had a management nightmare on our hands, and investors approached me with warnings about Dave that the mess was fully manifested.

3. RECOGNIZE THERE'S A PROBLEM.

Recognizing that there is a problem is all about you. If I think back to my relationship with Dave, I am proud that I actually chose to see the reality. I could have made any number of excuses why things weren't working without dealing with the truth that the partnership was causing a mess. I actually had a built-in excuse with the economy falling apart. However, I knew better. I also could have blamed property managers in the various towns and cities for not sufficiently managing my problem properties. Ultimately, though, I knew that the mess was caused by our purchasing of too many properties, in too many diverse regions, with too much leverage. I knew that Dave and I had conflicting visions for what Prestigious Properties® would look like, and I knew that if I was going to go forward with Prestigious Properties®, I had to take control of the good ship PrestProp and drive it back to harbor for repairs.

4. THINK ABOUT THE OPTIONS.

This step can be painful because when you first made the decision that got you into the mess you probably thought you were making a decision that would result in pleasure, not pain. But pain is what you got, so now your job is to think of how you're going to get out of the mess. Usually, there are several options out of a mess, so now is the time to list them all, discuss them with other trusted advisors or (new) partners and arrive at a decision of which option to take.

5. THE BROOM YOU NEED TO CLEAN UP
THE MESS IS NOT FREE.

Messes are often expensive to clean up. In my business breakup with Dave, this was certainly the case, but even the smaller messes that need to be cleaned up will cost you time, and often money.

If you're in the wrong job or business and forced to change directions, it will be costly to you, there's often a loss of income while you take further education or look for a job. Perhaps you go from a salaried position with a large corporation to a position in sales (as I did in 1995). In that case, you will most likely take a financial loss for the initial time.

Divorces are another example of costly messes to clean up as I have seen with many friends or colleagues who split with their spouses. Financial problems, children with two homes, relocation, health issues and stress are all associated with a divorce. I do not wish to belabor the point here as I lack the personal experience. (More on this later in the section called "Your spouse is your most important 50/50 JV partner.")

It may be a difficult pill to swallow, but spending the necessary time and money to clean up the mess is one of the greatest investments you can make because it buys you freedom of mind, a fresh start and far more energy. You will be ready to attack the next phase once you've cleaned up the mess.

I didn't say cleaning up your messes would be easy. I said it's important. Start today, and place a high priority on them. So get those messes cleaned up, and you'll have far more energy to create in your life.

LESSON 6:
BUILD A STABLE BASE (PART 1) – FAITH

Proverbs 3:5 Trust in the Lord with all your heart. Do not lean on your own understanding.

There are two reasons why having a faith is one part of what I call a stable base (the other part being family).

First, having a strong faith gives you courage and strength. When you inevitably have difficult days along your journey, you will need something permanent, and more important, larger, more powerful and more significant than yourself to fall back on.

Having a faith gives you a deep well of truth to draw upon when everything else in your life is questionable. It really doesn't matter who you are, you will have doubts and you will not always be certain of what you're doing, but if you have the stability of faith in your life, you can always count on the most fundamental truths, hence a stable base.

The courage and strength derived from faith will guide your decisions as well. Faith gives you the fortitude to make decisions for the right reasons. Let me give you an example. Before I ever started buying investment real estate I had been pondering the notion and studying how to do it for years. In fact, it was nine years from the time I first thought about investing in real estate (in Burnaby, British Columbia) until I finally bought my first property (in Calgary, Alberta) with big decisions and moves in between: three new jobs, two kids, two countries.

I was living in the south of Calgary when I bought my first property. After much research, I narrowed it down to a choice between two different properties. One was a single-family home in Crossfield (which was over an hour's drive away from our home, to the north of Calgary). The other property was a rental-pool condo in Calgary. Ultimately I chose the condo with the rental-pool structure, which didn't require any management on my part.

I did eventually choose to play an active role on the condo board, but I never had to worry about spending too much time or energy on the property. Everything was taken care of by the management company, and even if there was a vacancy, I did not have to be concerned.

The whole purpose of the rental-pool concept is to remove the risk of income loss from people by pooling all the income from the different units together and splitting the proceeds (after expenses) among the owners. As we will discuss later in the section on real estate lessons, impeccable property management is critical for real estate success. Property management is a time consuming and knowledge intensive task—and I possessed neither time nor knowledge at that stage.

My choice was between 1) a (potentially) time consuming real estate investment that would likely earn a very strong cash flow, and 2) a completely hands-free real estate investment that would return less cash flow.

At the time, I co-owned a business that demanded frequent travel between Calgary and the United States. I also had a young family and a wife that I loved deeply.

Ultimately, I chose the property that would be problem- and

stress-free with slightly lower returns over the property that would earn a bigger income but would likely take much more of my time and cause me more stress.

It was one of the best decisions I ever made as a businessman and a real estate investor. Over the course of my (many) careers, I've been witness to and have experienced different examples of success and failure. One of the most common ways in which people can fail is to choose greed over simplicity.

Yes, of course, I was trying to create wealth through real estate. I wanted to invest my money in real estate because I knew that over the long term it would help me build wealth. Ultimately, this has proven true, but there was no way I wanted to put my family in jeopardy. In that early stage of my real estate investing career, I would have done exactly that if I had chosen the Cross-field property.

Okay, perhaps it wouldn't have been a fatal choice, but I intuitively knew at the time that the extra effort of managing the property could have done a couple of things. It would have taken me away from quality time with my family, which both I and they needed, and it could have caused me stress that might have taken a negative toll on my business, which was producing all the cash that my family and I needed to live on. Yes, I wanted to invest in real estate and create long-term wealth, but I was also smart enough to realize that there was no way it would create enough cash flow for my family and I to live on.

I chose the path that was less about greed and more about long-term, sustainable growth. I credit my faith with helping me to make this principle-based decision.

I credit that grounding in eternal truths (which I spoke of above) with helping guide me to the decision that would ultimately be best for my family and myself. My faith is my guide through much of my decision-making process, and the first investment was no different.

So, faith can give you the courage and strength to make the right decisions.

The second major component of faith is the opportunity that

your chosen faith community provides. Of course, I'm not suggesting you take part in a faith community solely to seek material benefit for yourself. However, this might be one unintentional result.

I remember the first "big money" deal I did in real estate. Until that point, I'd been using my own money, and on one building, I borrowed some money from my father for the down payment, but taking the leap to a property where I needed to raise $250,000 in cash just to fund the down payment was a big deal.

I had raised $225,000 of the total from within my immediate circle of friends and family (including my faith circle) when I got the property under contract.

It came down to two days remaining before I had to remove the financing condition on the contract (and therefore would not be getting my deposit back). I'll never forget the day that I was driving to Edmonton from Calgary to take care of some of the due diligence for the property but was still $25,000 short!

In the car with me was a man from my church who I looked to as a Christian mentor. He and I spent a lot of time together, discussing our faith and how it affected our lives and the decisions we made. In addition, I'd traveled to Romania with this man on a mission a couple of years earlier. He was a major pillar in my faith community.

On the road between Calgary and Edmonton, I was explaining the situation with the apartment building. I told him that I needed an additional $25,000 and that I wasn't certain whether or not I'd get the money. His suggestion was unique and obvious at the same time. He said, "Why don't you pray?"

I had grown up "Christian," but it was more of a nominal Christianity. When I was younger, before I stepped more into my faith, I would never have considered prayer as a solution to a problem, but since I'd already been on a spiritual journey over the previous several years, and because my faith had deepened a great deal over those years, I decided that prayer was a fantastic idea. So, I prayed right there in the car on the way to Edmonton (thankfully, I wasn't driving).

The prayer alone was wonderful. Praying is an act that I have grown to appreciate and love. Thus when I finished praying I was already happy and feeling great.

What happened next was incredible. I received a phone call a couple of minutes later from David, an Irish investor whom I hadn't met yet, but who had committed $25,000 to the project already. He phoned me from Ireland. H e asked "Thomas, I have commited $25,000. Will you take $50,000 instead ?" I was blown away. It was an incredible moment of providence that I'll never forget, and it allowed me to close this deal. I only later learned that David is a strong Christian too. (As it turned out, when I finally met him several months later in person, I picked him up in Calgary with my newly acquired Lexus that I had bought after a successful flip of a house in Canmore. He asked me how much this kind of car costs in Canada. I answered: "About $50,000")

I believe faith forms a major component of the stable base. It's proven true in my life in the form of guidance and providence.

LESSON 7:
BUILD A STABLE BASE (PART 2) – FAMILY

I'm someone who has sought after business and monetary success in my life. I still seek it, and I will continue to seek it. However, I'm not someone who believes that business and monetary success trumps family.

I'm proud of what I've achieved in business, but I'm more proud of the stable family base that I've created through it all. Throughout my various business ventures and careers, I've had the chance to meet a lot of role models and anti-role models. I've seen people who appear successful with money, fancy cars, and a life in the fast lane—yet also leave several divorces and unhappy children in their wake. They have all the trappings of success, but in my mind that's not success, and I would never want to emulate that.

However, I have empathy for anyone who is in such a situation. I'm certainly not perfect, and I can see how it's possible to lead a life without the stable base that I value so much.

As I mentioned earlier, before I moved to Canada and eventually met my wife, Lynda, I had a long-term girlfriend back in Germany. She wanted me to settle down with her and get married, but something inside me knew it wasn't the best idea. I chose to move to Canada to pursue my MBA, and one result of that decision was that she and I broke up.

It wasn't that there was anything wrong with this former girlfriend; it's just that she and I were not a good fit. I didn't realize it at the time, but looking back I know that if I had stayed with her, I wouldn't have had the stable base that I now have. I might have fooled around on her, and I would not have had the strong and positive influence of my wife in my life. My ex-girlfriend did not have the personality that I need in my life, whereas Lynda is a very positive and strong influence in my life.

Perhaps it was luck, or perhaps it was intuition, or perhaps it was something more divine, but ultimately I made the move away from the unstable German girlfriend and toward the stable Canadian wife. I credit my wife with being one of the most positive influences in my life.

I met her at a time when I was seeking more meaning in my life. I had tried various types of spiritual practice, and eventually went to some functions at her church. I believe love and faith are very closely connected, and I came to my wife and my faith almost in unison.

The truth is that I could (and might) write an entire book on faith in life, faith and love, and love in general. For now, though, let me just put it like this: success is a holistic practice. Getting really rich without a stable base isn't real success. I can do anything for a while, but if I don't love it, I will not be able to do it really well for very long. When you do something out of love, you just have faith that the next step will show itself and that it will work.

A family is no different, and from a love for family, and the faith inherent in that act of loving, the more ephemeral aspects of success (such as money) follow. A stable base is real success, which leads to the other kinds of success that most people seek.

Build a stable base in your life, and you'll never be lacking.

LESSON 8:
YOUR SPOUSE IS YOUR PERMANENT 50/50 JOINT VENTURE PARTNER

"Love is not looking at each other, but in looking in the same direction." Antoine de Saint-Exupéry

When getting into any kind of partnership, you must be aware that you will be tied to the person you're partnering with—and untying yourself isn't easy. I was connected to Dave, my former partner, through the buildings that we owned together. Cleaning up that mess took significant time and money. When I purchased houses in Stony Plain with John, I was again connected through real estate.

In other business partnerships, I've been connected through software and restaurants. Each one took a different amount of work to extricate myself from. There are partnerships that I'm still in, and I expect to stay in them for the foreseeable future, but at some point, there's a good chance that those partnerships will end too.

My partnership with my wife, however, is different. A marriage is a different kind of partnership. You will remain (or at least attempt to remain) in partnership with your spouse through every decision that you make in your life and business. This means that what you do, in business or elsewhere, matters to your spouse, and what your spouse does matters to you. It also means that he or she has a say in what you do, and vice versa.

In addition, it means that you and your partner have to agree on many things. You certainly don't have to agree on all things, but you have to agree on the big things.

I recall working in Burnaby, British Columbia, as a software tester when we had a young family. I knew that I wanted to move on professionally and geographically, and I needed my wife to agree with me on this big decision.

At the time, I was still figuring out what I liked and what I was good at (a process that went on for a decade or more), and I still didn't know perfectly well what the end game was, but I did know that testing software wasn't it. When the opportunity arose to move to Munich, Germany, and take a position with IBM in more of a project management and technical marketing role, I was ready to jump at the opportunity. I'd always been an adventurer and a world traveler, ready to drop what I was doing and go off on another adventure, but this time was different. I wasn't looking for an adventure for the sake of adventure—I was looking for a career opportunity. But at the same time, I wasn't averse to the adventure of moving back across the ocean either.

There was just the small issue of our one-year-old son and my young wife who hardly spoke a word of German. Oh, did I mention she was pregnant with our second child at the time too? And did I mention the fact that we didn't have much money at the time? In fact, we had almost no money. Money was very tight, and we were facing the prospect of what must have seemed like a risky intercontinental move. I was asking my wife to sell our few belongings and start fresh.

I admire and respect my wife immensely for agreeing with this plan. She and I have always known that we don't have to agree on everything, but on the big things like this, we have been able to agree. I'm so happy that we agreed because the history of my professional life has shown that the move to Germany and into IBM proved to be a great success—in fact, it launched me into all of my future success.

Getting a foot in the door with IBM was what ultimately led me to learn sales, marketing, and presentation—skills that proved invaluable for all future endeavors. Improving at IBM was what gave me the expertise to manage skillfully. My management style at Prestigious Properties® is modeled to this day on the project management skills I gained at IBM.

I also became an expert on IBM's relational database software products, and it was from that expertise that I was able to join and profitably grow Lightyear Consulting (selling IBM software and related services in the emerging Java, Internet, handheld devices and wireless world) with my then-partner, Howard.

Finally, the income derived from Lightyear Consulting was the original seed money that I used to invest in real estate. My first several properties and even some of the smaller multi-family buildings were funded with cash that I earned through Lightyear Consulting. You could say that my professional move to IBM was a very important move in the chess game of my professional life.

Without my wife agreeing with me on this big decision, there is no chance I could have made such a move. Without her support, there is no way I could have made the high risk (but higher reward) move. She agreed with the bigger picture, that our family's prospects would be better if I took the position in Germany, and she supported the move. Without my permanent 50/50 joint venture partner on board for this move, it would not have been possible.

Imagine the opposite. She could have said, "Thomas, you're crazy, we have a young family, and we don't even have that much money. Furthermore, I don't speak German. There's no way we can move to Germany. There is plenty of opportunity in Canada. Let's stay here."

If she had done that, I would have missed out on several fortuitous events. But more importantly, what would have happened to my professional psyche? I had already known that I was in a position I didn't like. I did not want to continue testing software, and I knew it. I wanted to take a chance on a big move and improve my career prospects. If Lynda had denied me that opportunity, I can't actually imagine what might have happened to my state of mind. I know from experience that I can do almost anything, but if I have no love for what I do, I can't do it very well for very long. I didn't love software testing, ad I believe I was at risk of the malaise that so many workers find themselves in. I might easily have slipped into a kind of depression. I might have become the kind of person who hates his job yet stays out of a sense of duty. And inside, I might have questioned my marriage to a person who didn't support or believe in me.

But that is not what happened. My wife did support me, and rather than whither, my confidence grew.

Your spouse is your permanent 50/50 joint venture partner, and without mutual support and agreement on the big things, your partnership won't go very far. On the other hand, if you do agree on the big things, and if you do support each other, your marriage can be a great source of strength for the entire journey.

LESSON 9:
PRACTICE KAIZEN: CONSISTENT, INCREMENTAL PROGRESS

"Kaizen" is Japanese for "good change" or "small yet continuous and steady improvement." From its initial application to manufacturing and business practices, kaizen is now a term that is widely used to describe the philosophy of continuous improvement—whether professional, organizational or personal.

Many world famous and highly successful and dominant Japanese companies, most notably Toyota, have employed this business philosophy with great effect. Toyota's success has been copied by many other firms.

If you look at the Toyota Camry, one of the top-selling cars in North America for several years, you see a perfect example of kaizen in practice. The Camry was released 30 years ago, and every year since its release, Toyota has made small, incremental changes to the car. One year they would change the ashtray and the grille (for example) and the next they would change the lights and the rims.

Toyota never undertook a drastic remodeling of the car, and as a result, the customer always knew what to expect. Nevertheless, after 30 years of applying kaizen, the car is totally different from top to bottom. It's likely that there is no component that is now the same as on the original car.

Every year, the car is made slightly better. The progress was gained little by little. Toyota never tried to re-invent the wheel, but always made the Camry a little bit better every year.

I witnessed a similar phenomenon during my years at IBM. Originally, IBM sold what today would be considered crude machines, such as typewriters and time punch machines. From those crude machines, they have moved into some of the most complex and cutting edge machines in the world. However, they did not make those moves in giant leaps. They applied their own version of kaizen and continually improved and evolved from one phase of their business into the next, which has led them to where they are today—a massive company that is still cutting edge.

Bill Gates said it best: "Most people overestimate what they can do in one year but underestimate what they can do in ten. Don't let yourself be lulled into inaction."

Practicing kaizen means knowing that progress isn't always noticeable, but it is tangible over time. It means that, regardless of the fact that you can't see growth every single day, you know that you're still growing and therefore you take action that leads to growth every single day.

If you're feeling overweight and low on energy, you probably didn't get into that state overnight. It probably took years of eating unhealthy food and not exercising in order to get there. So guess what, you're not going to get out of that state overnight either. It's going to take kaizen in order to improve your level of fitness. Don't aim to drop 20 pounds this month; aim to drop three to four pounds. Then do it again every month until you are healthy and full of energy again.

Don't try to take your business from $80,000 to $80,000,000

in two years. Just go about your business methodically and continuously. When you lift your head up from your consistent toil to take a look at your progress, you will be shocked to see how far you've come. It's actually not as slow as you think. My team and I took Prestigious Properties® from $80,000 to $80,000,000 in about 10 years. That's a 1000-fold growth in a decade. What if you started today? What if you worked your way up slowly and surely, and didn't throw it all away and take some giant steps backward? What could you accomplish in the next five or eight, or 12 or 18 years? How old would you be when you get there?

If you're 40 years old, and you feel like you're just starting, how bad would it be to create something like your own version of Prestigious Properties® by the time you're 55?

I'm not even saying you have to work like a dog. Of course, you must work hard, very hard, but what's more important than hard work is consistency and gradually improving—every single day. Applying kaizen is important.

In Prestigious Properties®, we have a basic slide/PowerPoint presentation that we use to show prospective investors what we're about, and of course, to try and convince them to invest their money with us.

In the seven years that we've been using this presentation, we've applied kaizen to it consistently. We never make drastic changes, but perhaps we change one or two slides every quarter, or sometimes the fonts or a new logo or a new look. After seven years, we have a completely different presentation than what we started with. Nothing is the same, and that is as it should be. Just like the Toyota Camry, we've made the presentation better little by little, and what we're left with after seven years is a superior product.

Similarly, we own a building in Edmonton (Windsor Estates) that we improved from a rent roll of about $45,000 per month to more than $95,000 per month in about seven years—through incremental and ongoing changes. We added new doorbells, new hallway carpets, a new office, a new computer for the office, new voicemail, a new name (it used to be called Windsor Court so even the name change wasn't all that dramatic), new garbage bins, a new exterior paint job, a new paint job inside the hall-ways, in-suite upgrades by the dozens (five or six every year at most), and new windows. And this only describes what we have done as of the time of this writing (2012); I am sure in 2018 or 2022 we will still be upgrading and enhancing things. The slow, cumulative effect of the incremental changes is that the build-ing's value has steadily increased and it earns fabulous monthly cash flow.

As an immigrant (or as the Germans would say, "foreigner") living in Canada, one of my biggest challenges originally was verbal and written communication. I had a thick (some would say "sick") accent, and I couldn't decipher between my V's and W's. I used to say "Wolksvagen" when I meant to say "Volkswa-gen." It's a common affliction of the native German speaker liv-ing and working in a totally English environment. In addition, I had a firm grasp of German grammar and spelling in written form while in English, I was proficient but still clearly a foreigner struggling through.

It has been an ongoing process of improvement for the entire 20-plus years that I've lived in Canada to become very proficient in English. Many foreigners that I know improve a little bit, but then they give up, and they accept the fact that they will always remain at a remedial level in their English abilities. They don't re-alize that by applying kaizen to their language abilities that they can and will speak at a near native fluency.

Sure, it takes time, but why not improve continually? I per-sonally believe that my growth as an English speaker has helped me in life and business a great deal. When I give presentations, nobody is left wondering what I meant, and I can clearly express myself in such a way that I can be persuasive. The art of persua-sion is vital when you're trying to raise money, or even when you're dealing with bankers, lawyers, real estate agents, or any other professional that you may come across in business.

Practice kaizen. Don't think of what you can accomplish in one year, consider what you can accomplish in 10. Fight that seduc-tive tendency to seek immediate gratification. Know that your consistent and incremental growth will get you to where you want to be.

LESSON 10:
KAIZEN AS A STEPPING STONE FOR LARGER LEAPS

In addition to the slow and incremental changes of kaizen, one can occasionally take larger leaps in business and in life.

As we will discuss in the lessons on "Growth in Discomfort," there's a point where we must make a difficult leap into the next phase of our growth. Often when we make a big move (like going from software to real estate, as I did), it seems as though we grow quickly.

It's true that growth is exponential not long after making a big change, but what most people don't understand is that the exponential growth they experience in a fast-growth phase is a direct result of the incremental growth (kaizen) they made during a slower period.

We must make those "big leaps" from time to time. If we don't, we risk becoming stale. However, there is a type of person who is continuously trying to jump from one big leap into the next. They are prone to quitting what they're doing in favor of the next big thing.

This is a dangerous cycle because it brings people off the successful path that they were on to become a beginner again. The problem with always being a beginner is that it can cause a loss of confidence and momentum.

When I look back at my life, it is plainly obvious that I've often applied kaizen-like principles, which has led me to greater confidence and momentum. For example, when I purchased my first rental-pool condo for $80,000, I decided to go on the condo board after about a year of ownership—to understand the management aspects better.

It would have been easy for me not to join the board. I had more pressing matters to attend to with my family and my software consulting business, yet I joined the board to learn.

However, by joining the board, I was effectively studying how to manage larger buildings with all their social and often petty and mundane issues. After I had bought two more condos in two other complexes I joined one more board and later became the president of one board.

So, when the day came that I bought my first 15-suite building in the year 2000, it wasn't as big a leap as you'd think it might be (to go from managing single condos to multi-family buildings). In reality, I'd seen how management of multi-family buildings works from the inside prior to actually owning one myself.

People often look at what I've been able to accomplish as a real estate investor and they rarely understand what I've gone through to get there. I didn't simply leap into owning many large multi-family buildings, I applied kaizen, and each time I had to make a "next step," I was ready. I had the confidence and the knowledge (which are closely connected) to pull off the next (seemingly) difficult step.

On the flip side, there have been times when I didn't adhere as closely to the kaizen principle. The greatest example is with Prestigious Properties® when I let Dave (whom we discussed earlier) talk me into reckless growth of the company.

That reckless growth created a lot of mess in my life and in my business. In hindsight, I believe Prestigious Properties® would have been far better off by applying kaizen in one or maybe two of our core markets in Alberta. We could have accomplished far greater results by buying half or even fewer of the buildings than we did. In addition, we could have allocated more time and material resources to the properties that we already owned, and likely improved them more over the same time frame.

Rather than stick with kaizen, we went with a fast growth strategy, and in the end it put us in a big mess. In fact, it almost ended the company. But we survived, and I have a greater appreciation for kaizen and big leaps. I've seen the anatomy of how to pull off a big leap—by launching oneself through kaizen.

LESSON 11:
GROWTH IN DISCOMFORT – TAKING THE NEXT STEP

Fifteen years ago I had it all. I was working with a wonderful large company (IBM), had an exciting career, and I was making good money. My almost $100,000 per year salary was very good at the time, and I had the stability of knowing where the next paycheck would come from. My wife was happy with the income I was bringing in, and my kids were happily growing up.

In addition, I knew and understood my job well. I had already accumulated years of experience in IBM, and was actually a product expert in the arena of DB2 software. What more could I have wanted?

In reality, I wasn't wanting for anything in the traditional sense. I had a home, a family, and a strong income. However, I knew there was more in me than what I was doing professionally at the time. I often joke that if I had stayed with IBM, I could be earning $120,000 per year today. (People call this a "lifer" at IBM and many other large firms.)

That figure may or may not be totally accurate, but the principle is certainly correct. When you stick with the same path, even after you're ready to jump onto the next path, your potential stagnates somewhat.

It may seem that there is a contradiction between what I wrote before about the kaizen principle and now about growth in discomfort, but in fact, the two principles work together.

My method is to apply kaizen for many years along a certain path, but eventually make a change that seems drastic. I believe that eventually we have to opt for the uncomfortable change in order to grow into a more mature, possibly more successful and maybe even better person. If I had remained with IBM applying kaizen, and as a result had never joined a small, seemingly insignificant software consulting firm, then I'd really be nearing perfection in the IBM realm, and I might be one of the company's most overqualified employees.

However, I recognized that it was necessary (for me, at any rate) to make an uncomfortable change. As a result, I've achieved far greater financial rewards than the $120,000 per year that I would be earning if I'd stayed with IBM. I've achieved far greater in every other realm as well.

Perhaps you're wondering what was so uncomfortable about leaving IBM in favor of the software consulting firm Lightyear Consulting ("To Infinity and Beyond" was its motto then).

For this German lad, who'd always been an employee, switching to an entrepreneurial venture was indeed a big risk. The statistics clearly show that many, if not most, businesses fail within two years of startup—and I knew this. I did take some serious measures to mitigate that risk—most notably I went into business with someone who'd had success in the same line of business for years. This fact alone gave my wife and me a greater level of comfort than I could have achieved by myself.

Interestingly, it was my kaizen-like pursuit within IBM that made me a wonderful partner for Howard. I did much of the work, and Howard wrote the checks (see the section on partnering); it was a perfect partnership.

But there was discomfort in the fact that I was indeed taking a big risk. I started a company at a time when total failure could have had drastic consequences for the most important people in my life, and if I had been forced to re-enter corporate life, being away for a couple of years would have put me in a bad position to do so.

While I always knew that my technological and sales backgrounds could likely land me back in a good job, I certainly didn't want to have to explore that territory. I didn't want to take a step backward! The move to Lightyear represented a bit of a gamble, but I knew I needed to grow, and I knew that taking the uncomfortable step of leaving the security of IBM for the opportunity of Lightyear Consulting was the way toward that growth.

I was lucky on a few fronts when it came time to making the uncomfortable change between IBM and Lightyear Consulting. First of all, I had a wife who supported me. Oftentimes a spouse will disagree with their partner changing professions or starting a business. My wife agreed that the uncomfortable change would be best for our entire family, and she supported me in taking the step that ultimately led to greater success and provided the inroad to real estate.

I'd also managed to avoid many of the traps and pitfalls of over consumption. We didn't have an overly expensive house, and we didn't have large monthly bills for cars, quads, motorcycles or boats. We had lived a fairly frugal life, and when the time came to make a risky leap, I was able to because we weren't financially overburdened.

The uncomfortable change between IBM and Lightyear Consulting is very illustrative, but it's only one of numerous changes I made over the years. Each one of them was uncomfortable, and often they followed a period of kaizen-like dedication to a single craft.

Lesson 12:
Growth in Discomfort – The Anatomy of an Uncomfortable Change (The Stepped S-Curve)

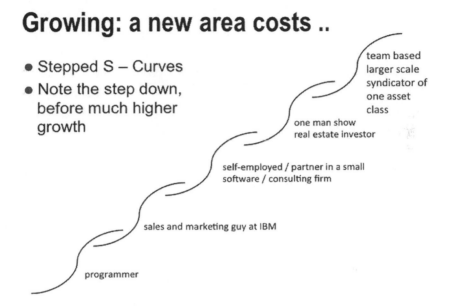

Growing: a new area costs ..

- Stepped S – Curves
- Note the step down, before much higher growth

team based larger scale syndicator of one asset class

one man show real estate investor

self-employed / partner in a small software / consulting firm

sales and marketing guy at IBM

programmer

Growing—that is, making necessary yet often uncomfortable change—resembles a stepped S-curve as shown above. I thought it would be valuable to walk through the process of the uncomfortable change step by step and give you a sense of what you can expect when you make a change.

When we want to make change, we're often faced with an old enemy named "fear." When we don't know what's on the other side of the change, and this side is cozy and comfortable—with a big-screen TV, a nice paid holiday, a big warm house, and a fancy car—it's easier to stick with what we already know instead of jumping over the other side and risking it all.

I commend you if you even recognize that you're ready for a

change that will undoubtedly bring you discomfort. If you identify it and want to make the change, I think it's valuable to know what to expect. Below is a step by step explanation of the phases of an uncomfortable life change:

1. AWARENESS THAT SOMETHING ISN'T RIGHT.

Whether you process based on rational thought or on gut feeling, you may be familiar with the feeling that something isn't right in your current life position. For me, there have been numerous times when I knew a change was necessary.

One that stands out was when I was working in my very first "real" job back in Germany, prior to coming to Canada to study at the University of Alberta. I was working in the software division of Siemens, a giant German company with more than 200,000 employees, a company that was into almost everything—from micro-processors, medical imaging systems, telephones, software, printers, and trains, and even whole nuclear power plants.

When I started there, my manager sat me down and showed me the income growth curve that I could expect. There it was, my entire life laid out before me (at least the income part), and I didn't like what I saw. I was in my early twenties, and I saw that my colleagues who'd been there for 15 or more years had already reached the top of their earning potential and the work they were doing.

For the most part, I was already doing the same work as them, namely programming. They knew their work better than I did, and they were more specialized and experienced, but essentially we were doing the same job.

Those points of awareness led me to believe that this was not the life for me. This realization was my first step toward making the uncomfortable change—moving to Canada to study for an MBA.

2. MAKE THE CHANGE.

I am no psychologist, nor am I a neuroscientist, so I won't be able to explain in technical terms how one gets one's mind prepared for a change. What I do know is that whenever I've known that I had to change in order to move forward, I've typically been able to gather enough courage and strength to make those difficult changes.

Don't ignore the awareness that something is wrong. Act upon your feelings and make the change necessary. You may not know exactly what to do, you may just know that you have to make a change (that's where Ready, Fire, Aim comes into play—more on that later). Even if you don't know the perfect next step, and you only know that you must make the change, it's best to act on that feeling.

The longer you wait in the stagnant position, the more you stagnate. Move, change, and see where the cards may fall.

3. FEEL THE PAIN. IT'S INEVITABLE.

It's inevitable. When you jump ship from that cozy lifestyle that you've come to trust, you will inevitably feel the pain of your change.

On the stepped S-curve, this pain is represented by the small drop-off whenever you make a change. What this means is that there is every possibility that you will go backward for a little while before you go forward to the desired result that you want.

In practical terms, it means that you will likely make less money for a while, you might sleep less, you might have less personal time, you might have to move, you might have to spend money, you might have to divorce your spouse, you might have to travel, or you might have to stop traveling.

Relax. All of those things are temporary, or at least they're temporary in the form that you're currently experiencing them. Either the experience will change, or your perception of the experience will change. You will adapt, you will grow into it, or you will stop doing it. But importantly, you have to give it some time, and you have to push through the discomfort.

4. SKYROCKET.

Just as certain as the fact that you will feel significant pain is the fact that you will skyrocket in your growth curve after pushing through the pain. Take a look at that stepped S-curve. It shows exponential growth after the initial phase of pain and difficulty. The growth in this phase is truly remarkable.

While on this part of the curve, it can be a remarkable emotional high. You will feel invincible, like you can conquer the world, and your outlook for your own future will be limitless.

When you make a difficult change, and you then experience the skyrocketing, feel free to enjoy the ride: you've earned it, and before long, the real work (kaizen-like focus) will come.

5. PLATEAU.

Soon you'll normalize all the incredible growth and change. What was incredible not too long ago is now normal.

Financially speaking, this is where so many people get themselves into trouble. They start making double, triple, or more than they were making in a previous position, and they believe that the natural next step is a bigger house, a nicer car, more trips around the world, etc. They think that there's no way they can ever spend all this enormous new wealth they have.

Before long, their new lifestyle is stretching their financial resources, and all of the old difficulties that they thought they were escaping come rushing back into their lives.

I believe the plateau phase is one of the most difficult to manage. It takes a special kind of focus to navigate your way through it. It takes a commitment to incremental growth, which unbeknownst to you may be setting up the next big change/growth cycle.

I credit my stable base with helping me to work through all the phases, but especially this tricky plateau phase. My stable base has helped me to refocus and grow incrementally through the plateau phase on each occasion.

Always remember these phases when you're going through or about to go through a change. Knowing which phase you're in will help you chart a safe and enjoyable passage through the change.

LESSON 13:
GROWTH IN DISCOMFORT –
CHANGE GETS EASIER EACH TIME

I'm not suggesting you should make uncomfortable change just for the sake of making change. In fact, momentum stops by making too many changes, so change is not always a good thing. However, it might take you a few iterations and a few years to really figure out what you're good at (see the lesson on discovering your strengths). Many people simply give up before they understand themselves well enough to know what they're bad, average, good, and excellent at.

Knowing yourself is key, but most people don't take the chance to know themselves really well. As a result, they decide to stay in a comfortable role rather than make difficult change.

If you're committed to knowing yourself, and if you have been on the journey of self-knowledge for a while, and you know that you have to make change, then it does get easier every time.

There is one strong caveat on the idea that it gets easier each time: you must give yourself enough time at whatever you are doing to feel some success. If you are constantly running from one thing to another, it's easy to feel that you're running from failures.

The constant questions from others within your circle about how you're changing (again) can be demoralizing, and you may start to wonder what's wrong with you.

On the other hand, if you've given yourself enough time to really feel the success, and you (and others) can easily see how you've succeeded, then it will be easy to justify the next uncomfortable change you're making. You simply say to yourself, "Well, look at the last time I changed, it was a big success, and this change is going to take me to an even better place." You can repeat the same conversation to yourself, your spouse, your partner, your kids, your friends and your family.

This is especially handy if you have a spouse who is resistant to change. If you can look back to the last change and prove clearly that it was for the best, then your spouse will be far more likely to believe that the next change is going to be a big success too.

When you have that track record of success, it makes each successive change that much easier. There was a time in my life when it seemed like I was moving every two years. This pattern was not a problem when I was a single man with no children and no real commitments. I was able to bounce around the world and do as I pleased, but once I became a family man, the moving became a problem.

Eventually, the every-second-year moves slowed down. Once I got to Calgary, my family and I stayed there for seven years. After that, we were in Canmore for 11 years, and now I live in Vancouver, and probably will stay for quite a long while.

Constant change might not be the best thing. It can stop your momentum, and perhaps make it seem as though you're not meeting with success along your path. Having success breeds a track record, and when it's time to take that next step up the ladder of life, you will be able to make the decision with relative ease because you will have a deep well of success to draw

LESSON 14:
READY, FIRE, AIM – TAKE REASONABLE
STEPS TO MITIGATE RISK

"Ships are safe in harbor, but that is not what ships were built for." – Grace Hoppern

When making any kind of decision your choice will always leave an impact on the world. This is inescapable. Your kids will be heavily impacted by your choices. Your spouse will be greatly affected. Your family, friends and business partners will all be affected. Your shareholders or your joint venture partners will be affected.

What you do matters and it will leave a mark on the world. There is no getting around that. Most importantly, you will be greatly affected by your own decisions. My decision to partner with Dave, my high energy but scattered former business partner, is still affecting me today. There is no getting around the fact that what we do will matter to us for a long time.

So, what does one do? Do we hide and never do anything different for fear of drastically changing our lives for the worse? Of course not.

With one or two different choices, I could still be a software tester in Burnaby, British Columbia. My software-testing self was multiple incarnations ago. I've made several large and seemingly risky life changes since then.

Changing your life does come with some degree of risk, and you may be negatively affected for years to come, but you may also be positively affected for many years to come too. To make a positive change, you simply must make a change.

My personal philosophy of change and growth states that we must take every precaution within reason to mitigate the big risks that may sink us in life.

If you value your marriage, then don't put the marriage on the line over a job promotion. That doesn't mean you can't try to push the boundaries of what is acceptable to your spouse, but don't act in a reckless way. Too many entrepreneurs can't seem to differentiate between taking calculated risks and taking needless risks. Just because your spouse has put up with your drastic changes in the past does not mean he or she will continue to put up with them in the future.

For example, I have moved for work or business several times in my life. My wife, Lynda, supported me on these moves. She and I don't and never will agree on every aspect of life, but we've managed to agree on the big things. I've asked her to support moves all around Western Canada, Toronto and Germany since the beginning of our marriage.

But what do you suppose she would have said if I'd have asked her to move to Siberia? That would have been pushing the limit too much, and I would have been risking my marriage. When I asked her to move to Germany, it was a risky proposition for her. She had to move away from her beloved Western Canada, to an environment far away from all of her family (who are her greatest support network), and to a country where she did not speak the language.

Yet she knew that there were benefits to living in Germany. She had the opportunity to learn a new language, and our children would live in the nation of their father and learn the language as well. In Germany, we would be close to my family, and it was important that she get to know my family better as well.

Lynda wanted me to be fulfilled and she wanted me to take the next step professionally, so she saw the value in moving to Germany for that reason as well.

In other words, the move to Germany was a calculated risk. It wasn't as though we were flinging the family across the world entirely without thought and into a totally unknown and dangerous situation.

At the time, I knew I wanted to advance my career, and I'd always had (and still have to this day) a very high regard for industry leaders, especially IBM, the King of IT (information technology). That did not mean at the time that I'd be willing to move to Siberia (or Sweden for that matter) for IBM. Why? Well, I wouldn't like Siberia enough for myself, but I also wouldn't want to risk my family life by asking my wife to go somewhere she would hate as well.

Before moving to Germany with my young family, I had considered all of these things carefully. I was confident that the move was the right thing and that I wasn't putting the most important things in my life at risk.

However, I was not 100 percent certain. In my experience, 100 percent certainty is impossibility. The man or woman who waits for 100 percent certainty will most definitely get stuck in the sorry state of analysis paralysis. They will not make the move, write the check, call the girl, or start the business. Hence the next lesson…

Lesson 15:
Ready, Fire, Aim – Leap Before You Look (sort of)

I started out on my professional journey as a nerdy, geeky kind of guy. I loved computer programming, and I pursued a career in that field starting from my youth, when I joined the German air force (Luftwaffe). My time there is a whole different story, but I joined the Luftwaffe so that I could get a university education in computer science as money was tight at home and I had two other siblings.

I have a deep understanding and respect for rigor and detail. I thrive in analytical situations, and I like partaking in analysis. Yet I realized at a very young age (during my time in the Luftwaffe) that I didn't want to bury my head in details for the rest of my life. I didn't want to be a small cog in a big wheel, programming for the rest of my days.

I eventually found that my sweet spot in the software industry was in combining my strong technical knowledge while using my communication and project management skills to interface with clients, designers and upper management.

So what's my point? My history in IBM demonstrates my philosophy of leaping before you look (sort of). I could have stayed where I was, ever so cozy and secure as a hardcore software guy, "nerding out" with my fellow geeks. I could have rejected the idea of transitioning from "tech guy" to "business tech guy" as too risky, involving too many unknowns. When I started making the shift, I wasn't certain that I would be good at business/technology interfacing (and later, sales). But in spite of that uncertainty, I made the change.

At the time I examined my position, and I found that indeed I was not too happy doing what I was doing. From an initial interest in software, I realized that a life spent buried in the details was not the life for me, so I took the first step—knowing something wasn't right.

Next, I did the necessary research and diligence to see if I could land a job in the business/technology interface sector. However, I did not quit my job in Burnaby testing software immediately; instead I applied at IBM in Germany to see if I could get the job! I was also prescient enough to play on one of my biggest strengths. I was German–English bilingual, and at the time IBM was investing heavily into UNIX and software, both areas I excelled at. My fluency in German and English and my technical knowledge were both assets for me.

When I consulted with my wife, I found that she supported me, and that she saw taking a career step upward to be a benefit, even though she was a Canadian who preferred Canada, and even though we had one young child and another on the way, and even though she did not speak German at the time. (It did help that her mother, Elfrieda, and to a lesser degree her father, Abe, knew some German as they grew up as Mennonites where prayer and talk at home was strictly Low German.)

Finally, I accepted the job and took the leap along with my

family.

What I did not do was know every single potential pitfall and problem. In a sense, I leapt before I looked. For example, we had to sell our car and my scooter, and move furniture with a pregnant wife (we didn't know about the pregnancy at decision time) with almost no money in the bank and a three-month no income hiatus.

When I was younger, I was more prone to leaping before looking, and I was more risk tolerant in both business and life. When you're young, you have less to lose, so you're often more likely to take risks. If you have little, you're risking little, and on top of that, you're young enough to start all over again. You also don't know what you don't know and thus, what could hurt you. You are unconsciously incompetent. When you're older, you often at least know what you don't know (that is, consciously incompetent).

What if Bill Gates and Steve Jobs would have been in their sixties when they started their respective companies? In all likelihood, they would not have been so willing to risk it all on their respective companies, both of which changed the world. To the chagrin of conservative parents everywhere, these two young men were perfect examples of young people taking the risky route and succeeding!

They most certainly leapt before they looked, and they succeeded in a big way. However, if they had been 60 at the time, they most likely would not have taken such risks. Oftentimes, the world of big risky ventures belongs to the young.

The people you rarely, if ever, hear about are the non-famous, non-successful versions of Bill Gates and Steve Jobs. These men and women are equally talented, they work equally hard, but they do not succeed so famously. The reasons why are often completely out of their control (see lesson one). Perhaps they come to the party six months too early, or six months too late, or perhaps their big idea is launched when the market is about to collapse. They lose it all, and they may (or may not) go back to the drawing board. (Perhaps this book is about one of them, as not many books exist that talk about these "almost" winners that disappear into the background.)

There's nothing wrong with the drawing board, especially when you're young, full of energy, and you didn't lose much in the first place.

For a more measured approach that is more likely to result in success, I recommend making prudent assumptions, doing prudent levels of diligence, thinking, and then leaping. I don't recommend leaping immediately. And I don't recommend over thinking and therefore getting stuck in analysis paralysis. I do recommend a balance between the two.

Successful people write down goals. Then they plan. Then they execute. I suggest the same. Setting goals is actually quite easy. Write them down. Revisit them every so often. They become ingrained in your brain. The harder part, where most people fail, is the lack of planning. What do I have to do to achieve the goal? Usually many little mini-goals are required. Do this. Phone that guy. Get a meeting here. Do a briefing there. Refine the message. Try a different way. Over and over again. Try again, i.e., execute. Execution is the hard part. All experts today were not experts in the beginning. They improved steadily, one goal at a time. One mini-success, or many mini-failures, at a time.

It would be easy to think this discussion only relates to business and professional pursuits, but it can be applied to all aspects of life. In love relationships it's highly recommended to take your time, learn about yourself, develop yourself, learn about your partner and ensure that you share similar opinions on the big things. It's important that you consider whether the partner is right for you in life, not just in lust.

At some point there it's necessary that you do leap in, pop the question, ask that person to be your husband/wife for the rest of your life. I'm a huge believer in the power of a strong marriage to a strong partner. Of the two main pillars of the stable base (family and faith), a strong partnership with your spouse is the most important. My wife, Lynda, has been a stellar influence on my life and a guiding light for me in many ways. She's helped me develop my faith, and she's been my rock at home as well as a capable partner to consult with on matters of business.

I could have thought and thought and gotten stuck in analysis paralysis about our marriage, but at the time I dove in, not knowing where it would end up, and not knowing every last detail about her (we had known each other barely a year), and whether or not we would be a great couple.

The same was true on Lynda's side. We both knew what kind of family we wanted to have. We agreed that we wanted a strong presence at home, and that Lynda would be the main keeper of the home, while I would be the main income earner. Lynda did not know whether I would be a professional success at the time, and she didn't even know if I'd be a responsible father, husband and man. She did her own level of diligence on me, and ultimately she leapt before she looked (sort of).

We make moves and decisions every day of our lives. Living life demands that we take certain actions in the faith that they will work out, without all of the information, and without knowing exactly what will happen. However, we ultimately must act or we never grow and never move toward what we want.

So go on, leap before you look (sort of).

LESSON 16:
ASK – LEARN BY ASKING QUESTIONS

I'm a big believer in failing your way to success. Sometimes life just demands that you make the leap of faith and jump into a story to which you can't possibly know the ending. The process of elimination will lead you to a higher place.

However, if a baby bird with stunted wings leaps out of the nest from a height, the fall might kill it. The same goes for your life. Failing is fine, but it's best not to let your failures ruin you. If you're a beginner at investing in real estate, you can expect to have your fair share of failures, but try not to make your failures so grand that they completely ruin you.

Believe me, I know quite a few folks who were wiped out in the North American real estate correction of 2008–09 after a decade of upwards appreciation. I learned in 2007 that we had reached a real estate peak of significant proportions and decided to sell 50 percent of our Alberta portfolio—realizing an insane profit, benefiting several dozen investors, my then-partner, my family and me. Without that leaping, life would likely have been vastly different two years later (more on this later).

You can eliminate many failures of trial and error by asking questions. For example, if I want to buy a property in a down-trodden neighborhood because I see big market upside in the future and massive cash flow, I would be well advised to ask an experienced real estate investor that I trust and respect—and who is an expert on the neighborhood—what he or she thinks of the neighborhood. They might alert me to the fact that most of the houses in that neighborhood eventually have foundation problems and the fact that no amount of potential cash flow can make up for the tenant problems I would experience by owning in the neighborhood.

There will still be times when you ask questions, think you're taking every necessary step of diligence and you end up making a decision that stings you, but don't let that stop you from asking questions in the future. When you do ask questions, something interesting will happen… you will get better at asking questions, and you will get more adept at hearing answers. The same experienced investor whom you thought was just a little bit too conservative before will suddenly start making sense after you've seen with your own eyes some of the issues that he or she told you about.

Children are famous for thinking, while in their teen years, that their parents are morons and then, when they reach their twenties, starting to see that their parents have a point. By the time most people are in their thirties, they've come to realize that their parents are pretty smart after all and a conversation with Mom and Dad can be a great source of wisdom.

Ask questions, not just of people you professionally admire, but also experts in related fields that you don't totally understand. Ask your parents, and even ask your kids. Even the young ones have much to teach you. But nobody can teach you anything unless you are ready to listen to them. That's why God gave you two ears, but only one mouth. In the words of Stephen Covey, author of (most famously) The Seven Habits of Highly Effective People, "Seek first to understand, then to be understood."

When asking questions you'll find that most people are receptive to answering your questions. If they're in an advanced position, it means they've worked very hard to get to where they are—and they often have a desire to give back and teach. It's the natural cycle of life. Why do you think I spend so much of my time blogging and helping tutor real estate investors? And why do you think I am writing this book? For me, I'm still enjoying real estate, but I'm also ready to give back. I want to share what I've learned and pass it along to others who might find some value in my experience.

People like to share their knowledge. However, please don't waste their time.

One method I have used (and still use today) is to take people whom I wanted to learn from to lunch. You ask them for a one-hour commitment of their time, and in exchange you buy them lunch. It might cost you $50 to $100 for lunch, but if you get four, ten or even just one or two questions answered, it's about the cheapest consulting you'll ever get.

Even if you don't meet people but just ask them questions by email, or standing around the front of the room at the end of an event, you will be shocked at how most people are willing to answer questions.

Before I bought my first apartment building, I spoke to real estate agents, property managers, and other apartment building investors. I asked them about different areas, the upside of each area, and the downside. I asked them about streets to avoid, how much rent I could expect, getting contractors to renovate, valuations of buildings, financials, and much more.

When you ask similar questions to multiple people, you will get a pretty good idea of who is off-base and who makes sense. If you ask five people about a certain area, and four of them say it isn't good but one of them says it's a great area, you can probably assume that the fifth person either doesn't know what they're talking about or they perhaps have a vested interest in the area. Either way, you're learning how to decipher what people say and what it means.

I'm a big fan of book knowledge, and I spend a lot of time reading. When I'm a beginner at something, I spend a great deal of time learning about the topic. However, beyond books there's real and gritty knowledge, which you get by asking real questions to real people. Some people call it the "10 feet" rule, that is, talk to people who have actually walked the last 10 feet from behind the curtain to the microphone. They know how it feels. At the same time, you're learning how to speak like an insider, a skill that will go a long way when you later find yourself doing the thing that you were learning about only months earlier.

I can't say enough about the importance of asking questions.

LESSON 17:
ASK – ASKING QUESTIONS SEPARATES YOU FROM THE CROWD

I learned this lesson somewhat by accident. In my efforts to learn by asking questions, I discovered that when you ask questions, especially in front of groups, you end up standing out from the crowd.

Whenever you ask a question, you're also taking a risk. Perhaps you will look like a little bit of a loser if you ask a question that has already been answered by the speaker. And this is probably the great fear of most people who refuse to ask questions in a group setting. There are risks to everything, but when you take the initiative to ask a question, you'll usually stand out in a good way. Asking a question in a room of 200 people, with a microphone, is like giving a mini-presentation. Some people are deathly afraid of that. Get over it.

Questioners stand out to the person they asked because you'll be one of the few people who took the initiative to approach them directly. You can start your email, phone call, or voice mail with something like, "I really enjoyed your talk about XXX on Wednesday at the YYY forum. It is always nice to hear from true experts in a field, such as yourself. You mentioned 'blah blah blah.' I wonder if this means that…" It's actually not that difficult to ask such questions.

An expert in any field will understand just how daunting it can be to approach someone perceived to be on a higher standing than oneself, so they often respect you for it. Remember, they usually like to answer questions anyway because they often like to share their knowledge, but on top of that they often think it's admirable that you might have the courage to step up and approach them. Opportunities often arise just from standing out in this way.

If you ask a question in front of a group of people, you will also stand out in the minds of most people in the audience. Whenever you say anything, you're selling yourself. So what are you selling about yourself when you stand up in front of a group of people and speak your mind? Whether you know it or not, you're telling everyone else in attendance that you are different. You're a leader, you're courageous, you're confident, you're curious, you want to learn, you want to advance, you want to grow. You're saying that you either agree or, more rarely (and you'd better be well prepared), disagree with the speaker.

Standing up and asking a question is like a policy statement, either in favor of what the speaker is saying or against it. You have a pulpit to speak your mind, and usually, in an effort to position your question, you will have a small chance to mention your experience and what you do, what you're selling, or what you're buying. You can actually say a little bit about yourself just by standing up in front of a crowd and asking a question.

Recently, I went to an economics talk put on by a major Canadian bank. There were a couple of hundred people in attendance, and at the end there was a question and answer period. I did as I normally do and I got up at the end to ask a question. I positioned myself as a real estate investor, specializing in apartment buildings in strong growth markets of Western Canada. I got a response from the speaker, and as always, I bolstered my confidence just by the act of speaking in front of a group of people.

More importantly, I attracted the attention of others in the audience whom I did not know. At the end of the event there was a crowd of people standing around the speaker and asking him questions, but lo and behold, there were also a few people who wanted to speak to me. They wanted to know more about Prestigious Properties®. They were interested in our track record and how we could help them turn their cash into more cash.

Standing up, asking questions, and standing out has its rewards. It doesn't actually matter if you're not driven by the desire for personal or business gain, you will gain personally and in business when you ask questions publicly.

I joined REIN (Real Estate Investment Network) many years ago, and even though I didn't know it at the time, REIN's network of real estate investors would eventually become a great source of not only knowledge, but also new friends, capital and deals.

Back when I used to attend all of the meetings (I can't make it to all of them now), I would take every opportunity to stand up at the open mic session and present my deals. I used it as an opportunity to sell myself. I used to stand up and say, "Hello, my name is Thomas Beyer, only sometimes a seller." I would then tell the assembled group of real estate investors about the latest investment that I was working on, what kind of an opportunity it was, and what kind of partners I was looking for.

We're always selling ourselves. In that environment I was selling myself, even though I could not have known how valuable that space would become for me and my business. In later years, when I lived too far away to reasonably attend every meeting,

I still wanted to maintain a presence in the powerful network of REIN members, so I went online. I started spending a fair amount of time on the REIN website and forum www.myreinspace.com. Thousands of investors visit the site daily. I wanted to give something back and get to be known as a trusted authority.

In the forum, I did ask questions, and I started interesting threads, but more often I commented on others' questions and tried to provide my knowledge to help others safely get through the inevitable hardships and difficulties that might arise on their real estate investment journey.

Again, securing investment capital was not my intent on the forum, but it was an inevitable consequence. There are often wonderful consequences from stepping up, speaking up, and standing out.

Lesson 18:
Know Yourself – Figure Out What You're Excellent, Good, Average, Poor, and Terrible at

Y ou may see a theme of awareness with many of my lessons learned. Before you're able to make a real change in any area of life, you must first have awareness around the problem.

Knowing yourself and what you're good and bad at is one of the most important areas to have awareness in, and it often takes time, a lot of time to gain this awareness. You can, of course, speed up the process of gaining awareness by putting a specific focus on learning about yourself.

I did this when I was working for IBM in Calgary (my third different position in my third different city while working for IBM). Through my awareness, I understood that my position wasn't a perfect fit for me. It wasn't so much that I'm not a natural born salesman (which I'm not), it was more that massive companies with all the politics and rules that come with them weren't my "thing". This "realization" may seem odd because I'd been with IBM for many years already at that point.

It's true, I'd been there for more than five years, and during that time I learned the many hard and soft skills that would serve me for throughout my professional life. To this day, I operate Prestigious Properties® with the same project management skills that I gained in my days at IBM. Working for others, especially large corporations with very strong systems, is a beneficial training ground for many budding entrepreneurs.

There's no doubt that I was honing my awareness around my own skill set all the time I was at IBM, but it's still a bit ironic that it was at a career counseling course, paid for by IBM, that I was told that my perfect niche was to be the number one in a small entrepreneurial venture.

It finally confirmed my suspicion that I didn't belong in a behemoth company such as IBM. While I was more than happy to learn from IBM and to give my absolute best effort to them, I knew there was something else for me. That's exactly what happened when I finally took the career counseling course and ultimately decided to strike out into an entrepreneurial venture with Howard, the man who eventually became my partner in Lightyear Consulting, an IBM business partner.

We were an IBM-approved sales company for a certain software basket within a certain territory, bringing IBM products to customers across the Western United States and Western Canada.

I was number two in this venture, providing most of the leg work, with Howard providing the money and some of the connections. With the move into Lightyear Consulting, I was almost at my ultimate destination— being head of a small entrepreneurial venture. Working with Howard was the final step in my training to become my highest professional self. It was the last step in getting to truly know what I was excellent at.

Self-knowledge has paid off in numerous ways in my life. For example, it took me several years, but I finally learned that I didn't like working in a busy office environment. Currently, I live in Vancouver, even though the Prestigious Properties® office is in Canmore, Alberta. Moving to Vancouver was a personal choice based on the love we have for the area, and being here affords me the opportunity to work from home in a way I love, with more space and freedom.

The Prestigious Properties® office in Canmore isn't the busiest office in the world, but just being in an office with a bunch of people—speaking on the phone, chatting, typing, occasionally yelling, moving about, people visiting—is highly distracting to me. I love quiet. I love being able to set my own schedule, and I dislike being distracted.

The physical space between me and the Canmore office can be an inconvenience at times. For example, when there are a large number of legal documents that need to be signed, they all have to be couriered to me in Vancouver where I sign them all and send them back. However, the separation from the day-to-day distractions works for me, and I wouldn't change it for the world.

If I didn't know that about myself I might be plugging away in an office somewhere and not enjoying my business or my life nearly as much.

The rewards of knowing yourself are enormous. It's worth dedicating yourself to the effort of learning self-knowledge. It will change your life.

There is a large movement of people who advocate total life planning and envisioning of every step. As you know from Lesson 1 (Man Plans and God Laughs), I not only believe that it's not possible to plan every step of the way, but that it is actually not desirable.

Every day, people follow certain predetermined paths. They take the necessary education for a specific profession only to find out that in fact they're not good at it, or that they don't enjoy it (which is usually related).

How many mediocre lawyers are there out there? Many thousands, I would say. Self-knowledge can help with this. Knowing that you're a mediocre lawyer and that you actually love something else, you can then make an informed decision.

Quitting a law practice, however, and starting a new profession might mean taking a financial step backward. Many do not want to do this, so they remain a mediocre lawyer making $150,000 rather than an excellent base-level accountant (which they might love) making $60,000. They don't see that eventually they will make $350,000 and have fun in the job and make a positive impact on others.

If you know what you're good and bad at, you can at least make an informed decision about what you want to do. If you want to be a miserable lawyer instead of a happy accountant, that's your choice, but at least you know where your true strengths lie

LESSON 19:
KNOW YOURSELF – EVERYONE IS GOOD AT SOMETHING

When I first came to Canada, I was stunned to see other young adults in my late-twenties peer group studying at the University of Alberta in the MBA program who already owned their own house.

I was shocked because I'd lived my whole life as a renter and it had never occurred to me that all of those rental houses in Germany must have been owned by someone.

Finally I realized they were owned by someone, and all of the commercial buildings must have been owned by someone as well. The idea of real estate ownership was not even on my radar to me at the time, not even a blip. Given my current position as a full-time real estate investor, this story might be hard to believe, but it's true.

Looking back, I commend those young Canadians for owning homes at such a young age. Home ownership seems to be a rite of passage among young Canadians. Years later, after we returned from Germany, I was shocked at how easy it was to get my first mortgage when I bought my first home in Canada. Home ownership is also an important cornerstone of financial security in Canada.

However, my German upbringing brought me one advantage over the young Canadian homeowner. Since I had little to lose, I was more willing to take chances and try different things.

While I commend young Canadians who buy homes, I think that often these same people are getting financially stuck at a very young age. Home ownership can actually stifle creativity and the ability to change. Too many Canadians own too big a house, at too young an age, with too big a mortgage.

The ability to change directions is essential when you're trying to seek out what you're good, let alone excellent, at. Everyone is good at something, but if we're financially saddled at too young of an age, we might not have the freedom to try new things.

Freedom is essential when seeking out the best version of you, and youth is the best time to be experimental with life and to be seeking out one's talents. When you're 40 years old and you have children to support, it becomes more difficult to seek out your highest self. It's not impossible, but it is far more difficult.

Everyone is good at something, but the rewards are not always the same for being good at different things. Perhaps you're an excellent painter or poet, but in your own lifetime you'll likely never be hugely financially rewarded for your endeavors.

Does this mean you should choose to be an impoverished painter or a wealthier "something else"? I'm not sure, and you have to make that decision for yourself. But knowing that everyone is good at something can be incredibly powerful knowledge to have.

How do you know what you are poor, good or excellent at ?

Post this list on your fridge and give a blank copy to people who know you well— your friends, your spouse, your parents, and your co-workers. Ask them to add several activities on this five-item list, several per category:

Excellent at: _____

Good at: _____

Average at: _____

Poor at: _____

Terrible at: _____

By doing this exercise, you will realize that several things stand out, and your goal over the next few months (and even years) is to eliminate as much as possible on the average and below lists and keep focusing on the things you're good or excellent at. The list might change slightly as you age, but only marginally. For example, I was poor at English and history and almost failed a grade in high school, but today I am probably above average in English and at least average in (some) history.

Knowing that everyone is good at something might be the piece of information that gives you faith in the road you're travelling. Certainly my own life is a great testament to this. The winding path that I took to arrive where I am now might not look perfectly sensible. If I was going to end up as a full-time real estate investor, shouldn't I have started in real estate in my twenties?

I didn't start young in real estate, but I still ended up where I wanted to be, from a financial, physical, family and lifestyle point-of-view. What I did was continue to take the next step, and the next step, and the next step. I continued to move forward with my understanding of myself and of the knowledge I needed—day by day, week by week, month by month, and year by year. It was not perfect, but it was progress.

I can't say why some people don't or can't muster up the desire or courage to move forward. I can't say why some people settle. I'm suggesting that for a happier, more fulfilled, more successful, and wealthier life that you should continue on your path, and never give up learning about yourself, how you can benefit others and what you're good at.

Even if it seems like you're a long way from it right now, there is something out there for you, and even though it might not make sense right now, what you're doing right now is the right thing, and the next step that you will take is the right one. Developing the faith along with good judgment will be critical, but this one piece of information above all else might be the only thing you need to know when you're trying to figure it all out: everyone is good at something.

Please note, not everyone is equally good at something. Some people are massively talented, and others are not as naturally endowed, but this matters not. What matters is what you do with the talent you have. You and everyone else are good at something. You can do whatever you like with that information.

As I mentioned before, you may choose to be a mediocre lawyer instead of a happy accountant (or whatever your version of lawyer and accountant are). Whatever the case, I want you to know that everyone is good at something, including you. It might be the most important piece of information you ever have, and it might be a great source of faith and eventual progress for you

LESSON 20:
KNOW YOURSELF – PATIENCE

I t's ironic that I am writing on the virtue of patience, because I'm a notoriously impatient person. Like most entrepreneurs, I'm always looking to make things happen right now.

I don't like waiting for results and I rarely do. Sometimes it's worked out well for me, but other times a little more patience might have helped.

For example, when I sold the first ever multi-family building that I purchased back in 2000, I sold it for $50,000 per door in 2002 two and a half years later and made a $100,000 profit. At the time, I was very happy and thought I'd done extremely well. That same building just sold for $104,000 per door. If I had waited to sell, it would have meant an additional $750,000 in profit on the sale (plus cash flow and mortgage pay-down). This building alone could have made me a millionaire had I been a tad more patient. (This is why I now often use the tag line "My name is Thomas Beyer, only sometimes a seller." As I am a lot more patient seller these days, usually to my benefit, my partners benefit and those that co-invest with us.)

In that instance, perhaps patience would have been a valuable asset. However, I sold the property to generate more cash to purchase a larger deal, and to build a track record, so perhaps my impatience was a virtue because it allowed me to take the next step. It's an interesting question to which I'll never know the answer.

However, I do know that patience is a virtue when it comes to knowing yourself and what you're excellent, good, average, poor, and terrible at.

Don't be surprised if this process takes you a long time, perhaps many years, decades even. If you are by chance able to know yourself very well at a young age, then I commend you, and good luck to you. There's a good chance that you will flourish at that young age.

However, if you don't know yourself perfectly well yet, and you're already beyond your youth, don't despair. Have patience with yourself. Keep looking until you find what it is that makes you different and special.

Remembering that everyone is good at something is a good start.

Patience is great, but I want to caution you against settling. If you went into a certain field of study at a young age and you learn that you are not a good fit for it, there is no reason to stay in that field for much longer. That's not patience, it's self-torture.

The lesson is to have patience with yourself. It's not to settle on one thing. By all means, when you identify that change needs to take place, then jump on that change, and go out there and make a difference. Take proactive steps to learn what you're good and excellent at.

There are aptitude tests that can point you in the right direction. It's a good idea to take one in high school, and then another one in university, and then another one in your late twenties or early thirties. It's important to do them multiple times because you're a different person when you're 17 than when you're 22 or 30 or 45 or 58.

These kinds of tests can help you decipher roughly what box you fit into. Of course, no test can give you all the answers, and ultimately, you will have to make the difficult decisions, but patience is not the same as apathy. Take proactive steps to learn about yourself.

I don't want you to get the impression that sitting around doing nothing will help you find what you're good at. You have to do things, and you have to try things, otherwise you will never learn about yourself. That's not patience, it's just being lazy. But be patient with the process of you. Remember what Bill Gates said: "Most people overestimate what they can do in one year and underestimate what they can do in ten."

Be like Bill Gates and recognize that your life will look different from a decade perspective than it will from the micro scale of one year at a time.

Do this little exercise: Imagine yourself in 10 years. How old will you be? Where will you live? How old are your kids? Your parents? Some things are rather predictable, such as this: in 10 years you (and your parents, kids, spouse) will be 10 years older (or dead).

What kind of different life do you envision living then? If it's vastly different, ask yourself what steps you can do today to get there. For example, if you always wanted to run a marathon by age 40, and you're now 30, then you cannot just go out tomorrow and run one. If you try to do it that way, you will fail, but in a year or two you can, if you honestly train and follow a fairly regimented and proven system. (By the way: I do not want to run a marathon, as I am far too lazy for that and never had the ambition to finish a marathon. However, I did look up the regimented and proven system and decided it wasn't for me. I am more of a sprinter.)

Or perhaps you wanted to play the piano or the trumpet. Again, you cannot just wish that and start playing Chopin tomorrow. It takes years, but it is doable, and if you plan carefully and set time aside and a separate room in your house or condo and rearrange your working profession you can become a fair trumpet player or pianist.

People with extreme impatience are inclined to give up on themselves, which causes them to settle on something they're not excellent at. When you do that, you don't give yourself a chance at becoming the best version of yourself.

Be active, try things, take clues, follow hints, but be patient with the process, and if patience is an impossibility for you, then just know the pain is temporary, and that you are in fact moving to where you must go.

The most common cliché about patience is the famous maxim, "Rome wasn't built in a day." Or this one: "Even God took seven days to create the world." Or this one: "It takes 10,000 hours to be an expert at something." But we don't need to go back to the ancient times to draw inspiration.

Think of your own life. If you're over 20, then you probably remember a time when email wasn't widely used. If you're over 30, then you probably remember a time when computers weren't widely used. If you're over 40, then you probably remember a time when there were almost no computers. And if you're over 70, you probably remember a time when electric lights, flush toilets, automobiles, commercial flights and telephones were uncommon.

Getting to where we are now technologically took time, but now the new technologies are a common part of our daily lives. Taking things day by day, or even year by year, you might not have been able to see the technological changes happening.

Your life is the same. You're evolving even when you don't know it, and it's vital to your growth that you give yourself the credit, even when you don't think you're moving closer to knowing yourself (and therefore becoming the highest version of yourself).

Having patience with your path (or at the very least an understanding that you're growing along the painful path) is vital to your success because it will help you understand that you're getting closer and closer to knowing what you're excellent, good, average, poor, and terrible at. From self-knowledge, you must simply execute.

LESSON 21:
DELEGATION – DON'T CONFUSE GETTING THINGS DONE WITH DOING THEM YOURSELF

O f all the lessons in my life, this is probably the one with the most impact. So simple, yet so powerful.

Part of the awareness of knowing what you're excellent and good at is that you will also know what you're average, poor, and terrible at. This is a wonderful thing, because then you can know what you must delegate or eliminate and what you ought to focus on and not delegate.

Delegation is an absolutely key component of success in business and in life. I could write an entire book on this topic alone. You simply cannot do everything yourself. Even within a marriage, there will often be a partner who is more adept at one task than the other. Cooking is a great example. At best, I'm an average potato peeler or omelette maker, but my wife is an outstanding chef. She has all the technical expertise of putting together flavors and creating exquisite cuisine. I'm a simpleton when it comes to cooking. If I was forced to cook I could, but the dishes would be without much flair. I'm a subpar chef. However, I eat well because my wife is an excellent chef who loves to cook.

The whole story of Prestigious Properties® and getting to well over $80,000,000 worth of assets under management is largely a story of delegation. I've been delegating in that business since the beginning and have been deepening the level of delegation since the beginning.

At first delegation meant that I put systems in place for everything, and whatever step was in front of me was quickly sent off to whoever I was delegating that task to. I didn't have any of my own staff in the beginning, so it meant outside professionals.

When I received receipts, they went to the bookkeeper. If there was a maintenance issue, I sent my handyman. When I was buying a property, I sent it to my lawyer. When a property went vacant, my property manager took care of it instantly.

All of it was part of the system, and even from an early stage of the business, I had a high level of delegation in place. The only two things I didn't delegate initially were the area researched, finding and purchasing great properties, and raising money.

It's difficult to delegate those tasks when you're starting a real estate investment business, but even still, I can't help but think how I could have been more successful early on if I had been able to delegate those tasks.

Look, for example, at the time frame when I sold a small multi-family building and used the proceeds to purchase another building. At the time, I was in charge of raising all the money for purchases, and I did not want to wait to purchase another building, so I sold one, and the financial impact of selling too soon was significant.

I earned $100,000 in profit. Not bad, but not even close to what I could have received if I had held onto the property for an additional 10 years. If I had done that, I would have made an additional $750,000. Doing some simple math tells you that I could have earned $75,000 per year (tax preferred, by the way) from that one building alone just by holding onto it!

Again, I don't think there was any other way I could have done it. The truth is that there was not enough income in the company to afford paying for someone else to raise money. However, it's still a stunning example of how delegation would have been highly profitable. It certainly would have been more profitable than selling to release equity for the next purchase.

A few years later, however, I began to delegate even the money-raising task. Scotty Grubb came on board in late 2006/ early 2007, and since then, he's done the lion's share of raising money for Prestigious Properties®. Scotty is a natural-born salesman who loves to talk on the phone with people. He likes the challenge of breaking through the voicemail barrier, and he likes closing sales. Scotty is excellent at sales, whereas I'm merely proficient. Making the decision to delegate the task of raising money was a huge step in the right direction for our company.

I used to do all of the property acquisition as well, but now even that task is delegated. Mike Hammerlindl came on board around the same time as Scotty, and now I have more of a leadership/ enabler role. Bringing on an acquisition specialist has pushed the company even further.

I'm like the Elton John of Prestigious Properties®. Does that seem like a silly comparison? While I don't sing well, I do operate like Elton John in my delegation.

Elton John doesn't move his own piano. He doesn't sell the tickets. He doesn't book the concerts. He doesn't do his own hair. He doesn't do any other of the many thousands of tasks involved in putting on concerts and recording music.

Yet every time one of his songs is played on radio or television, he gets paid. He gets paid every time someone purchases a song or an album from iTunes as well. Elton John just sings and plays the piano; that's all he does.

I show up to important meetings and give important presentations. I speak to important investors, and I look at buildings after Mike has filtered them out. If a building is good, it will make it to my desk. Otherwise, I don't even see it. The truth is that Mike will know more about any building than I will, but I may be able to give him a perspective he hasn't thought of, or I can ask him a question that might make him see the bigger picture since creating the culture of the company and steering the ship is my job.

I don't do Scotty's or Mike's job for them, but I can facilitate for them and everyone else in the company.

Delegation allows you to accelerate your growth because it's a form of leverage, but also because it puts more qualified people into positions where you don't belong. I'm no accountant, I'm only a decent salesman, and I don't have the inclination to do building acquisitions full time anymore, so each of those positions is delegated within Prestigious Properties®.

I'm a B player in many aspects of our business, but have learned to surround myself with A players in each of the important aspects: fundraising, asset acquisition, property management, web presence, accounting, securities regulations and document management. This is the essence of delegation. Bring the A players on board and let them do what they do best. Actively support them and do what you can to make their jobs easier, and you will reap the rewards of delegation.

LESSON 22:
DELEGATION – YOU CAN'T (AND SHOULDN'T) DELEGATE EVERYTHING

D elegation is hugely important, but you simply can't and shouldn't delegate everything.

Let me give you an example. I feel like getting stronger, so why don't I hire someone, perhaps a strong young man to do 200 push-ups for me each morning? While the example may seem a bit ridiculous, you must admit that it's a good one: push-ups are a task that you cannot delegate.

Personal health and wellness are obvious example of activities you can't delegate, but there are many others that aren't so obvious.

Education is probably the biggest example of something you can't and shouldn't delegate. It's important to know what you should and should not learn about, but if it's essential to your success, then you must take the time and effort to learn about it from the bottom up.

When I purchased my first ever rental property in 1997, I chose a condo in a rental pool. What that means is that I purchased a property in a large building that was part of a system called a rental pool. All of the units in the building were owned by different owners, but they all participated in the rental pool. The whole building and all of the units were under professional management, and all of the rental income of each unit was pooled into one fund, as the name suggests.

Then the management fees, condo fees, and building expenses are taken from the big fund, and what's left over is then paid out to each individual owner based on the unit factor (percentage of what they own) of their condominium. The individual owner then has to pay their own mortgage after receiving the monthly check.

The biggest benefit of this arrangement to a new investor, or any investor, is that it does not matter if their individual unit is rented for the month, they still receive income. In addition, they don't have to worry about the difficult aspects of property management, especially filling vacancies. The profits are often less on a rental-pooled condo than on a single-family home, but the amount of effort required to pull it off is so much less than a single-family home that it is often a worthwhile set-up for the investor. It's as though you buy into a streamlined system that would otherwise take you months or years to build.

If you're a busy professional, property management is often more hassle than it's worth, especially when starting out. Buying into a rental-pooled condo is like doing a massive delegation from day one.

I chose a rental pool for my first, second, and third properties over potentially more profitable single-family homes, and it was the right choice for me at the time because I had a young family as well as a busy software consulting business that demanded my time and produced all the cash that I needed to live on and for my early investments.

The rental pools I bought were plug-and-play, and I could have completely left them alone for years without worry. In fact, the one I purchased in Edmonton is still in my portfolio (although it produces a tiny negative cash flow now because I refinanced it and converted a bunch of equity into cash a few years back). The fact that I still own it is testament to the uncomplicated manner of this type of investment. Why would I keep a single individual condo (when I specialize in large multi-family projects) unless it was dead easy to maintain?

Despite the fact that it was so simple to own the rental-pooled condos, I did have a larger idea of wanting to expand my holdings. I saw early that to receive larger benefit through real estate that it was going to be necessary to buy units in bulk and capitalize on economies of scale of price and management efficiencies. I had the idea (I wouldn't call it a plan) that I wanted to buy buildings at some time in the future.

I had a problem, though: I did not know how to manage a large building. On the positive side, I did know that I didn't know how to do it. When you know that you don't know something, you're in a lot less danger than when you don't know that you don't know it. And I knew that I didn't know how to manage a multi-family building, so I started taking steps toward it.

I joined the condo boards of the condominiums that I owned. By going to the regular meetings, and by making decisions on the boards, and most of all by seeing how the management of large buildings was done I received insight into how to manage a large building before the task would be mine.

You might be thinking, "I don't need to learn how to manage a building, I just need to hire a management company and let them do their thing." That's true to an extent. I knew when I eventually purchased my own multi-family buildings that I would hire professional management companies. As it turned out, I later decided to open my own property management firm, though I decided early on not to be the president but to hire someone for that role. This firm today has morphed into Fireside Property Group, managing more than 1600 rental units in British Columbia and Alberta, with another A player, Keith McMullen, at the helm.

Unless you know what to watch for and how to direct a professional management company, you will have a hard time fully delegating the task of management. I'm not saying you have to be the world's foremost expert, but this is one of those cases where it truly helps to know the business from the inside out in order to achieve positive results. In other words, you can't delegate learning about building management.

I needed to educate myself from the bottom up, and the best way to do that without taking a big risk was to join the condo board of my rental-pooled condos. This allowed me to see how the management was done. It required the gritty kind of education that I'd come to know and love, asking questions, sitting through long and tedious meetings, and reading boring documents where one paragraph or phrase would later turn out to be worth tens or hundreds of thousands of dollars in price reductions or negotiating power. It was valuable and powerful knowledge that could not have been delegated.

It was an advanced property management class but better than any theory class. I had a financial stake in it, and I had a practical interest in learning all there was to know about it.

I could not delegate that kind of learning to anyone else; it was well worth the time I spent at it.

I'm a huge believer in delegation. You must delegate to be successful in business, but on this occasion, I did not delegate so that I would know how to delegate later when I owned my own buildings.

LESSON 23:
DELEGATION – KNOWING WHAT YOU
DON'T KNOW, AND "THERE'S NO
HYPHEN IN 'MICRO-MANAGE'!"

There's a great cartoon that depicts a manager standing over the shoulder of one of his staff members and pointing at the computer screen as he screams, "There's no hyphen in 'micromanage'!"

Micromanaging and not knowing what you don't know are diseases that can seriously inhibit your success. People often get confused by their own success and think because they were successful in another business or even sector of the same business that they must be extremely brilliant and therefore cannot fail at a new endeavor.

I see this all the time with doctors, dentists, lawyers and other assorted professionals who want to invest.

They have gone through long and rigorous educational programs to arrive at their high social position, and society, or their colleagues, or their spouses, or their bank account, tells them that they're brilliant to be in the fields they're in.

They then falsely believe they will also make brilliant investors based on this. They probably could if they'd follow the proper steps and apply the same kind of rigor. But since many of them are far too busy, and some far too arrogant, from their own past successes, or just too tired in the evening to do the proper due diligence work, they frequently get slaughtered as investors.

Entrepreneurs are susceptible to the same disease, perhaps even from within their own niche, when they make a slight shift and don't account for the different knowledge and skills necessary.

When Prestigious Properties® made the move from our core markets in Alberta to some of the other places we went, we were guilty of this very problem.

Whether it was micromanaging, or just not knowing, we made a mistake in Dallas, Texas, that has cost us hundreds of thousands of dollars because we negotiated a poor mortgage.

You see, we were great at doing due diligence on buildings, and our system of diligence actually filtered out some dogs in the Dallas market. We ended up with a great property, and this great building has saved us in our Dallas venture and is the reason we're profitable there.

However, we made a mistake with the mortgage that almost erased the wonderful advantage that the building gave us. We did not properly understand the mortgage market in the United States, we researched it poorly and we ended up stuck in a mortgage that was not right for us.

The problem was that we did not know what we did not know, and rather than delegate to a trusted professional to help us, we simply pushed through with the deal and thus ended up with that bad mortgage. We were specialists in the Canadian market, but not the U.S. market, or the U.S. mortgage market.

It's true that you can't really delegate things you don't know exist, but you can employ professional third parties to advise you. Their job is to identify blind spots due to your lack of expertise and notify you of them.

In the case of the Dallas purchase, we could have sought out a professional real estate entrepreneur, or a second mortgage broker, or another experienced U.S. investor, and paid him or her a small sum to analyze the entire deal. A real estate lawyer, commercial real estate agent, an independent commercial real estate broker, or a business consultant all could have worked as long as they had a deep knowledge of all aspects of commercial real estate transactions, and had we specifically asked them to analyze every aspect of our deal and our position. Our Dallas deal would have been significantly more profitable if we had done this.

In business, consultants are a viable avenue to find out what you don't know. It takes a level of humility to hire one, though. At the time of the Dallas purchase, we might have been a little bit overconfident, given our own track record of success in Alberta.

We had forgotten that we were moving into a different market with different considerations. We knew that we didn't know the neighborhood or the economics of the region, so we paid careful attention to those aspects and did very well with our diligence. However, we did not know that we didn't know about the US mortgage market, and we got slaughtered there.

In addition, the only person who was advising us on the matter was a mortgage broker who had a vested interest in us getting a certain mortgage. He did not notify us of better options. It was a terribly short-sighted business move on his part to simply treat us as a single transaction rather than do his best to take good care of us, but that was his decision and we made the mistake of trusting his advice wholly.

Had we thought to delegate the analysis of the deal as a whole to a true and independent professional, we potentially would have saved hundreds of thousands of dollars over the course of holding this property.

It's probably one of the most striking and painful cases of non-delegation coming back to haunt me that I've ever had, but the root problem was not knowing what we didn't know and therefore not hiring someone to eliminate that problem.

This issue is not such a big problem if you're operating in a realm where you're one of the preeminent experts, such as Prestigious Properties® is in the Alberta real estate market, but when you make the move to another realm, not knowing can be a big issue.

Just like a successful doctor making the move from the medical realm into investing, you can be fooled by your own success and not take the time to find out what you don't know.

Whenever making a change into something new, it's best to delegate the task of helping you understand what you don't know to an independent professional. Lose the arrogance and be open to the fact that you just might not know. If you do this you will be far ahead.

(Of note here is: had we actually obtained a one-year mortgage in fall 2007 we would likely have lost the asset, since the credit market froze completely for several months following the collapse of Lehman Brothers in September 2008. Of course we did not know that then. Today we still own the asset with a $100,000 or so annual cash flow and far higher value. See also Lesson 1 of this book.)

LESSON 24:
DELEGATION – DON'T DELEGATE YOUR STRENGTHS, WORK ON THEM

Delegation is a wonderful thing. The story of Prestigious Properties® is really a story of delegation and the successes of delegation (and, in some cases, the failure of delegation).

However you can't (and shouldn't) delegate everything. To be successful in some ventures, you first have to learn how to do the thing yourself. This is the same concept that I employed (whether fully aware of it or not) when I learned how to manage large buildings long before I could ever delegate the management of large buildings.

You also should never delegate what you're excellent at. It simply doesn't make sense, and it will take away a whole lot of the enjoyment of life if you let others do what you could do better.

Each person has different talents, and if you spend your time working on weaknesses you'll end up with a bunch of strong weaknesses. There is a big difference between a strength and a strong weakness. It can take time and awareness to learn what your strengths are.

Imagine looking out over a river valley. When you look down upon it, you can see geological formations and different kinds of soil and rocks. You see several different kinds of trees and grass. You might see several different animal species. You see water flowing along. You see a bridge crossing the river, and you see traffic driving across that bridge.

Depending upon who looks out over that valley, each of those aspects and probably many others will be highlighted. The geologist will focus upon the topography and the various rock formations. The botanist will see the plant species. The zoologist will focus upon the animals. The engineer will see the bridge. The canoeist will see the gently flowing river, and the city planner will see the traffic moving across the bridge and how it relates to the overall flow of traffic within 40 kilometres.

You would not say that any one of these different people has a better understanding of the valley, but they do each have a different view of the same valley.

People have different talents and therefore see the world differently. You would never counsel the botanist to go and learn everything about bridge construction or the zoologist to study traffic patterns in an attempt to be a better city planner.

Changing the course of their specialized knowledge simply does not make sense for the specialist. It would be foolhardy and wasteful for them to go out and expend energy just to strengthen their weaknesses. On the other hand, it makes great sense for these people to continue to practice their own specialities and deepen them.

Furthermore, it would not make sense for these specialists to seek out others to delegate the job of their specialty.

Once you know what your strengths are, by all means spend your time there, as much time as possible. Delegating is counterproductive when working on your strengths.

I took a while, but I did find my sweet spot in terms of professional strengths. While I started out from my early days of education as a geeky programmer, I realized that I wanted a bigger picture role soon thereafter. After many iterations, I found myself at my best when interfacing between clients and production teams.

The specialization of customer/technical team interface is really quite unique if you think about it. It's not a position they tell you about when you're studying to be a programmer. It took me effort to get there.

But in my subsequent positions (which were suited to me), I found that I've been doing a role similar to this. In Prestigious Properties® I often joke that my main role is "chief bottleneck remover." I make stuck things get unstuck.

Another way to say it is that I'm an excellent enabler. In fact, I'm delegator-in-chief. Enabling is advanced delegation. To delegate effectively, you first need to put the right people in place and then give them everything they need to get the job done and then to connect them to others they might not be aware of.

With IBM, in my sweet spot doing technical marketing (client/ technical team interface), I did not seek to delegate any further from the role that I had undertaken and where I actually found a great deal of joy. Once there, I focused in on actually doing the job and not delegating further.

The same pattern repeated in Lightyear Consulting where my role was often similar to the technical marketing role I had with IBM. Again with Prestigious Properties® as the chief bottleneck remover/enabler/head delegator, I relished the role and continue to excel in it, although my company may have outgrown me somewhat.

Nowadays Prestigious Properties® is on the edge of being a small to medium-sized entrepreneurial venture and it could go public, or at least go far bigger, far more corporate. I'm a little bit ambivalent about that prospect because I don't believe my skills would be best suited for either of those kinds of positions.

I would not be able to continue what I do best, and I would be forced to delegate some of those things that I'm excellent at.

Getting to an awareness of yourself can be a long and hard-fought battle. When you arrive there, please do not throw away the joy and efficiency you capture by working within your greatest strengths.

Don't delegate away your strengths, and you will find that life and business becomes more joyful, and you will be more effective. But in order to get to a powerful position of being able to choose to do what you're excellent at, you first need to identify those things you're excellent at and be aware of them. Take the time to get to know yourself better and better.

LESSON 25:
DELEGATION – YOU CAN'T DELEGATE
RELATIONSHIP BUILDING

There is one more realm where delegating is not recommended. You cannot delegate relationship building. In fact, I would question whether you can even leverage relationship building.

You can leverage it in a way; for example, you can build more relationships by joining clubs, groups and associations. That's growth by breadth, but a more important kind of growth is growth by depth, and to do that, you must spend the time. Growing an email list of contacts is another great way to grow by breadth, but again, I don't think any amount of social media or Internet wizardry can help deepen relationships.

You can't leverage relationship depth, nor can you delegate it. If you delegate it, the relationships will be built between the people that you have tasked with building relationship and the other party.

In business we do this all the time. Scotty Grubb is Prestigious Properties' main salesperson, and in a way I am delegating him to develop relationships on behalf of our company with investors, but this is not the same as building relationships that necessitate my participation.

The best example is parenting. You can't delegate parenting and developing relationships with your kids. You must spend the time with them, putting in daily effort to build a strong relationship.

The whole notion of "quality time" is actually bunk when it comes to kids. They don't need quality moments with their parents; they need quantity time with their parents. In some circumstances, the difference between quality and quantity is a valuable distinction to make, but when it comes to parenting, it's not a valuable distinction. More time = quality time. That's how you build a relationship with your kids.

What if I had charged someone else with the task of putting my kids to bed when they were young? What if I had hired someone to give them hugs when they scraped their knees? The result is obvious. My kids would have a great relationship with someone else rather than with me.

My kids would have learned to trust someone else with their feelings and their sacred moments. My kids would have grown up with a great relationship with their minders, but would have thought of me as something different than a parent.

Please note: I'm not criticizing people for hiring nannies or maids. Many families are very busy, and even though my family's choice was to have my wife be a full-time mother in our house, some families don't make that choice. Nannies and maids can take care of much of the cleaning and cooking, but the strictly parental tasks such as comforting and teaching children has to come from the parents. I will criticize anyone who thinks that it's a good idea to delegate the task of raising children, especially for the sake of a bigger house or intense dual careers.

Recently, a young friend of mine told me a story about how his kindergarten-aged son had fallen and smashed his head at school. This friend was able to go down to the child's school and collect him. He then took him home and cared for him for the day. This is a wonderful example. What if he had hired someone to pick up his son and care for him for the day? Again, the child would start to develop a trust relationship with the helper rather than the father. Relationship building can't be delegated.

The same rule applies to business, but as mentioned, it's not as hard and fast as with personal relationships. Like I said before, Scotty Grubb does most of the money raising for Prestigious Properties® (now through a third party called an Exempt Market Dealer, or EMD, due to legislative changes). This has been a very successful delegation on my part, and a big part of his job is to develop relationships with our investors.

However, there are times when I, as the big cheese, still need to speak with investors. This happens either face to face, on the phone, or when giving a presentation. These interactions can't be delegated.

Recently, Scotty's hard work garnered the interest of a large institutional investor based in Toronto. Scotty did his job admirably in getting us in touch with this investment group. Indeed, he built a relationship on behalf of Prestigious Properties®, but the time came to deepen the relationship and our potential large investor wanted some face time with me, so I went down to Toronto to make a presentation and see if there was any possibility of a good fit between their firm and ours.

This is only natural. If you want to know about a business, especially if you might be investing big money with them, you will want to know more about the company, and a big part of that is knowing and understanding their leadership.

It was a case where I could only delegate relationship building to a certain extent. There came the time when I needed to be there personally to deepen the relationship.

With personal relationships, the difference between building relationships by breadth vs. depth is even more pronounced, but even in business relationships the same message holds true. You can't delegate relationship building!

LESSON 26:
DELEGATION – EMPLOYER/EMPLOYEE RELATIONSHIPS MUST BE WIN/WIN

The term "win/win" was made famous by Steven Covey, and at first glance, it's such an obvious principle to follow in all relationships. It simply means that both parties benefit from a relationship or transaction.

The problem is that many (if not most) people don't know how to do win/win properly. It's a lot harder to do than it seems at first glance.

In the relationships we have with our onsite managers at Prestigious Properties® we strive to develop a culture of win/win relationships. Our business demands that our onsite managers be top-level performers in the industry. It's absolutely essential to a smoothly running real estate investment business.

We actually pay our onsite managers very well, and that's a big part of the win/win arrangement. They feel valuable because they are valuable and because we pay them like they're valuable. In an industry where it's not uncommon for an onsite manager to earn $25,000 to $35,000 or less per year, we are paying our onsite managers as much as $40,000 to $60,000 per year. And we're happy to pay them that much—but believe me, we demand that they perform too. Our buildings are very well managed; it's what has allowed our business to flourish. On the pay scale, the relationship between company and onsite managers has to be win/win. We win with great management, and they win with better pay.

But it takes more than money to make the relationship as a whole win/win. We also give them bonuses such as spa packages, gift baskets, vacations and cash. A bonus is different than pay. It's a way of saying thank you. The excellent pay is a way of saying "You're worth it," but the bonuses aren't strictly necessary because we already pay them well.

When our excellent onsite managers receive a nice little bonus, it's our way of saying "thank you." Feeling appreciated is a human need that our onsite managers feel. They're human, after all, something a lot of apartment building owners forget. Sadly, the bigger travesty of relationships between owner and onsite manager is not the lack of pay that's almost endemic to the job, it's the demeaning way in which the "big boss" often treats the onsite managers.

Above all, we strive to treat our onsite managers with dignity and respect, and giving them a nice bonus is one way to do this. By treating our onsite managers with dignity and respect, and by saying thank you, we expect loyalty and diligence in return. We believe that through deep trust, our bottom line results improve.

Dignity and respect are important components of creating a win/win relationship with our onsite managers.

But perhaps the most important way in which we create a win/win relationship with our onsite managers is through the education that we give them. When we're first beginning the relationship, we'll sit down with the manager and ask them what they think their job is. They often say something like, "Cut the grass, vacuum the hallways, etc." And then we'll say, "Yes, that's part of it, but your top line job is filling vacancies with quality tenants, and secondly, collecting rent checks from existing tenants."

So we instill in them a sense that the revenue is the most important thing in managing an apartment building. By educating them on salesmanship, and teaching them the system of bringing in leads, when an initial phone call comes in, they know that the first job is to sell the caller on making a visit to the building. We teach them to build a rapport with the caller from the start, get their name, ask where they work, and pre-qualify them. We teach them to ask the right questions. Should the prospect be allowed to live here?

We teach them to be professional sales and marketing people. The gift for them is to see the power of applying the training in their everyday job. Rather than their work being a difficult struggle, it's a joyful creation.

Our property managers feel empowered by their education, and of course we end up with lower vacancies, more rent checks collected monthly, and a stronger business. Providing education is a big win/win. It's fantastic to see our onsite managers feeling so empowered in their jobs, and on our side, there's no way we'd have experienced the success we have without the impeccable management they provide: it's the number one component of successful real estate investing. All the acquisition strategies and all the money-raising abilities are useless unless you have impeccable property management.

One of the most important aspects of creating win/win relationships with employees happens before the employee is hired. Just as knowing oneself is a hugely important component of life success, business success, happiness, and fulfillment, it's equally important to know which kind of person should do which kind of job. We carefully select our onsite managers, searching only for those who are actually cut out for the job in the first place.

It's not an accident that many of our onsite managers are mothers of grown-up children. It's not that we specifically look for someone in that specific life circumstance, but it does happen to be a fact that women who've already raised children are uniquely qualified for the job of managing a large apartment building. In a sense, each tenant is like a child. That is not a statement on the immaturity of tenants, it's simply a useful comparison.

We ask our onsite managers to treat the tenants with respect and love. Just as we treat our onsite manages with respect and dignity, we ask them in turn to treat the tenants in the same way. We ask them to care about the tenants somewhat like they would care about a child.

On the other hand, living in the close confines of an apartment building necessitates a certain adherence to the rules, so we need an onsite manager who will be able to uphold the rules, be stern with the tenants who break the rules, and at times do what must be done for the good of the whole and evict the odd unruly, drug-dealing and/or non-paying tenant. We call this principle "tough love."

We choose onsite managers who can care about the tenants, treat them with respect, but at the same time be in charge of the building. By choosing the right person to begin with, we're going a long way toward having a win/win relationship in place with our onsite managers from the start.

Win/win relationships are an essential component of successful delegation.

LESSON 27:
POSITIVE FEEDBACK – REACH OUT TO
EMPOWER YOURSELF USING MENTORS

One thing I never did when I worked for IBM was to reach out to a mentor from within the company. I don't exactly know why I didn't, because I'm a big believer in the power of mentoring. Perhaps I was more self-assured and arrogant when I was of that age.

In hindsight, not having a mentor might have been a good thing, because if I had had a mentor, I might still be with IBM, moving up the ladder. Perhaps I would have been influenced by a good mentor into seeing the value of staying with the mother ship.

That is not what happened, though. Instead of a mentor, I took a career direction course that told me I belonged in a small entre-preneurial venture (something I already knew deep down inside) and ended up leaving the mother ship for my own ship.

But while I was with IBM, and later with Lightyear Consult-ing, I spent a lot of time in the company of more senior business people. Over those years, this time adds up to a lot of business lunches, meetings and customer presentations. There are many words spoken, jokes cracked and questions asked over the years in business. I saw a theme where the senior people had a great deal of wisdom. By listening to them and asking questions I found I could take what I learned and apply it in my own life, with excellent results.

I learned over the years that the value of that kind of relation-ship lies in the fact that these people are not attached to the out-come of what I'm trying to achieve.

In a sense, they were detached from what I was going through, so it enabled them to speak directly to me. There was no need for them to sugar coat anything, they just told me what they thought based on their experience. Many people within the day-to-day run of life will not speak in this way. Your spouse will rarely tell you that you could stand to lose some weight. Your kids won't often tell you that you're overbearing, and your colleagues won't usually tell you what you're lacking professionally.

Your boss may tell you what he or she needs done, but even that is often driven by the internal pressure that they are feeling to meet a deadline or complete a project.

An independent mentor is not constrained by any of the same issues that a colleague, boss or business partner is.

When Prestigious Properties® was growing, I engaged the help of an outside consultant/mentor to help structure the company. He engaged the business and learned all about us from the inside. When he told me that one member of our executive was not a good fit, I thought he was crazy.

When that same member quit a few months later because he felt the company wasn't a good fit for his goals, I started thinking the consultant we'd hired was onto something.

In fact, he saw through an issue that I did not see, even though it was right under my nose the whole time. I was simply too close to the issue, and whether I wanted to or not, I'd become attached to the team member.

I wanted him to be someone that he wasn't, and I wanted there to be a fit between him and Prestigious Properties® even though there wasn't. I like people and want them to succeed, and once they're inside my world, I don't easily want to send them out. I couldn't see that this team member wasn't a good fit because I was too close to the situation.

It's like watching television. When you sit the right distance away from the screen, it's easy to see and comprehend everything that's going on. However, if you sit two inches from the screen, you can't see what's going on. You're just too close to see the bigger picture. The same issue was at play with the ill-fitting team member. Since that, I've been more of a believer in the power of an outside mentor, and I've engaged a mentor for the past 10 years.

Mentors will not always be exactly right in their assessment of your situation, but they will help you see something new, a way in which you couldn't see by yourself or that people attached to the outcome might be.

Most importantly, a mentor may be able to give you something that you'd otherwise overlook. Having a paid mentor is like systemizing the positive feedback loop that is so important to build on success. Just as someone can be too close to a situation to see their own problems clearly, we can also be too close to our life situation to see how we're growing, progressing and improving. A mentor can show you how far you've come.

Being resilient against the vague feeling of stagnancy or failure is a large component to overall success, and one of the greatest ways to build resiliency is to consciously surround yourself with people who will see the progress you're making and share it with you. We tend to focus on weaknesses, problems and difficulties.

However, we tend to not give ourselves credit where it is due. If you're working hard on yourself, your business or your relationships, you will undoubtedly be growing.

Whether or not you see the growth is unknown, but seeing it is essential! It will drive you to continue building upon what you've already started. Sometimes all it might take is a mentor to point out what the stepped S-curve of growth looks like. Then you will be able to identify where you are on the curve. This can give you a perspective and spur the next stage of growth.

A mentor's perspective is valuable for pointing out both what's working and what isn't

LESSON 28:
MENTORING – THE VALUE OF
INFORMAL MENTORS

We live lives, we don't just live businesses, and that's why informal mentors from different walks of life can lift you up in ways unimaginable.

Formal mentors and consultants are great. They will be able to help you analyze your business in a way that perhaps you could never do by yourself. I highly recommend using them.

Informal mentors may help you synthesize. They will help you see the bigger picture and to put your various pursuits and beliefs inside a larger context.

Analysis is highly effective, but to develop a perspective and a sense of well-being in life, it is essential that you spend a great deal of your efforts on synthesis.

Analysis is the taking apart of large and complex things and looking at all the small pieces as individual parts. Synthesis is taking all the disparate pieces and seeing how they all fit together. If I spent all my time inside my business and never engaged the other components of myself, I wouldn't be a very interesting or well-rounded person.

I'm not just a businessman, I'm a whole person. I believe in family, in God, and in Jesus Christ. I have beliefs beyond just improving my own bottom line. I believe that we should all do our very best to leave the world a better place than how we found it, and I believe in providence. I believe in having fun and in having strong and fulfilling relationships.

Engaging informal life mentors helps to bring together (synthesize) these diverse aspects of life.

For example, I have a good friend named Paul. He was a pastor and also the Christian coach for the Calgary Stampeders. He's not a business minded individual, and therefore I usually don't discuss business specifics with him. Yet he is and has been a very strong mentor to me over the past several years.

He and I don't talk about ROIs and profit centers, but we do discuss the role of faith in our daily lives and communion with God. He helps me see the value in what I do and he helps me to develop connections between my work and my faith.

I recently undertook a political role with the University of British Columbia Residents Association. The residents who live on the UBC campus elect five directors to represent them on council along with various other stakeholders who live, work and study on the UBC campus.

I'm a complete newbie when it comes to political matters. I've been reading and commenting on politics for many years, but to actually be a part of the process is new to me. On the council, I have a friend who is my political mentor of sorts. Speaking with him on a regular basis affords me a completely different perspective on my political views, and the way my political views mesh with my life and business.

I'm a businessman. When there is a strong business environment, I believe it benefits all Canadians, so I'm often outspoken on political issues that affect business.

On the UBC council, I find myself being in the minority in many of my views. Many of the people who work on the council alongside me place business as a low priority, and my views have often clashed with theirs. That's not such a bad thing; people are obviously entitled to their views and their opinions. What I wasn't aware of before joining the council is just how we affect others by making our opinions known.

My political mentor is a man who once worked for the UN. He comes from the Philippines originally and has lived a much different life than I have. Normally, I would not really grasp his world, but because I respect him and see him as an informal mentor, he has helped me see how my words and opinions affect others. I'm still processing what this new realization means to me, but I simply was not aware of that impact before. As a result, I would speak loosely about my political opinions, just stating them without too much thought for what others might think.

How will I move forward with this understanding? I'm not totally sure, but for certain, I'm learning that political process and consensus building is unique and important. Running a small or medium-sized entrepreneurial business (especially with an uneven number of directors, less than three) is not the same as running a political body with many committees and consensus building ad nauseum. My mentor has helped me see that.

The value of informal mentors is derived from the simple fact that everyone we come into contact with on any given day is a potential teacher. Everyone we encounter can teach us some-thing! Imagine that! But there are many things that I'm just not that interested in, so I filter them out immediately. My wife loves fashion, but I do not care about it. As a result, I don't learn from her or others on fashion, and I remain a fashion dunce.

I'm not suggesting that you should have a mentor for each and every aspect of life, but it doesn't hurt to have an informal men-tor in each area that is important to you.

Think about it right now. What areas of your life do you have an interest in changing? What areas of your life do you have a gen-uine interest in? Do you care about fitness, spirituality, healthy eating, wealth, investment or travel? There's probably someone in your life who would make a good informal mentor. Go ahead, ask them some questions. You might be surprised at the response you will get from them and the value they can impart to your life.

LESSON 29:
LIVE BELOW YOUR MEANS –
YOUR CAR IS A MONEY PIT

I grew up in Europe where the culture is vastly different than here in Canada. It's a mixed blessing. When I put my life in perspective and think of the lessons and cultural lessons I took from my upbringing in Europe, there are aspects of it that I almost had to overcome in order to find the kind of success that I have in my life.

There are other aspects of my old-world culture that I took with me that I believe have served me very well and the youth of Canada would be wise to learn from Europeans.

One such example is the automobile culture of Europe. Cer-tainly there are a lot of cars in Europe and Europeans love cars as much as people anywhere in the world do. But many people in Europe live without a car. Having or not having a car is really not that big a deal in much of Europe. Growing up in Germany where I did, there was never any sense that having a car is an important thing. For many people who do have cars, they think of it as an object of utility rather than an object of status.

In addition, the public transportation system in Europe is better. There are plenty of options for traveling around cities and long distance by bus and train. Due to the lack of parking spaces in Europe, it's often easier to take transit!

The car culture of North America is much different. In many towns and cities, it's simply impractical to not have a car. You rarely see people walking in some North American cities, and many places the transit systems are insufficient. When it takes three or four times as long to get somewhere by bus as it does by car, then it truly makes no sense to not have a car.

In the biggest Canadian cities of Toronto, Montreal and Vancouver, it's more practical to rely on transit, but probably not quite as practical as in Europe.

I see the car culture of North America as an impediment to many North Americans, especially young people because it is wise, if at all possible, to live without a car when you're in a certain position in life. Or, if it's not possible to live without one (as in many Canadian locations), then it's best to limit oneself to a cheaper, usually older and less sexy car.

Here's why: cars are the single biggest money pit we are exposed to. Most people don't know the true cost of a car. Do you care to take a guess just how much a car costs? It's between $600 and $1,000 per month.

HERE'S A LIST OF MONTHLY COSTS TO CAR OWNERSHIP:

Payment/Lease Payment: $300+

Maintenance: $50 (new car)

Gas: $100-$500

Parking: $50

Tickets: $10

Depreciation: $200

Insurance: $100

For many people, it takes one week out of every work month just to pay for their car! It's an incredible drain on finances, one that only promises further expense down the road. Unlike a house, from which you can reasonably expect to make money eventually, a car just costs you more and more money with each passing day, week, month and year. Repairs pile up, or if you get a new car (usually a nicer car) then your payment will grow. You will never recover your costs on a car.

Please note: I'm not anti-car. I like cars, and now finally after many years of driving junky cars, my wife and I own a nice little convertible BMW, but we're at the phase of life where we can afford it.

When our children were young, we drove old, often ugly, cars for years.

The best example was when we moved to Munich from Burnaby, British Columbia. It was not too long after the reunification of Germany, and at the time there was a shortage of reliable cars available. With the reunification there was suddenly a massive untapped demand from our East German brothers and sisters.

The price of a normal car in Germany at the time skyrocketed. It was simply outrageous how much a car cost then, and it was difficult to find one even if you did have the money.

When we arrived there from Burnaby, we most definitely did not have a lot of money, so we were left looking for an affordable option. We eventually found an old beater. The previous owner had massive speakers in the back (which he took out when he sold it to us) and the seatbelts were some kind of suspenders. No matter, we covered the big holes left when the speakers were taken out with a carpet, and we found some seatbelts to replace the missing ones.

It's important to note that we survived with our beater of a car for the two years we lived in Munich. We were cost conscious and when we returned to Canada two and a half years later we had some money saved up to purchase a home. It was the first home we bought, and even though we lost money on our original purchase, we did make $50,000 on our second home (in Calgary) and over $600,000 on our third home (in Canmore). That's right, our home appreciated over $600,000 during the 10 years we lived in Canmore. One could argue that in a roundabout way the cheap car we drove (and therefore the money we saved) ultimately led us to earn well over half a million dollars a little over a decade later.

When you're at that formative phase of wealth building, the true cost of an expensive car can be immense. You don't really know what the money you save by either a) living without a car, or b) driving a cheap car will do for you if you were to invest it in something else such as a home or rental property.

Whenever possible, it's best to live without a car, or to save money by owning a used car that's really good on gas.

LESSON 30:
LIVE BELOW YOUR MEANS – A PENNY SAVED IS TWO PENNIES EARNED

You're probably familiar with the old saying "A penny saved is a penny earned." Well, in fact, it's better than that: a penny saved is actually two pennies earned.

You might be wondering how one penny saved could be worth two pennies earned. The answer lies in life's largest expense— tax. We pay more tax than we're typically aware of in life, and if you aren't completely aware of how much you're spending on tax then you need to give it careful consideration.

In any society, you will pay an exorbitant amount of tax in relation to what you earn. These taxes are charged in two major areas. The first is taxes on employment income. If you earn $50,000 per year, you will likely pay about $15,000 in taxes on that. And the higher your income is, the higher the percentage you pay, usually approach or exceeding 50 percent in most industrialized nations. Pretty much everyone is aware of income tax, or should be.

However, most people don't think about the amount they spend on taxes on their purchases. In Europe, the combination of sales taxes is typically in the range of 20 percent. In most of Canada and the United States, you will spend a minimum of 10 percent on point-of-purchase taxes, with many jurisdictions being significantly higher than that. The notable exception is Alberta where the lucky residents only pay the federally mandated 5 percent GST.

If you purchase a computer, for example, and you spend $2,000 on that computer (expensive computer, I know), you actually have to earn closer to $3,000 or more to pay for it.

Here's why: you pay for everything you buy with after tax money. This means that to pay for the original $2,000 price tag, you've already had to earn significantly more than $2,000. If you're in the lower tax bracket, and the government takes "only" 30 percent of your income, then you would have had to earn just under $2,900 before tax to buy the base item. Except the item will then be taxed an additional amount, let's say 10 percent. So rather than paying $2,000 for the item, you're now paying an additional $200 for a total of $2,200.

Effectively, you've paid $1,100 in taxes in order to buy one item for $2,000, and you had to earn over $3,000 to be able to do it. If you work for $30 per hour, it means you would have had to work for over 100 hours in order to pay for the item, rather than the approximately 67 hours that you originally thought.

Not spending money on this computer would have meant not only saving a bunch of money, it would have also meant saving a bunch of your time. Buying it also means that you never saved that money you needed to in order to invest, which is something you must do in order to create true wealth.

Am I saying that you should live life as a miser? No, but what

I am suggesting is that you should develop a resilience to over-spending. We undoubtedly live in a time of chronic overconsumption. The prevailing attitude is one of entitlement.

Many people do not know what it's like to go without, and at the same time, they have unprecedented access to credit. The topic of credit and debt is a whole different discussion, but on the topic of living below your means and therefore saving money, it's an absolutely essential skill to step off the ladder from "paycheck to paycheck" into wealth creation and ultimately generational wealth.

This is true for most people. Some will be lucky and therefore able to skip this difficult process, but for most it's essential to learn early how to save more than you earn.

Saving is not a be-all-end-all. You will also have to learn how to invest the money you save wisely, but being able to save more than you spend is the essential first step to wealth creation. The biggest reason for this is that taxes eat away at everything you earn and get piled on top of your consumption as well.

Saving money is a way to make more without having to make more, because you will pay less tax, and on top of that, you will be spending less on the actual stuff.

I was raised in a postwar German rental apartment. Austerity was part of life. Many people didn't have the need for a lot of expensive stuff and expensive trips. My family was like so many others at the time in that we didn't overspend. I shared a bedroom with my brother for most of my upbringing.

Even my own kids grew up each with their own bedrooms and en suite bathrooms. They didn't know the kind of austerity that I experienced, and I believe many thousands of young North Americans shared a similar experience to my kids.

They've never known tough times, and if they're not aware of this fact and vigilant about their spending, it is easy to get caught in the trap of overspending. When you're young and you move out of Mom and Dad's home, suddenly you have to pay for all of those small luxuries you became accustomed to. It can be a shocking experience that many don't easily recover from.

When you experience austerity, you understand that in fact, all of the stuff isn't so important. The best things in life can't be bought, and you can live with a lot less than you thought.

At the very least, I think it's valuable to travel to places that do not have all the economic advantages that you are accustomed to in life. It will provide you with a perspective that will probably be able to help you live below your means. My son David did this in 2011 when he spent a few weeks in Ethiopia—it was a truly eye-opening experience for him.

"A penny saved is two pennies earned" is a powerful way of life. Learn that lesson, and learn why it's a powerful thing. Living below your means will serve you well, especially in the formative years of wealth creation.

LESSON 31:
LIVE BELOW YOUR MEANS – EXCEPT WHEN IT COMES TO YOUR HOUSE

Y ou might be surprised that I would suggest you live to your highest means when it comes to your house. For every rule there is an exception.

The reason for this exception is simple. A house is usually an appreciating asset, and it's the best tax-free savings account you will ever keep. If you maximize your buying potential on a house, you will profit from long-term appreciation more than if you had purchased a cheaper house. The math is simple. Imagine two scenarios:

SCENARIO 1

Purchase value: $300,000

25-year appreciation: 80%

After appreciation value: $540,000

Total appreciation: $240,000

Money down: 20% or $60,000

Monthly mortgage payment: roughly $1,280 (using a 4% mortgage with a 25-year amortization)

SCENARIO 2

Purchase value: $400,000

25-year appreciation: 80%

After appreciation value: $720,000

Total appreciation: $320,000

Money down: 20% or $80,000

Monthly mortgage payment: roughly $1,700 (using a 4% mortgage with a 25-year amortization)

In the first scenario, the buyers thought they'd live below their means and they earned $240,000 worth of appreciation with a total equity gain of $480,000 (namely $540,000 minus the initial $60,000 investment), whereas in the second scenario the buyers decided to live within their means, but not much below it, and they ended up earning an additional $80,000 on appreciation alone, plus they own a free and clear house worth $720,000, 50 percent higher than the first scenario.

The key difference? Couple B didn't have a second car!

It's as easy as that. See how expensive one additional car really is? In this scenario, it's a difference of almost a quarter million dollars and a nicer house for 25 years.

I'm not suggesting people take unnecessary risks with their lifestyle, and certainly I would still caution anyone to make prudent assumptions. Is there any chance that one spouse might lose a job or have to reduce their workload for any reason (for example, because of having and raising children)? People must calculate what they can truly handle. The advice is not to live above your means, just to live to your highest means when it comes to a house. Buy the biggest house you can truly afford.

When Lynda and I bought our first house in Toronto, we wanted to live in a nicer neighborhood and we wanted to live to our highest means. At the time, we were able to do that. However, we cut back on other items. We were still spending below our means on cars. We drove only one car, and it was an older one, a lovely Ford Aerostar (my wife might disagree here with me on the car quality). A nice neighborhood was more important to us than a nice car (or two) like most of my IBM colleagues then. Creating long-term wealth was more important to us than short-term status.

Beyond appreciation, a personal residence is like a massive tax-free savings account. Every dollar the property appreciates (see above) and every dollar that you pay down in mortgage, and every dollar of value you add through renovations and taking good care of the home, is all accumulated in that big bank account until the day you sell, then you take all of that money out of your big bank account. But you don't have to pay taxes on it!

In Canada, we're exempt from paying taxes on the sale of our personal residence. How else would you be able to earn $400,000 and not pay tax on it? There's no other legal way to do that.

Any other scenario where you earn $400,000 would involve you earning the money either through a job, business or investment. The three of them are taxed at different rates, but they're all taxed. When you get up in the realm of $400,000, they're taxed heavily.

You might be asking: hey, who can guarantee property values will actually go up over 25 years?

That's a good point; there is a very small chance that they won't continue to rise. But there are really good reasons to think that home values will continue to go up.

Inflation is the biggest reason. We live in a democracy, and in a democracy, politicians have to tell people things that will make them happy in order to get elected. We don't elect the most realistic politician, we elect the one who promises us the most, and typically the one who promises us the most has to spend the most. In order to spend the most, governments have to create debt. It's highly uncommon that a government at any level doesn't run a deficit.

Since debt keeps rising, and since paying down debts with hard cash is very difficult, governments will keep eliminating debt in the only way they know how, through future money with less purchasing power, also called inflation, or quantitative easing. Governments create inflation to pay their debts, and in the process cause inflation across the board.

In an inflationary environment such as the environment that we live in, and will likely continue to live in, you don't want to be in cash for very long. You're better off to have your money (and the bank's, if possible) in a hard income-producing, inflation-protected asset (such as real estate). Hence, it's a good idea to live to your highest means when it comes to owning a home.

The caveat to living at your highest means is if the day comes when a house is simply no longer affordable.

Vancouver is the best example in Canada of a phenomenon that other parts of the world experience. The difference in how much you'd have to pay for a mortgage vs. rent in Vancouver is often so great that it's impossible to justify buying a home.

If rent is $2,500 per month and a mortgage would be $4,000, the numbers just don't make sense. Take that money you saved on a mortgage and put it into real estate somewhere else where the numbers still make sense, or invest it elsewhere in a way that earns you income.

Other than places like Vancouver, go ahead and live to your highest means when it comes to a house. You will profit from appreciation and at the same time earn from within the best tax-free savings account you will ever find.

Don't be silly though and live beyond your means, that's a recipe for failure, regardless of how good an investment a home typically is. Live to your highest means instead.

LESSON 32:
CHALLENGE YOUR BELIEF SYSTEM – ADHERE TO THE EVIDENCE

A m I married to the right person? Am I actually happy in my life? Am I on the right path financially? Am I spiritually aligned? Was Jesus Christ a lunatic or was it true what is written? Was it smart to buy these four rental properties? Is the climate really warming, and if so, what percentage is man-made? Is this current career really where I want to spend the next 20 years ? Am I healthy enough? Do my kids like me? Am I an engaged parent? Why did I gain 15 pounds? Is there a real estate bubble? Is gold a good investment?

There are many such questions that we can and must ask ourselves regularly in order to grow as human beings, partners and businesspeople. But how many people really ask themselves these kinds of questions regularly? How many people examine their own beliefs in detail?

The common practice around beliefs is to accept as fact whatever we are handed. Many, if not most, people will never question what they've received. Diet patterns, sleep patterns, behavior patterns, parenting patterns, relationship patterns, religious patterns, financial patterns, and every other kind of pattern is potentially rife with false beliefs.

When we have false beliefs, we cannot move forward. You've heard the expression "the truth will set you free." It's the truest truth in the whole history of truths. Without truth and the right knowledge that comes from truth, we cannot effectively act in the world.

Conversely, without action, we cannot know the truth. We must act, evaluate, change where necessary and then act again. We must apply the process of kaizen to our inner belief system, throwing out the bad and moving ever closer to the good.

Can we ever arrive fully at our destination of complete perfection? Probably not in our lifetime, but we can strive to become continually better. The greatest people of all time are continually trying to improve their lives, both the outer and the inner.

However, I would contend that the inner is more important, and there is simply no way to improve the inner game without paying special attention to our beliefs. What we believe will be our basis for the next action, therefore the better our beliefs are, and the closer they are to truth, the better our next action will be.

Just because we believe something does not mean that it's true. There was a time when the commonly received wisdom said that the earth was flat. This belief is simple logic. You look out across the earth and you see that generally speaking, the earth is flat. Sure, there are some big bumps and some small bumps, but it always flattens out on the other side of the bumps. Hence, based on this observation, the earth must be flat.

However, believing that the earth was flat did not make it true, and eventually explorers sailed around the earth, proving that the earth was round. At the time of this great discovery, only about 600 years ago, there were many dissenters, people who did not believe the great new findings, many of them in authority positions such as ministers or popes.

No matter, the evidence continued to grow, and finally one day, man flew into space and took a photograph of a perfectly round and beautiful blue planet. Today, you'd be considered a nutcase to believe that the earth is flat. There is simply too much evidence to the contrary.

What are the "flat earths" in your life? What do you believe that might actually be false?

I think entrepreneurs and investors have a special advantage in this because adjusting our actions based on correct beliefs is precisely the skill that will allow us to thrive or cause us to perish.

Imagine if I thought a certain neighborhood in a certain city was poised to be the next best thing in real estate. Imagine that I raised millions of dollars to purchase buildings in that town or city, and then imagine that the city's economy simultaneously tanked. Imagine that 20 percent of the jobs left town and 20 percent of the people left with the jobs. Now I've purchased a whole bunch of property, and I'm stuck with an asset that has suddenly halved in value. My vacancy rates skyrocket, and the rental income is not enough to pay for the expenses of running the building.

My false beliefs would be what caused this unmitigated investment disaster. The problem with investing is that you never know the exact future of any town or city, so having perfect beliefs isn't possible. However, we can make prudent assumptions based on the history of a region and the history of industry in any region, we can look at migration patterns, we can look at taxation levels, we can look at transportation improvements, we can look at the growth or decline of certain industries, etc. Having evidence-based beliefs will give us the best chance possible to get it right.

Prestigious Properties® has mostly gotten it right, but some of our most troubled buildings, and the few disasters that we did have, have all been the result of false beliefs, coupled with sloppy research.

We falsely believed that the baby boomer demographic would push our Powell River investment value up. We falsely believed that $13,000 per door was a good deal in Detroit. We falsely believed that we were getting into a good mortgage in Dallas.

We didn't have the evidence to prove that we were right, at the time of decision making, primarily because we did not do enough primary and secondary research.

Don't worry, I don't beat myself up about it. I know that sometimes you have to act, and only after you act can you get the whole picture. After you take action, then you can adjust your beliefs to the evidence.

Today at Prestigious Properties® we run a tighter ship. We are more fundamentally sound in our investments. We seek markets with stronger indicators, and we take more prudent steps toward finding out what we don't know and fixing it.

We've improved our beliefs, we do more due diligence and we will continue to improve based on the evidence that has arisen.

If you're walking around with beliefs not proven by evidence, then you're a disaster waiting to happen. If you take action and don't adjust based on what the evidence tells you, then you're in for an arduous life. However, if you can learn to graciously and quickly integrate the evidence into your beliefs and adjust accordingly, then you're in for a long, prosperous and happy life.

One of the key questions I ask prospective employees is, "What do you believe?" and the answer is always astounding. I should write another book about this... but I digress.

Challenge your beliefs and find out what your "flat earths" are. There's a great chance you've been carrying them since birth. Identify them and eliminate them for your best life.

LESSON 33: CHALLENGE YOUR BELIEF SYSTEM – YOU'RE NOT THE BELIEFS THAT YOU INHERIT

Taking evidence as your starting point to changing false bTaking evidence as your starting point to changing false beliefs is an absolute must. After that you must actually make the change in order to meet with success around whatever belief system you're looking to change.

Change will be a very personal thing, however, and what's true must be true for you. Often people look at what they have in life, what they're doing, and what they want to do, and ultimately, their assessment bears out the fact that they don't want anything to change.

I have no problem with that. If you've fully assessed your situation, and you find that you're happy with exactly what you have and that there's no need to change anything, then by all means stay the same. What I do have a problem with is when people rightly identify that something is wrong, and then they choose to not change. They choose to live in misery and unhappiness because the task of changing is too difficult. This does not sit well with me. I believe we're all here to leave the earth a little bit better than how we found it. It's not possible to do this if you're unwilling to change your bad situation!

For me, change and improvement are givens. I like to always change and improve. There was no grand plan, but I always believed in the notion of moving toward something greater for myself and my family. The best world wasn't always the one I was currently inhabiting at the time. So changing my life, and therefore my actions, and therefore my beliefs was a common occurrence in my life, and it will continue to be. It's the way I'm built.

The commonly received wisdom of my upbringing and of my education told me that it was best to get a good education and then ensconce oneself in a massive corporation and stay there for the majority of one's career. I'm not sure that it was a German thing, because massive corporations and the large fleets of workers they employ is a global phenomenon, but it might be a little more prevalent in Germany than in some nations. Germany probably has more than its fair share of successful multinational corporations. What is also has, of course, is the "Mittelstand," i.e., small to medium-sized enterprises that employ the vast majority of workers. But for some reason I was never exposed to that world; it was not in my belief system at the time. My first "real" job is a great example of such a successful German multinational corporation: I worked for Siemens while at university.

And it was with Siemens that I had my second real wake-up call about not wanting to be a small cog in the big wheel. The first time was when I was still in the German air force (Luftwaffe). I saw that it was a very top-down, rule-driven organization and knew that something about it didn't resonate with me. At that age, I was still learning a lot about myself (as I am now) and I didn't quite know that the same experience would translate into large corporations.

At Siemens, I again received clues that the large organizational lifestyle wouldn't be my ultimate goal, but it wasn't until years in

IBM that I finally placed my finger on the real reason why it was not a fit for me.

I didn't like the petty politicking and the necessity to hand over my own personal progress to others. I had my own agenda for life, and I didn't like the fact that to advance my own agenda in a large corporation I had to win the favor of my higher-ups. In some cases, I didn't even respect the people who held the keys to my future in their hands. Furthermore, I wanted to be the boss in a fast-moving and flexible entrepreneurial venture.

So how did I manage to free myself of that received belief in the life path that was laid out for me? It wasn't without significant effort, but again, it was not a master grand scheme.

However, it was the sum of many hundreds and hundreds of small efforts and small realizations. More importantly, it was the result of awareness about who I was in relation to this received belief and awareness of my abilities.

Whatever the case, I was able to throw off the received belief around sticking it out and climbing the corporate ladder. I can't imagine where my life would be today if I had stuck it out there based on adherence to a false belief that I belonged in a large company.

Please don't get me wrong. I don't think large corporations are wrong for everyone, just me (and others like me). I learned a great deal from all of my stints with massive organizations, especially IBM (because I was there the longest). I learned about systems, processes, marketing and, most importantly, sales.

Another belief system that I had to change in order to be who I am today was the belief system around real estate ownership. It's not that there was an anti-real estate sentiment in my home growing up or in the broader Germany of my youth, but there was just an overriding culture of renting for life. It wasn't that anyone was against real estate ownership per se, it's just that it wasn't really considered in my circle of friends or parents' friends. Real estate-owning folks were usually seen as "rich."

When I arrived in Canada in my mid-twenties and saw young people my own age who owned their very own houses, it was like a slap in the face (the kind that wakes you up). It took me some time to comprehend just how that could be possible. But it planted a seed inside my head, a seed that grew and grew.

Several years later, while working with IBM in Toronto, Lynda and I purchased our first home, which was the first of a whole string of real estate purchases.

But seeing those young Canadians was the beginning of a shift inside of me. I slowly but surely processed the idea of ownership and replaced my original belief system around real estate.

Truth and belief systems are often constrained within our received culture. I don't begrudge my parents for not teaching me to own real estate. The German experience at the time dictated that home ownership wasn't necessarily the great idea that it was in Canada. When I changed my life to a new continent, I had the chance to change my belief to fit the evidence, and I was able to.

We're not constrained within the belief systems we inherit. I wasn't then, and you're not now. Make a progressive and consistent effort toward the right beliefs and their corresponding actions that fit for you.

LESSON 34:
THE NOBLE ART OF LEAVING THINGS UNDONE

B esides the noble art of getting things done, there is the even nobler art of leaving things undone.

We rightfully place much prestige upon getting things done, and on people who get things done. However, there are plenty of times when the best course of action is inaction. Doing nothing is a kind of action, the act of changing nothing and just leaving things alone.

When I'm faced with a decision, and I don't know what to do, the first question that I always ask myself is, "What would happen if I did nothing?" Try it sometime. Doing nothing is harder than it seems, especially for the real go-getters, those type "A" personalities.

The power of leaving things is derived from a few simple facts:

SUCCESS TAKES TIME

No doubt you've heard of a famous person, probably someone you admire, who spent years, and likely decades working hard and grinding to get their way to the top. Malcolm Gladwell discussed the 10,000-hours phenomenon in his book Outliers. The basic premise of that section of the book is this: the common denominator among the majority of experts (across many different fields) is that they all practiced their skill for at least 10,000 hours. It takes 10,000 hours to become an expert! That's five and a half years of five-hour days!

If you keep interrupting your progress, then you're continually starting from scratch each. Please note that some disparate paths are actually contributing to the 10,000 hours you may be working toward. For example, I worked in project management, client/team interface and sales. Each of them were related within IBM, but more importantly, they were all critical skills that I needed to develop in order to be an effective entrepreneur in real estate. I was practicing and getting my 10,000 hours on someone else's dime!

There were times when I was with IBM when I wanted to make a drastic change, but I bided my time and continued to rack up my 10,000 hours. I knew I had a different end destination, but I also knew I had to be continually paid while I was learning, and my time at IBM was a perfect bridge from 0 to 10,000.

EXPONENTIAL GROWTH

I love real estate as a vehicle for creating wealth for a number of reasons, but one of them is the semi-forced waiting it imposes upon the investor. I'm a notoriously bad stock picker, and the main reason for that is my impatience. A stock is a liquid asset.

When I buy a stock, it is simply too easy for me to sell the stock on a whim if I don't like the stock's performance.

Real estate is fairly illiquid and even though I've often felt like selling assets in real estate, I've at times been forced to keep them. And often, after having to keep the asset, perhaps after a collapsed sale, I've been able to wrap my head around keeping it for longer. Typically, the asset will begin to perform better, and ultimately I'm happy that I held onto it. In those cases, I'm very happy that I was forced to keep the asset rather than sell it. I was happy that I was forced to leave things undone, rather than doing anything.

The real estate example demonstrates the concept of exponential growth. Think back (better yet, look back) to the stepped S-curve that I showed you earlier in the book. Notice that the curve shoots up drastically after a time? I've found this rule to be almost universal. It takes time, but with most ventures, a consistent effort over time will eventually create a drastic jump in result. Sometimes, the best action you can take is to just continue doing the same. Exponential growth often takes time.

Leaving things undone allows you to plod along, putting in the work that you need to in order to get to the big jump. You may have to make small changes or tweaks, but you will experience big leaps by staying on a consistent path. Of course, sometimes you must change, and there's nothing wrong with that, but other times the desire to change for change's sake should be muted in favor of the noble art of leaving things undone.

You won't always know whether you're on the plateau of the stepped S-curve or stagnating. Sometimes it may feel like you've hit the wall and that your current path is no longer fruitful, and in some circumstances you may be right, but generally you might just need to redouble your efforts, or find a way to delegate part of your current project, or tweak something small, but for the most part the noble art of leaving things undone rather than making drastic changes will eventually lead to a big leap.

The true art of living well is in knowing when to make big changes, when to make tweaks, and when to completely keep your hands off and leave things alone.

There's no better proof than my first ever apartment building. Leaving things undone and keeping the building until today would have meant an increase of three-quarters of a million dollars to my bottom line.

I'm proud that I'm an action taker and that I'm able to get things done, but in that instance, I wish I had been able to practice the noble art of leaving things undone for another decade.

LESSON 35: PRINCIPLE-BASED DECISIONS LEAD TO BIG RESULTS

Making decisions on a whim or because of fear means choosing to struggle. On the other hand, making decisions based on principle leads to fulfillment, success and happiness. If you scan through your thoughts, you will probably find that you already make a great deal of your decisions based on principle.

How often is there opportunity to steal or cheat others in life? Most people simply don't do it. The principle of "Do not steal" is stronger in our society than is commonly believed. If it weren't, we'd have total breakdown in our society. In general, people are good, and they don't steal or cheat.

Let me give you an example of how principle-based decision making provides long-term positive results.

Back when I was with Lightyear Consulting, I was about to purchase my first ever investment property. I'd been searching for a good deal on my first investment property and found a couple of prospects.

The first one was a single-family home in a town called Crossfield, which was about 40 minutes north of Calgary. The deal was a good one, and the property would have cash flowed very well.

The second one was a rental-pooled condo in Calgary. The deal was not bad, and it cash flowed. The property did not promise as much of a return as the Crossfield property.

I'm a successful real estate investor, so I must have picked the one that provided the strongest return, right? Wrong. I chose the rental-pooled condo with a smaller return.

You might ask why. Well, at the time, I was a very busy man. I had young children at home, and I had a business that took me around the Western United States and Western Canada. I didn't want, nor did I have the time, to drive to Crossfield every week or even every month to fulfill property management duties, and I was untrained to select, then manage, a property management firm to manage the asset.

I had a background in project management, and I knew that even a tiny software development project with only three developers has to have a project manager. Every boat, no matter how small, must have a captain, and I knew that every property, no matter how small, needed a property manager.

The question I had to ask myself was this: Who will manage this property impeccably? Since I couldn't answer that question, I knew the answer was: me!

My wife had no inclination to manage the property and I had no idea who else would do it. I knew I couldn't do it, so the property would have been left without a manager.

On the other hand, there was a rental-pooled condo in Calgary (which was also about 40 minutes closer to my house than the Crossfield property). The rental-pooled condo promised a smaller return, but it came with a built-in management system. There was a professional property manager who was paid by all of the owners to take care of all the little things that the owners did not want to do. They even took care of filling vacancies! And if there should happen to be a month when my property wasn't occupied, I would still get paid through my share of the pooled rent in the rental pool.

The decision turned out to be a really good one. I was able to experience the upside of owning real estate and at the same time learn about property management (without doing it myself). I joined the board of the condo corporation and was able to see how the operation of a large building worked. I was on the board of that condo for three years, and in addition, I joined the board of the two other rental-pooled condos that I purchased in the next couple of years. That insider training (with no risk) served me well when I began purchasing my own multi-family build-ings.

So, what are the principles I applied when choosing the rent-al-pooled condo over the Crossfield single-family home?

1. FAMILY FIRST.

Of course I wanted to profit and create wealth. That's obvi-ous; otherwise I wouldn't be doing it in the first place. But I knew I wouldn't be able to take good care of the rental prop-erty in Crossfield without neglecting my family.

2. EVERY SHIP NEEDS A CAPTAIN.

To bring any project along from infancy to completion suc-cessfully, there needs to be a head man or a head woman. Jobs and projects don't organize themselves. Luckily I knew that and applied the principle of successful management to my de-cision making on which property to purchase.

3. PROFITS FOLLOW GOOD BUSINESS AND SYSTEMS.

Too many people just starting out in real estate and busi-ness are seeking a quick buck and immediate success. In some ways, the Crossfield property would have been a better pur-chase because there was more opportunity for profit. How-ever, purchasing the Crossfield home would have meant I wasn't purchasing a system. I couldn't manage that property, let alone more of them. The rental-pooled condo, on the other hand, was a turnkey investment. It was easily repeatable, and even thought the profits were smaller, my ability to stay in the game made it worth its weight in gold.

Let's go back and reimagine history for a minute. Here's how it could have gone, had I not based my decision on principle:

I purchased the Crossfield home and threw myself into learning property management in my spare time (or alternatively hiring and supervising, then firing and re-hiring a property management firm), between flying to San Francisco and spending time with my family. My wife got upset with my absenteeism and my kids forgot my name. My first tenants were good, but they moved out after six months. In those six months, there were three significant repairs that needed to be done on the house. All of my cash flow was eaten up on those repairs because the contractor overcharged me. I struggled to attract a tenant after the first tenants left and I had a difficult time finding the time, between traveling and family obligations. Finally, I found a tenant after the property had sat vacant for two months. I paid the mortgage and bills out of my own pocket for those two months.

The new tenants started causing problems two months into their tenure. It took me four months to get them out, and in the end, I didn't get paid any rent for the last four months they were there!

I sold the property at a loss after I finally got the tenants out of the property and got it cleaned up.

I hated real estate! I never bought another property again!

Does that seem extreme? It happens to new investors all the time. People buy real estate or start businesses without fully considering the consequences and in the end, they throw their arms up in the air and quit.

They only see the money at the beginning, and they don't base their decision on the broader principles they want to live their life by.

Basing your decisions on principle might seem to be a hassle at the beginning, but it is the only path to long-term success, happiness and fulfillment.

Lesson 36:
Principle-based Decision Making
– Know Where You Stand, or Be
Pushed Around

The power of principle is enormous. Being conscious of your own principles and following them on purpose is the process that unlocks the power of principle.

Have you ever had an uneasy feeling about a decision you made, but didn't quite know why? That's your conscience telling you that you're doing something that goes against your principles, even when you don't know what your principles are. Your conscience is a powerful thing. It's a good idea to listen to it and try to understand what it's saying to you.

But when you're consciously aware of your guiding principles, it enables you to make decisions before the bad feeling kicks in.

Living unaware of your principles or, worse yet, not having any, is a recipe for utter failure, humiliation and feeling bad in general. When you stand for nothing, it can seem that the whole world knows where it's going, and you're just a passenger. It may require digging deep, but the rewards of knowing, and then living by your principles are so plentiful that the effort expended to get there will seem puny once you have the clarity of your principles.

As with most areas of self-improvement, the power of the pen is mighty. Get one out and start writing what you stand for. Post it on the fridge and consider your principles every day. Do they really belong to you? Are there any missing?

Getting to know what you stand for will be a lifelong process. As with all lifelong processes, the earlier you start, the better off you will be. I can happily say that I know much of what I stand for, but I'm always open to tweaking and improving. Some of my principles stand out more than others:

1. HONESTY.

Seeing people dance around the truth really bothers me. I truly can't stand it, and therefore I always seek to not only tell the truth, but to be direct with the truth. Dancing around the truth is just as bad as lying, to my mind. It's masking and withholding what needs to be said, and it does two things.

1A. It postpones the inevitable. The truth always comes out eventually, and there's great power in the truth. Dancing around the truth, or worse, outright lying, is an enormous waste of time.

1B. It creates false beliefs. It obscures the evidence, so it does not allow people to adjust accordingly. We can only adjust to the evidence at hand, and with only partial evidence, we can only partially adjust.

Honesty and forthrightness are principles that, once known, understood and followed, are truly empowering.

2. WIN/WIN.

There's no such thing as the successful lone wolf. In the human world, we're totally dependent on other people not only for our success, but also for our happiness.

Successful marriages, employment, business partnerships, even casual encounters, all require a win/win. Too many people are trying to "win" while others lose. You see it in real estate sales all the time. A seller lists their property well above market value in the hope that someone will be uninformed enough to make the purchase. When this happens, the buyers do themselves a huge disservice: they get stuck with a property that will take them years of ownership and market appreciation just to get to the point where their property is worth as much as they paid!

Thankfully, most people don't fall for such win/lose pricing schemes.

What about employers who try to get as much as they can from their employees, squeezing them for all they're worth without providing benefits or fulfillment? Ultimately, employers like that will fail, or they live a life of suffering with high employee turnover rates and low morale. When I speak to other business owners they often complain, "It's hard to get good help these days." I usually reply, "You are probably not paying them enough as it is easy to find very good talent, but you have to pay them well and treat them well." Most of our onsite managers, as an example, make good base salaries, get a bonus for performance and trips to Mexico or the spa, in a business notorious for poor pay and lousy customer service. It reflects eventually on the customers and the asset performance.

If you feed peanuts, you get monkeys.

Living the principle of win/win is a winning approach to life in every aspect. Adhering to it will yield excellent results.

3. REPETITION IS THE MOTHER OF SUCCESS.

In many ways, this book is a big statement of my principles.

One principle that you've seen before in this book is kaizen, the idea of consistent, incremental progress.

Another way to say it is that repetition is the mother of all success. In other words, practice and keep getting better.

When I bought my first property, I remember being incredibly nervous at the prospect of writing offers and especially removing conditions. Both of those steps, but especially removing conditions, represented making a commitment. Once the conditions are removed, the deposit money is forfeited. This act of commitment is significant.

Today, when we remove the final condition of an offer on an apartment building I feel none of the fear or nervousness that I once did.

I've repeated the process of purchasing real estate so often now that it's not difficult anymore. This does not mean that I take it lightly, but it's simple to me now. I know my contract, we have done our intensive due diligence and I know what kind of result the action of buying will yield.

Applying repetition makes everything easier. If you need to learn how to have difficult conversations with your spouse, doing it often will make it easier each time. If you are starting a career in sales, repetition will make it easier to close sales.

I've applied the principle of repetition to every aspect of my life to great effect, and so should you.

Repeat, and then repeat again, tweak, repeat, tweak, repeat. Now do it again, and you're building a recipe for success.

Above is a sampling of some of my principles. More importantly, though, what are your principles? The time it takes you to know and understand your principles will serve you for the rest of your life. I recommend that you start the process of figuring them out now.

LESSON 37:
COMMUNICATION – CONTINUAL GROWTH

P erhaps I have more respect for this than most people. Communication comes easy for some people, but for me, it hasn't always been a cakewalk. It's still not a cakewalk today, but it becomes easier and more natural as I get further away from a couple of the bigger roadblocks that I had to overcome in order to become a proficient communicator.

The first major roadblock came about when I was a teenager. At that time, I was going through some stressful events in my life, the most important of which was that my parents were undergoing marital difficulty.

That had a profound effect on me, and the overall anxiety that I was feeling caused me to develop a stutter. I can remember putting my hand up in class to answer a question that the teacher had posed, and I could not get the answer out. That was when it struck me that it wasn't enough to know the answer in my head, I would need to communicate the answer or else there wasn't much value in my knowing the answer.

At that time, I undertook a program of self-improvement in the field of communication, especially spoken communication.

I still stutter and have difficulty formulating clear verbal thoughts when I'm overtired, or perhaps if I've had too many glasses of wine. However, as long as I'm energetic and aware, I can speak clearly.

But going through the experience demonstrated that merely being able to speak without stuttering was only the first level of improving my communication skills, and it was the beginning of my lifelong pursuit of better personal and business communication skills.

When I joined the German air force, I took courses on public speaking and presentation. Again, when I studied at university, I continued to study these topics. And, when I came to Canada to study for my MBA, I joined Toastmasters to improve my spoken communication skills further. The Real Estate Investment Network offers a course called "REIN Speak" to improve presentation skills in a variety of formats. There are other firms too, such as Dale Carnegie or Toastmasters. Speaking with clarity and impact is vital in business, to individuals, small groups over lunch, in the board room, or to groups at large. As someone once said, "Who is paid the most in industry these days?" Answer: "People who flap their lips." Actors, salespeople, CEOs, musicians, politicians, they all communicate (i.e., connect with others) exceptionally well.

Alas, when I came to Canada, I experienced the second major hurdle of the communication dilemma. While I could survive in the English language at that time, I was in no way proficient at a professional level.

I had to study and practice English intensively in order to reach professional level proficiency. I have endeavored to improve my English ever since, and now I'm proud to say that many people can't even place the German accent on me when we speak. They know there is an accent of some sort, but they aren't able to immediately know I'm German, as was the case back when I first came to Canada.

Whereas a native speaker is able to simply say or write what they feel and clearly express it, I often have to undertake a period of study in order to write or speak clearly. It's much easier now, but back when I first arrived in Canada, it was painstaking.

It's often true that whatever you must overcome becomes your biggest strength. I had to overcome a couple of different setbacks regarding my ability to communicate, and perhaps it gave me a greater sense that improved communication is important.

When I finished my MBA and had a strong grasp of English, I continued to practice my communication skills, both formally and through practice.

With IBM, I consistently gave presentations to groups that numbered between five and 500. The early days of high school and the Luftwaffe were an excellent start, but the practice of giving presentations to large groups was a truly advanced step in my communication studies.

There's a chance you might think it's not that important to improve your communication skills. Perhaps you don't really have any problems communicating, so you don't see the point.

Take a lesson from someone who has actually struggled with this aspect of life. You can always improve! And it's this improvement that might eventually be your greatest tool for advancement.

Think about it: can you imagine a CEO, president, or prime minister of a nation who can't communicate well? Do you think they became such proficient communicators over night? Or do you think they had to continuously improve? Since you are the CEO of your own life, learn to communicate well, both orally and in writing!

When Apple was launched, Steve Jobs was a smelly hippie. He succeeded despite his smell and looks due to a great product designed by Steve Wozniak, his own tenaciousness and his excellent communications skills. The first computer was not a great seller. What changed was the marketing for the Apple I and II, becoming slicker, with a backlit Apple logo and black velvet-draped tradeshow booth, for example, with far better computer packaging in a slick box and in a specially designed case.

Over time, Steve Jobs also cleaned up and became a much smoother salesperson and presenter—i.e., a better communicator. To this day, product quality, product design, packaging and marketing are what sells Apple products; a sales person is almost never involved actually. The packaging and the ads and the website communicate clearly. Apple's continual growth and success really is a communications story.

If you want to improve and find success in life and business, always practice and improve your communication abilities.

80 Lessons Learned:
From $80,000 to $80,000,000

PART 2 :
BUSINESS LESSONS

LESSON 38:
COMMUNICATION – SELLING AND
MARKETING

Marketing is getting the horse thirsty; sales is leading the horse to your trough.

One of the deadliest beliefs for any entrepreneur is that a top-quality product alone will create a successful business. Of course, the product has to be good, and a garbage product won't last too long, but a great product alone doesn't equal business success. For any business to be successful, excellent marketing and sales are also required.

Marketing is not the same as sales.

Marketing is a form of one-to-many communication. Marketing is your website, television commercials, newspaper ads, pay-per-click ads, trade show booth, blog posts, advertorials, billboards or radio ads. It's speaking to many people in an attempt to get them interested in your product. While it is one-to-many, in reality it is one-to-one, as a person looking at your TV commercial or your brochure or your website is looking by her/himself. Thus, the messaging needs to speak one-on-one while keeping in mind that there will be tens of thousands of website hits or TV viewers.

Selling takes the next logical step from one-on-many communication down to (usually) one-on-one communication. Selling is done on the phone, or in person. Selling is about understanding a client's needs, matching your product's attributes against those needs, and then getting the prospect to actually open up his wallet and spend some money with the reasonable expectation that he will have his needs filled.

Both marketing and selling are key aspects to a business's continued success. Without one or the other of the two, businesses will struggle. If cash is the life blood of a business, then marketing and sales are the heart: they actually pump the blood and keep it moving so that it can sustain every other aspect of the business.

Marketing and sales are vitally important in your business. Never underestimate the significance of marketing and sales. Whenever you say anything, you're sending a message about yourself. You're marketing yourself. What is the message you are sending? Does it match with the customer's needs?

Perhaps it came from my early realizations about the importance of communications and the necessity to continually improve in that realm, or perhaps it came from my time with IBM, which not only had good products but also strong marketing and excellent sales, but I have long understood the value of marketing.

I realized early on that business is only partially about the product. I knew that the best product in the world wouldn't sell without the right marketing and sales of the product.

In the seminal days of Prestigious Properties®I created a website to showcase the power of real estate investing as a method to attract money. It was rudimentary, but I did it at a time when websites weren't common. The bigger players had websites, but small companies didn't have them. Just having a website back then was a point of differentiation. It made my little investment company stand out over the others trying to do the same thing as me. It made me look professional at a time when I didn't feel totally professional.

Over time, when you create a professional image, you have no choice but to become more professional. It's a self-propagating cycle. First you make a professional move like buying an apartment building (as I did), and then you tell the world about it through your marketing. The marketing makes you appear more professional, so it attracts more clients (or, in my case, investment capital). The additional clients (or investment capital) force you to become more professional.

One begets the other. We're still tweaking the system at Prestigious Properties® to this day, and following the rule of kaizen we will continue to tweak as long as our shop doors are open. However, we have a fairly good handle on it now. We have a system that keeps working. Certain people in the business have the job of marketing & lead generation, others focus on product, and others on sales. Keeping them cohesive and removing any bottlenecks is my job, but generally, they all supplement each other.

Sales is the component of the (almost) holy trinity that came least "naturally" to me. At Prestigious Properties® we're blessed to have Scotty, and now also Denise and Christine, who love to talk to prospective investors on the phone all day long. For Scotty, for example, it's just the way he's built, and I have to commend him, because sales can be a demoralizing profession. Rejection is common, and persistence is necessary, often demanding calls in the evening or weekends even. Scotty has the persistence and desire to break through the mighty voicemail and "no" or "not yet" barrier.

I'm not built as Scotty is, and to this day, if I were to call Prestigious Properties' 50 top investors, I could probably help raise significant capital, but whatever the reason, I just don't enjoy that job.

Still, I must give myself credit because even though it's not my favorite job in the world, I did understand the value of it and even forced myself to do it for a couple of years with IBM, then Lightyear Consulting and in the early years of Prestigious Properties®. It was tough sledding for those two to three years at IBM, partially because I was breaking into a market that was heavily penetrated by a powerful and successful rival company (Oracle), but to be honest, it was also hard because the sales profession is just not my forte.

It was from this experience that I developed the understanding that I can do anything well for a while, but if I don't love it, I can't do it well for very long. I survived in sales and even thrived somewhat financially, but at the end of those few years (all at or above quota), I was at the end of my rope, and luckily, a new opportunity that was more suited to my unique personality presented itself just at that moment.

The fortuitousness of that timing is part of the reason I believe so firmly that man plans and God laughs. Where would I be now, or what I would have done at the end of that three-year stint in sales, if the opportunity to start Lightyear Consulting hadn't arisen? There is no way I can know, but it's not unreasonable to imagine a scenario in which I returned to a salaried position requiring my core skills.

Sales and marketing are distinct entities of equal importance. In essence, they are complex types of communication and are as elemental to business success as anything else, including product. It's important for entrepreneurs to understand the importance of each and improve their abilities in each of these types of communication, especially at the early stages of an entrepreneurial venture. At that early stage, when you ask yourself "Who will market and sell this product?" the answer will inevitably be "me!"

Yes, you can eventually (hopefully soon) hire those positions and outsource, but understanding them is key for the entrepreneur.

Marketing and sales are vital for any firm's success. Learn those skills, practice them for a while, and if you're not an A player yourself, hire someone who is and pay that person very well.

LESSON 39:
COMMUNICATION – KNOW YOUR
ADVANTAGE AND COMMUNICATE IT

One of our trademarked phrases at Prestigious Properties® is: "Become a landlord without the hassles.™"

We use that phrase on much of our marketing material because we know that systematically researching, acquiring, improving, managing and ultimately executing the exit strategy on a property are all difficult, time-consuming and knowledge intensive endeavors. It takes a lot of hard work to succeed as a real estate investor, and we've done it successfully for years. I know that many, many people understand the power of real estate and that they have a strong desire to participate in the wealth creation that real estate can provide.

I also know that many people have tried their hand at real estate investments on their own, and that they have hated the amount of work that it actually takes to be successful. For most people it makes more sense to focus their energies on the job or business that generates cash rather than spend their time do-it-yourself investing. I also know that there is a great deal of dislike for the "toilets and tenants" dilemma of rental property investing.

That's why we market ourselves as the answer to their problems. We bring a system of real estate investment that takes the pain away, while still providing the advantage. We allow people to invest without experiencing the hassles, and we let people know it. It's one of our advantages and we capitalize on it.

Another of the advantages that we market is that we don't earn any significant money unless our investors earn money. Many people are completely fed up with the investment industry. The fees payable for the "privilege" of investing your money with a mutual fund, combined with the low returns, are driving sophisticated individuals toward alternative kinds of investments, also referred to as private equity, or exempt market securities, often real estate.

On our website (and all of our marketing) we make the point that we don't make money before our investors. First of all, we don't inflate the value of our assets going in, which is a tactic that many syndications use to earn profit from their investors.

In addition, we don't charge exorbitant fees as mutual funds do. Our strategy to earn a profit is to earn a profit from our investments. Our business is not primarily the business of fee collection; it's the business of real estate investment return. When our investments earn a return, then our investors do, and only then we do too.

We communicate this advantage to prospects, and it differentiates us from many of the other investment options that our investors have. We capitalize on this difference and let our prospects know, and it helps draw them in, but we still have to close the sale.

Track record is another advantage that we enthusiastically communicate in our marketing. It's one of the advantages that we have worked hard for. The simple fact is that once you've shown you can do something many times, there's every chance that doing it again will lead to success again.

You might be thinking, "What if I don't have a track record, Thomas?" If you're new to this game, you have no chance of communicating a track record, right?

Yes and no. It's true that you can't communicate what you don't have. Doing so would be deceptive, and I would never counsel you to be deceptive in your marketing. However, what you may not know is that you likely have more of a track record than you think.

Back when I'd only done one apartment building deal, my track record was short, to be sure, but it was still a track record. I didn't hesitate to tell people that I was an apartment building investor. It was true, and I was successful with my single apartment. I never lied and said that I had invested in many apartment buildings, but I did not shy away from telling people that I had successfully invested in an apartment building.

Humility is a virtue, but being overly humble can be a detriment when it comes to marketing. If this is a mental block for you, you might just think of marketing your advantage as this: simply telling people what you've done.

Don't think of it as tooting your own horn. Most people desire to be humble and would feel bad about telling others about their own success. Don't let your desire to be humble be a detriment to your marketing efforts.

Developing a track record is one of the many reasons why I recommend doing your first deal or two in real estate with your own money, but that's another topic for later.

But what if you don't even have a rudimentary track record? How do you tell others about your track record if you've really never done it before?

There are a couple of ways:

1. FOCUS ON A DIFFERENT KIND OF MARKET.

When raising money, this is very common. Many people will raise money from people within their circle first before they seek it from strangers. The people in your circle might know that you've never invested before, but they might know from your past and your personality that you'll make it work no matter what.

2. FOCUS ON THINGS YOU HAVE DONE THAT CREATE A TRACK RECORD OF SUCCESS FOR YOU AS A PERSON.

Again, maybe you've never been successful in the field you're moving into, but maybe you've had a successful business venture in the past, or perhaps you've been successful at another job.

If you don't have a track record in the actual thing you're marketing yourself for, you can still market your personal track record.

Whatever you do, figure out your advantage and tell the world about it. This is the most fundamental aspect of marketing.

Lesson 40:
Communication –
Speak Their Language

I may not be a natural born salesman, but I do know the principles of the job, and I've made it my business that all my onsite managers also know how to sell. When learning to sell, there is one simple rule that makes a big difference to sales communication.

You must speak their language.

One of the most important strategies we employ with Prestigious Properties® in our marketing materials and online is to speak to the prospect in the way that they like to be spoken to.

Some prospects don't like too many numbers when researching their investments. This may come as a shock to the detail-oriented person, such as an engineer or an accountant, but some people just want to know the basics.

We might write, for example, "We project that you will earn 10 percent per year with this investment." These people may be looking for a high level of trust and integrity first and foremost, and excessive number slinging might even leave them wondering if you're trying to bamboozle them.

So we don't cram numbers down everyone's throat with our marketing. Instead, the person who doesn't seek numbers for assurance will find a checklist showing the benefits of investing with us. We tell them, with words, why we've been successful over the years, and why we expect to remain successful going forward.

Other prospects are more humanitarian focused, and want to talk about tenant relationships, relationships with the onsite manager, and the property manager. They want to know all about the human elements of the building.

Do these unique ways of speaking to certain clients mean we neglect the numbers-oriented person? Not at all. On our website, they can click to their heart's content and find the numbers they desire. Perhaps they don't only want to know what we project for a return, they might also want to know what the average rents are in the area for a similar type of property, and by contrast what our average rents are.

They might want to know what kinds of renovations will have to be done in the next five years and how much we expect each of those renovations to cost. How much per square foot will it cost to replace a floor? How much will cost to paint a suite? How much will it cost to replace baseboards and trim? Approximately how many suites will need work? All this information is available to the numbers-oriented investors, and this knowledge reassures them that we've thought of everything.

The numbers-oriented person might want to know five different scenarios based on mortgage rates, amortization, raised rents, lowered rents, market gains and market losses. We endeavor to provide as much information to the numbers-oriented person as we can, but not at the expense of the word-oriented person.

Then there are visually oriented people. They will be moved by seeing a picture of an ugly building beside a picture of a nice building. They will be happy to see that we're buying buildings near river valleys or amenities, or those in-suite upgrades, or of happy tenants. Happy faces always help, just don't overdo it.

You might be getting the idea that it is tough work balancing all the various desires of potential investors in marketing materials, whether online or off. We try to appeal to the different types of people and speak to them in their language as much as possible, but at best, marketing can only attract; it can never close a sale.

That's where a trained professional salesperson comes into play. They are adept at figuring out which type of person they're speaking to and can quickly start speaking that language. If they're speaking to a "people person," the salesman can highlight the people aspect of their business, and if they're speaking to a numbers person, they can go over the numbers in greater detail.

In extreme cases, the salesperson might have to actually hand the prospect over to one of the specialists within the business. Recently, Scotty attracted the attention of a large institutional investor from Toronto that was interested in investing money with one of the lead players in Western Canadian apartment buildings. As you'd expect from a large investor looking to invest millions (rather than the normal $20,000 to $150,000 investors that we attract), they were very numbers focused.

The stakes are a bit higher on this kind of deal, and Scotty did a wonderful job of bringing them into the fold, but there came a time when the investor wanted a higher level of detail from our end than Scotty was able to provide.

He's the sales guy, not the numbers guy, and to his credit, he's able to speak numbers in most situations. In fact, he had to in order to hook these large investors. To his even greater credit, he knew when it was time to call in the numbers guys. So Mike, our acquisitions guy (and numbers hawk), and I went down to Toronto to speak to the investors.

These kinds of cases are extreme, and when you're starting out, seem rather remote, but the point remains that you must speak in the language of your prospect, both in your marketing materials and in your sales approach. It's one of the most important aspects of business communication, and one that you'd be wise to heed as early as you can.

We don't yet know whether the hard work that Scotty, Mike and I have done will pay off with a large investment from the Toronto players, but what we do know is that through our marketing, our professional sales, and our top-notch product, we did attract a major player to the table.

The same hard work and professional communication that has been bringing us smaller investors for years was what brought us the larger player. We speak in their language wherever possible, whether the player is large or small.

LESSON 41:
COMMUNICATION – SALES PROCESS

Whether you know it or not, you're always selling yourself. If you put photos of yourself drunk on Facebook, then you're representing yourself as a drunken person who doesn't mind showing it on Facebook.

You might only drink once every six months, but the fact that you post those photos of yourself means you're representing yourself as a drunk to a large group of people whether you like it or not.

If you dress like a slob and fail to shower or clean yourself, then you're communicating that you don't care about your appearance.

Over the years, I've written many thousands of posts on some online forums, especially the REIN (Real Estate Investment Network) forums. As a result, I've had many people—often newer investors—approach me to ask for advice, or show me their real estate investment projects, or their sales pitches. People have seen that I have experience and am a leader in that community, so I've heard from many.

I think it's great. I'm generally pleased and happy to read what they send me and spend a few minutes giving feedback. The presentations range from very slick, glossy and professional presentations to two lines of email written with poor grammar, typos and spelling mistakes.

I don't believe that every aspect of a communication has to be totally perfect and completely polished, but I have to wonder what the people are thinking when they send the messy stuff. If they're sending that message to me, then what are they trying to send to their prospective investors? The truth is that they're selling themselves as incompetent and sloppy. The written word is equally important as appearance or oral communication. When writing to someone, you must make a point of representing yourself well; this is part of selling yourself.

HONESTY AND INTEGRITY VS. AMPLIFICATION AND MODIFICATION

If you're selling me an apple (a fruit, or a computer), then I believe you're allowed to amplify and modify the message about the apple, but you're not allowed to lack honesty and integrity.

You're allowed to shine the apple so it looks nice, and you're allowed to turn the bruised side down, so that the first impression I get is the nice bruise-free side. I still believe that you shouldn't actively hide the bruise from me, and you should give me a chance to see the bruise before I buy the apple, but you don't have to make a point of telling me all about the bruise, and all about how bruised all your apples are (which could potentially be by having been shipped here over 3,000 kilometers in a dirty truck), and how you just hate your apple delivery people who always bruise the apples.

Selling is partially the art of showing the good side. False and excessive modesty or actively tanking deals by telling only the bad side of the story is not necessary, but it's not dishonest to highlight what's good about your product.

The product has to match your description, and it's not acceptable to mislead about your product. I named my real estate investment Prestigious Properties®, and we always aim to have prestigious properties eventually—after a few months or years of ownership. We wanted to create an image of tidy properties that a tenant can be proud of. We would have called it sloppy properties, as many assets we buy often are quite sloppily managed (before we take over) and look the part, if we wanted to portray that part of the business. But I called the company Prestigious

Properties®, and we always seek to have our properties match that name. That's honest and integral.

You can represent the best side of your apple when you sell it, but you can't pretend it's an orange. And if your apple is a run-of-the-mill apple, you can't sell others on the idea that it's the best apple in the world. There is a market for run-of-the-mill apples and people will pay the right price for that, but it's not okay to tell people that a run-of-the-mill apple is the best apple.

This is especially important in real estate investing, or any sort of investing, because one is always dealing with new investors. They are often not sophisticated about investing, but they have some money that they want to invest. It is certainly not okay to mislead them or be dishonest with them.

It's just not okay from a human standpoint. Do you really want to be responsible for taking someone's money for your own profit in a misleading way? Even if the investment works out and they make money, if it hasn't been done in an honest way, it's not okay.

The truth will always be discovered. That bruise that you actively hid from an apple buyer will eventually be found. If you painted over the bruise, they'll taste the paint when they bite into it.

If you tell an investor that they will receive regular cash flow checks and then they don't get regular cash flow checks, they will notice very soon, and they will be very angry. This puts your own future at risk because these angry people will tell everyone they know that you're dishonest and that you'll do anything, even lie, to get investment money and that you won't deliver on your promise. The truth always comes out, so you can't mislead people, even if you had the inclination to, which you should not because it's not okay to do.

It is acceptable to accentuate your best qualities in the selling process, but it is not okay to mislead or lie.

LESSON 42:
COMMUNICATION – RELATIONSHIPS
COME FIRST

I just finished telling you that the sales process is all about communication and that everything you do and say communicates a message about yourself. I've also told you that to sell effectively, you must first seek to understand, and then to be understood.

I believe that improving salesmanship skills is so important to the entrepreneur that I'm stressing the point. I really could write an entire book on the importance of sales to the entrepreneur. You may think you're in the business of delivering some product or service, and you are. However, any entrepreneurial venture must specialize in how to sell that product. If you or your organization don't know how to sell, then you will not do any good to anyone else.

I understand this lesson so well, primarily because of having worked at IBM for more than seven years. I learned that in order to succeed you need a good (or great) product and you need to sell it well. IBM's focus, like most successful firms that have been around a few decades, such as BMW, Apple, Coca-Cola, McDonald's, etc., was on sales and on product.

I knew early on that I had to represent myself well and sell what I was doing. Taking it back to the late 1990s, I even had a website, which was only common among larger companies at the time. At that time, just having a website was an excellent sales tool because it made me stand out above the rest of my competition.

I was communicating a cutting edge and forward thinking image. The content on the website was rather rudimentary considering I hadn't done too many deals at the time and didn't have a substantial track record to fall back upon. Still, I shared what I had done and what I projected to do going forward.

Such was my sense of salesmanship. It worked, yet I don't consider myself a gifted salesman. My partner Scotty Grubb is a gifted salesman, and he has a track record to prove it. Wherever he has taken over sales, the top line (revenue) numbers have improved dramatically. This trend continued when he joined Prestigious Properties®.

I may not have been that gifted at sales, but I understood the importance of it and I can do it when I must. That's exactly what I did in the early days when it wasn't possible for me to hire an expensive sales specialist like Scotty. This same lesson must apply to you in your entrepreneurial adventure (assuming you have such ambitions). Learn this fact early, and you will do well— the product is important, but it must be sold and marketed as skillfully, or better sometimes, as it's developed.

Salesmanship is about communication. However, communicating the story of you and the story of your product assumes that you have a relationship with someone to begin with, because communication is about tailoring a message to an individual. Individuals are just that: individual. They are all slightly different.

A relationship doesn't have to be a personal relationship, as in Joe your neighbor, or Tina the girl you went to middle school with. These days relationships are created all the time online. You write a blog post that resonates with a few people and they take an interest in you. Then they continue to read your blog regularly and they make a comment on your blog. You respond to the comment and suddenly you're in a relationship with them.

To consummate the relationship you become Facebook friends or you start following them on Twitter. Now you're interacting regularly. Every time you make a post on social media, they see what you say. In a way, relationship building is easier than it's ever been, but of course there is a lot more noise in the world now, too.

This is one way to make a relationship, but it should not be the only way. If you cease making real world connections, you might lose touch with what it's like to actually stand in front of another person and talk. Networking and developing relationships is important. I recommend you do it regularly. Just today, I went to a networking event in downtown Vancouver to meet some new faces.

To the outside observer, this might not make sense because in the eyes of many I've "made it." It could be said that my years of hard work in business mean that I don't have to network any-more. I disagree. I might not be looking to get the same result out of networking that I once was when I attended a networking meeting, but I still seek to develop new relationships. It is only from those new relationships that I will have someone to com-municate with.

It's all a process. You can't jump straight to sales from hello. Nothing feels more awkward than being sold to immediately af-ter meeting someone. First you must develop a relationship, then you must communicate, then you must understand the other person's needs or issues, and then, and only then, can you sell. You start the sale through your communication. Eventually you have to close the sale. That's a whole different skill.

Selling is about solving someone's problem or pain. Therefore, to sell well, you have to understand their problems first. That takes a while. No one, after a quick "hello," will tell you that their RRSP performance over the last decade has been lousy, or that they took a 30 percent pay cut or just got divorced. Once you understand their issue, then you can relate what you want to sell to their circumstances.

You want to increase sales? Meet people, lots of people, and be yourself. Don't be fake or gimmicky. Don't over-sell yourself at the start, just develop a relationship. Primarily, people want rela-tionships with other people. They don't want relationships with a caricature of a salesman or saleswoman.

Get started now, and do it all the time. Spend valuable blue dol-lars (see below—blue dollars are time invested) creating relation-ships. Sales develop out of relationships, and the simple equa-tion is that the more relationships you have, the more sales you will get. It's also referred to as "prospecting." People die, existing clients move away or buy from the competition. You must con-stantly replenish the customer base, no matter how loyal (yes, it's true for Apple fans, too, as Google, Sony, Blackberry and Nokia have ever-improving products also).

LESSON 43:
COMMUNICATION –
PRESENTATION SKILLS

D eveloping presentation skills is essential to your business, especially in the formative years, and whether you try to or not, you will get better just by discussing your business and what you do. You will inevitably have many hundreds and thousands of phone calls about your business, and you'll have to explain yourself to each person you're speaking to. Each of these phone calls is a mini-presentation.

Then there's the elevator speech. Sometimes, you want to leave a very short and succinct impression, and you might only have 20 seconds to do it. When you're doing an elevator speech, you need to tailor your "presentation" to the circumstance.

As always with communication, your context matters. Who is seeing the presentation? If I'm presenting to a crowd of real estate investors who understand the buzz words and terminology of the industry, I can create a presentation that is more technical in nature and explain what I do in a technical and detailed way.

If I'm presenting to a room full of teachers or civil servants who might be looking to invest their money, I have to give a more top-level and usually more conservative view. I have to understand that they don't care about apartment building investments per se and that they are more interested in what happens to the capital they will invest and the returns they will receive.

And if I have one hour to present to each of those crowds, I can go into more detail than if I only have 15 minutes. The audience is a major piece of the context, but so is the amount of time that I have allotted for the presentation.

Is it a big room or a small room? If it's a big room, there might not be much use in trying to have a question and answer period. Your body language has to be big as you are far away, bigger than in a small room or in a restaurant where exaggerated gestures, such as waving your arms, might look downright silly.

If it's a small room, a question and answer period might be the most effective way to use your time. The context matters for how you will tailor your presentation in every way, and this rule stands whether it's an official presentation or an informal presentation such as a phone call.

The biggest benefit to mastering the art of presentation is not even found in the conversion of audience to client/investor. It's in the learning you will receive from the process of preparing for the presentation.

To prepare an effective presentation, you have to start from the audience and work backward. Once you understand the audience, you have to ask yourself what kind of data and visuals to include.

As you start building it, you will likely have to learn a bit more about the topic that you are trying to convey. You will likely be a little bit nervous about your presentation, so you'll want to take the extra step and make sure you understand your information well.

You will also have to ask yourself what will move this kind of audience, which will force you to think about motivation. Thinking about motivation means considering what will be important to the audience. If you're presenting to a specific customer, perhaps there is a way you can add value to your product or service and charge more as a result. Often, money is not the most important consideration to the customer, and if you only focus on providing a cheap product, you'll fail to impress your customer.

If you were a car dealer in Germany and you were making a presentation to the Taxi Cab Owners Federation of Germany (if such an organization exists), you would want to understand the motivations of taxi owners in Germany. Not knowing could mean spending a 30-minute presentation telling the room about the benefits of cheap cars and how much they can spend. The truth is that taxis in Germany are almost all Mercedes because of the legendary reliability of Mercedes cars, high availability and low downtime.

So knowing your audience well and working backward from there can be the difference between a successful or unsuccessful business.

However, you will learn your market well by having to put together a presentation and then taking the time to learn what drives the audience.

Of course, you could go into your presentation with the taxi owners in Germany and just build the presentation with no regard for the audience or what motivates them. When presenters do that, they often present the information that they think is important. This means what is important to the presenter without regard for the truth of what the audience wants.

This is really about selling to your advantage. If you don't know what your advantage is, then preparing presentations is a certain way to learn. The thought of standing in front of a group of people and looking silly is a very strong motivation to make sure that you can present well.

Often this means searching within for your own worth—both as a person and as a business. When you stand in front of a crowd, you want to show your worth, and there is no better way to do that than to know your worth by thinking about it and then studying how you can apply it to the specific audience you're presenting to.

All presentations, even the 30-second ones, have four elements: an opening, a body with content, a summary and a call to action. Tell them what you are going to tell them. Tell them. Tell them what you told them. Ask for an action such as, "Phone this number, go to this website, come talk to us at the booth, or fill out this form." It is really not all that complicated, and in time, with practice, you will get better.

Speaking to a large group is exactly the same as talking one-on-one or one-on-three. I think I should repeat this as it is so critical. You speak exactly the same one-on-one as one-on-500.

Why ? Because the audience listening is not an audience, but a collection of individuals. You talk, you present a message with empathy and conviction, you smile, you make gestures, you tell a joke, just as you always would face-to-face or in a very small group. Don't ask "Where are you all from?," since this is not how you would address an individual. Ask instead: "Where are you from?" or "Are you from Atlanta?"

In a big room you will use bigger gestures and hand motions as you are far away and appear smaller to the audience. That's the only difference. Pick three or four folks in the audience, and speak to the first person for 15 to 25 seconds. Then move on to your next point and talk to another person, perhaps in the front; then on to another thought and another person in the far back, and so on. In a big room of 200 people you can cover the entire audience by talking to three or four people dispersed in the room and it almost feels intimate, like sitting at a table.

Presentation skills are essential to the businessperson. Spend the time and the effort to improve yours, and you will see incredible results.

LESSON 44: PARTNERING – DON'T PARTNER IF YOU DON'T HAVE TO

Partnerships are an incredibly important aspect of business, and as you move through your business life, you'll almost certainly have to partner at some point. But what is a partnership? In a sense, any time you bring more than one person together to complete a project or achieve a goal, you're in a partnership.

When speaking in this broad sense, you could include employees as partners. If you have to borrow money from the bank for your business (as is usually the case in real estate), then you could consider the bank to be a partner.

However, for the purpose of this discussion, I'm speaking more specifically about a partner as someone (or some group/company, etc.) who will take a share of the profits (or equity) in the business. Having a share of the equity is an important distinction because whenever a person or group owns some of the equity, it also means that they have some right to make some of the decisions, or at least have a say in the decisions. How often do supposedly silent partners suddenly gain their ability to talk when they perceive there's a problem?

Even in a legal structure such as a limited partnership, in which the general partner (which Prestigious Properties® always is in our LPs) has all the legal right to make decisions and the limited partners are relegated to a silent role, the investors (silent partners) can speak up when they believe they ought to, but they have no decision-making powers. Of course, they can talk with their feet. They can choose not to invest with you anymore and they can also tell their friends to not invest with you.

Equity partners always have a say of some sort.

I've made a wonderful business (or rather a series of businesses) out of partnering with people. I've already told you about some of the trials and tribulations I've experienced in partnerships as well as some of the successes within those difficult partnerships.

My partnership with Dave was an example of such an internal contradiction. On one hand, Dave's footloose and fancy-free style brought about a lot of headaches. From the day we went into partnership together until the day he left, Dave ran headlong into new investments that my more conservative self probably wouldn't have. At the time, I knew I needed a more aggressive partner to push my boundaries and therefore grow the business.

There was a series of inevitable headaches from that mad rush into real estate, but at the end of the day, some of our greatest wealth was created by some of those investments. We bought apartments in places I never would have, and by timing the markets well, we made a significant profit in many of those places. We also made a significant loss in some of the others, but on balance, we profited from that crazy and stressful time.

There was a point where I was prepared to put all the assets up for sale and walk away with the entire business liquidated. That's how stressful it was and how bad things had gotten.

The partnership ended when I bought Dave out after a lengthy and very expensive legal process. I was able to structure the business in the way that I wanted to rather than the default way that we had done through the partnership. My stress was brought back to manageable levels and I eventually thrived again, holding the properties in the business longer. Things have worked out well, but my point is that the partnership cost me more than money, it was costing me happiness and peace of mind.

Did I have to partner with Dave at the time? Well, with what I'd created in Prestigious Properties® already I'd put together enough assets and involved enough investors that indeed I needed an infrastructure around me. This started with property management and other administrative tasks, but ultimately I needed help raising money and with all of that money raised I needed to buy more buildings.

The slow and deliberate pace with which I acquired buildings was not going to keep pace with the money we had in the business, so in hindsight, yes, I did need to partner with someone more aggressive, like Dave, at the time.

Hindsight is usually 20/20. But in this case, I'm not sure that it is. The stress of my partnership with Dave informs me that I didn't need to go into that partnership with him, but when I look at it again, I'm not sure I had a better option at the time.

In this case, hindsight is muddy, but I'm certain that I did the best I could with my decision-making capabilities at the time.

All things considered, though, you should not go into partnerships unless you need to.

Taking the real estate example, if you were an up-and-coming investor with a desire to acquire many valuable real estate assets, and you had unlimited access to funds (or at least a lot of money), and if you had the knowledge to make those investments, why would you partner with anyone?

The two most important factors (and those that rightfully earn a partner equity) are knowledge and money. If both knowledge and money are present in the same individual, then there really is no reason to partner. Such an individual is better off to hire employees.

There's some argument to be made that even employees are partners, but I'm referring to equity partners here.

Don't take on partners unless you have to because there is a far greater likelihood of experiencing business hassles, confusion about who is owed what, fighting between you and your partner, and a whole host of other potential issues.

Please notice that I'm not categorically saying that you'll experience difficulty in every partnership, but what I am saying is that you have a far greater chance if you partner with others than if you do it on your own.

Don't take on a partner if you don't have to for the above listed reasons, but more importantly, why give away part of the ownership of an asset or series of assets unless you have to? You stand to gain more if you own the asset by yourself, and on top of that, you will retain total control about where you're going in your business if you don't have to partner with anyone else.

LESSON 45:
HOW TO CHOOSE A PARTNER

I f you've already determined that you're going to have to partner with someone else, then your next step is to choose the partner. Too often, people (especially beginners) choose a partner based on who they see immediately in front of them. They often don't think strategically about these partnerships and they just partner with a friend or a colleague.

That's why in real estate, you'll often see two young go-getters partner together. In reality, these youngsters will be happy and excited to shake the tree in order to dig up deals and make things happen, but almost invariably neither of them has money.

A young go-getter needs nothing more than a slow-moving, cautious, conservative old partner with loads of money. I'm now further on the other end of that curve, and I now seek youth and energy, or deep institutional ties to complement me in a partnership.

Prestigious Properties® is set up such that we're the experts, and we raise money from within our LPs, so that makes us the expert partner. However, within Prestigious Properties® we have a partnership setup in addition to the company's partnership with the various money partners (investors).

Within that framework, I am not the only player with an equity share. I also have Mike, Scotty, and in my property management company, Keith. These gentlemen also have a significant equity stake, and I act more as the senior member holding it all together. It's their individual bits of expertise that I've partnered with in Prestigious Properties.®

Complementary skills are critical; in fact, it's the first question I always ask myself when I'm looking for a partner: Do they have the specific skills needed to do the job? Keep in mind that if it's a money partner I'm looking for, the specific "skill" is simply having the money (besides some other security regulation imposed rules).

Just as important as complementary skills, though, is the next question: Do I trust him (or her)?

Some people are exceedingly talented, and there is no doubt that they could have the talent to help me, yet I would never partner with them because I don't trust them.

Of course, the trust muscle is not 100 percent accurate. There are times when you analyze your feelings of trust and find that you do trust someone—only to find out later, through painful experience, that they're not totally trustworthy. There's nothing you can do about that except raise your ability to sniff out an untrustworthy person. I've learned to ask my wife for a second opinion, and usually she is right.

When I partnered on the houses in Stony Plain, I believed I was partnering with someone I could trust. I did my best at the time to understand what I was getting myself into, and when I look back at the deals with the advantage of hindsight, I can see that it was a failure on my part to decipher that the person I was partnering with wasn't trustworthy.

I couldn't know with 100 percent clarity that my partner was going to have marital difficulties, nor could I have known that if he did have marital difficulties he would allow it to affect him so adversely.

In addition, I didn't know he had a drinking problem and that his drinking would escalate and cause him to lose the ability to properly manage our shared projects.

The lesson was driven home that I need to do more due diligence on the people I partner with. If I had done more due diligence, I perhaps could have found out that my partner had a history of broken relationships and that he had child support payments from his previous relationships that didn't end too well.

That mess, which I'm still cleaning up, taught me more about what it means to trust. How well do I really know someone? How do I know I can trust them? These are the questions that you have to ask yourself in order to truly know if you can trust someone.

The third major aspect of a partnership is perhaps a little bit unexpected. I ask myself the question: Do I like them?

This may strike you as a little bit odd because business is sometimes thought of as the absence of sentiment and emotion. Whether or not you like someone is definitely a matter of sentiment and emotion, so where does it fit in?

There are a couple of reasons it's important that you like a potential business partner.

Throughout the course of a business relationship there will be plenty of time spent together.

Right now, I'm involved in a land development project in Cold Lake, Alberta. Since Edmonton is the nearest major airport to Cold Lake, and since Cold Lake is three hours away from Edmonton by car, this means I spend significant hours in a car on my way to Cold Lake. Several times I've had the occasion to drive there with some of the other players involved.

Going both ways, that's six hours' worth of driving. If I don't like the person I'm partnering with, there is no way I want to spend six hours with them. I can endure that, but do I honestly want to work with people I'd rather not spend time with? It just makes business far easier if you like the others involved.

Perhaps more importantly, though, getting to know partners better means that you have a better chance of learning enough to know if you can trust them.

I didn't hate my Stony Plain partner, but we just didn't spend enough time together for me to know if I could trust him. If we'd spent more time together, perhaps I would have found out about his past problems.

If you know the potential partner has the necessary skills, that you trust them, and that you like them, then you're on your way to having a successful partnership. Thus ask these three questions before you decide to partner:

1. Do I respect this guy (for his chosen skills)?

2. Do I trust this guy?

3. Do I like this guy?

Could they answer yes to all of those questions if they put you under the same scrutiny? Ensure that you're worthy of partnering with too, and you'll have a real foundation for success in the partnership.

LESSON 46:
IMMEDIATE AND DELAYED INCOME

When I was at a critical growth stage with Prestigious Properties®, I took out an advertisement seeking a partner. In my ad I wrote, "Low salary, high equity."

Most of the people that called me for that ad were thinking that I meant $100,000 when I said "Low Salary." Most of the respondents were coming from the high salary world of big corporate investing and were accustomed to salaries of a quarter-million dollars per year, plus similar bonuses.

They weren't prepared to take a low salary in exchange for a significant chunk of long-term equity. Time and time again, I had to tell them that low salary meant more like $20,000 per year, and that I expected whoever was to join me to have a separate source of income (or a spouse or a semi-retirement income stream from pensions or investments) so they could focus their energy on building the business.

In real estate, the problem between immediate and delayed income is universal, which is why I always say that to profit from real estate you have to be in it for the long term. This implies that you have to be able to hang in there for quite a while, both emotionally and financially, before you will see a profit.

This implies that to profit from real estate, you need a system to manage your properties and your cash flow well so that your life doesn't become a cascade of toilets and tenants issues, and that you have some means to support your life while your real estate churns little or no cash.

Cash flow is an often ill-understood term. This is where the misunderstanding takes place most commonly: people think cash will be flowing out of the property and into their pockets, but the truth is that cash flow flows out of the property and makes a brief stopover in your bank account before flowing back into the property. This is the real meaning of the term "cash flow."

In a single-family property it goes like this: you have a nice little rental property that cash flows $200 per month. From the day you purchase it an excellent tenant occupies the property and continues to do so for 18 months. Good for you, you've now earned $3,600 of cash flow.

After 18 months, the tenant moves onto greener pastures, and now you are faced with your first vacancy. You also realize at the time that the property needs to be painted, and the floor newly carpeted. By the time you've spent the money on painting the property, repairing the carpet, and finding a new tenant, two and sometimes three months have passed.

This means that you're also spending two months' worth of mortgage payments out of the "cash flow." Reinvesting that money into the property is not an unexpected outcome, it's totally expected and necessary. Doing so will continue to ensure that your asset holds its value. It's the cost of getting another tenant in the property.

The "cash flow" is gone and hopefully the real estate investor didn't rely on that money for anything other than reinvesting back into the property.

Most businesses are similar to real estate in that there's always a balance between immediate income, which we need to live on, and long-term income, which produces long-term wealth because it is tax-deferred and tax-preferred.

Let me explain briefly: a gain on an asset—equity creation—is long-term income, but of course it's not cash. However, it is net worth improvement, taxable only when crystallized, usually many years or even decades later. The taxes payable in Canada are only on 50 percent of the gain, thus roughly only 19.5 percent to 24 percent on the entire gain depending on the province you live in—a very powerful wealth creation strategy. To this day it's my preferred way to make money, in your sleep, with few blue dollars invested (see Lesson 49), and low taxes payable later only. Far better than employment income, which is taxed immediately and at a rate twice as high.

When I was early in my real estate investing journey, I owned a software consulting company that provided me with the immediate cash that I needed to live and actually funded my early real estate investments.

As I moved into real estate full time, in about 2005, I still needed to earn immediate cash to finance my lifestyle, and that's the best reason I can think of to sell buildings every now and again. If it wasn't for this fact, I would prefer to hold all of our buildings forever. Other than selling, the main option for generating immediate income is to refinance properties, pull out the excess cash and then continue holding them into the future.

I utilized both the sell option and the refinance option to earn income as I moved along my business and real estate journey. Of course we also take management fees, and the property management firm throws off some significant cash now that we manage more than 1,500 units, but it wasn't always so.

Having a long-term income is important for building long-term wealth, but without immediate income, you'll never have a chance to realize the long-term wealth.

Always, always ensure that you don't make the mistake that thousands of investors do in every boom time economy and forsake the immediate in favor of the delayed income. The delayed may never come, especially if the immediate is not cared for. Thus, take some chips off the table once in a while.

LESSON 47:
MOVE UNDERSTANDING FORWARD

Too often people think of a successful businessman or businesswoman as a hard-nosed, hard-negotiating kind of person. There may be some of those types who are successful, but in my experience, a far more valuable trait of the successful business person is the ability to truly understand others. It's the communication ability, and the successful negotiator, manager and owner has to be able to push the understanding to a further depth whenever they interact with others in a business capacity.

Typically when we buy buildings, we will never see or meet the owner of the building. Therefore, it's difficult to get a good read on their motivation for selling.

Knowing the motivation is important because it allows the buyer to craft an offer that's tailor made for the seller. When we know the motivation of the seller, we can perhaps give up something in order to get something else.

Often, since we don't know the motivation, we write two offers for the seller. One will include all cash (to the seller; to us it is cash and a new mortgage usually) and is for a lower purchase price, and the second will include a vendor take back (VTB) mortgage portion and a higher price.

This is our attempt to offer the seller something that might suit them more than a single offer would. We want to work with the sellers in such a way that will get them thinking about their motivation a bit more. It's a useful and effective technique as it gives us a better chance to hit on the seller's motivation.

However, there was one building in Edmonton I purchased back in 2004–05 when I did meet the owner and had a chance to speak to him face to face for many hours. Before I made a decision to buy, I wanted to do a building walkthrough, as usual, and went ahead and booked it.

Typically, when doing a pre-offer walkthrough, the onsite manager or the property manager will accompany the prospective buyer through the property, but this was our lucky day and the actual owner walked me through the property.

It was a building walkthrough like no other. Usually when you're looking at the building, the onsite manager will take you through the boiler room very quickly just to show you that there is a boiler there and that everything appears to be in good shape.

As a buyer, you want to take note if there are any leaks or if the boiler appears to be about to collapse, but the boiler is never a marquee part of the tour. Boilers are considered big money expenses in an apartment building and 99 percent of buildings have old boilers. If the building is 30 years old, the boiler is usually also 30 years old.

When we walked into the boiler room in this building, we saw two shiny new boilers. It stood out to me because of how rare it is, so I began asking questions (one of my core success techniques, since talking gains you no new knowledge, only listening).

It turns out that the second boiler was on the property strictly for redundancy. The owner very proudly told me about how he replaced the boiler and added a second just in case the first one breaks down. I was more than a little surprised, with the second $20,000 boiler.

The next thing that shocked me was to see a fully plumbed-in and functioning toilet right there in the boiler room beside the boilers. The owner informed me that he spends a lot of time at the building fixing things up. As there was no separate bathroom in the building that he could use, he put one in his boiler room so he had a toilet to use should the need arise.

We found out that he was an engineer and had a background in HVAC (heating, ventilation and air conditioning) engineering and that this building was kind of like a fun hobby to him. I knew the lingo of HVAC engineering because my father was involved in the same industry, and the owner and I chatted at length about related HVAC topics. The owner liked having the building because it gave him something to tinker with.

We kept our discussion going, and by moving the understanding forward, I was able to unearth the fact that the seller's brother had recently suffered a heart attack and was incapacitated as a result. This event was what led the seller to put his beloved building up for sale. He enjoyed the building, but at the same time he'd realized how short life can be upon seeing his brother get ill, so he also wanted to take more time to relax and enjoy life with his family.

By the time we left, I knew the seller well enough, and I decided that I was going to write an offer. In my cover letter for the offer, I discussed many of the things that we'd chatted about during the walkthrough. Specifically, I mentioned the value of his life decision to get out of the business.

This offer was unique in that it was the longest closing I've ever written in an offer—one year! I reasoned that the seller liked to tinker, so the one year would give him a full year to tinker. At the same time, I was totally honest with the seller and told him that I still had to raise some of the money to buy the building, and that I was buying another building at the same time as well (Windsor Estates). The one year between offer and closing would give me the chance to raise that money.

My offer was accepted by the seller, and the realtor told me that when the seller read our cover letter, he almost started to cry. He was very touched by the way I reached out to him as a person, and he was willing to work with me on the long closing.

I purchased that building for $1,900,000 and when I sold it four years later it went for $3,900,000. Between the time I made the offer in early 2004 and closed on it in early 2005, I had already achieved a large value lift through appreciation.

There is no way we would have been able to craft an offer and cover letter tailor-made to that seller if I hadn't moved our understanding forward during the walkthrough. I truly knew him well enough that I was able to give him what he wanted.

In business, moving your understanding forward should always be your goal. At the end of the day, you're dealing with people, and people like to understand and be understood. Often the best deal will go to the person who understands best, listens most and talks least.

LESSON 48:
HAVE A CASUAL DISREGARD FOR MONEY

The title of this lesson might shock and surprise you. Aren't entrepreneurs and business people supposed to be tightwads, closely and religiously guarding their money? Well, in some sense, yes, I mean nobody likes to lose money, including me.

But in another sense, all the money you spend or invest in business is an act of faith. Every day you spend money or invest it to further your business, with the belief that the money will either come back to you or that the money spent will provide some benefit to you and/or your team. In some way you expect the money you spend to be worth it, but you can never know with 100 percent certainty.

It's a simple fact that sometimes you spend money and it never pays off in any noticeable way. Sometimes it appears that you threw the money away. Business always involves risk, and there's always the risk that you will spend money that doesn't come back.

Over the years, I've attended dozens of conferences, sometimes as a speaker, more often as an attendee. Whenever you go to a conference, especially conferences away from your home city, you end up spending hundreds if not thousands of dollars. In fact, I often spend $2,000 on a weekend conference by the time I pay for accommodations, transportation, food and the conference fee.

It's not an insignificant amount of money to spend. I always go to conferences with the intention to learn, but also to meet someone who will push my business, network and knowledge further. Perhaps I will speak to a quiet guy who secretly has millions of dollars of investment capital and is looking for a good vehicle to invest it. Perhaps I can chat up a young go-getter who will eventually become a business partner. Perhaps I learn a new management technique. Perhaps I find a mentor for one aspect of the business.

There are so many opportunities to meet people with whom to build a relationship and thereby further your business, network and knowledge.

I often return home from a conference and when I think about it, I haven't really met anyone who specifically stands out as someone that'll be helpful to me in my business. I understand that the result of such encounters might pay off months or years later, and for that reason it's difficult to track the value of going to conferences, but still, some conferences don't result in any tangible forward growth with a lot of money spent.

Does that mean I stop going to conferences? Of course not. I know that I must have a casual disregard for money and that taking risks is part of business.

I may come home from some conferences without any tangible results, but I also come home sometimes with excellent results. I've met some of my biggest investors at conferences, and I've learned tips and tricks at other conferences that were worth way more than the money I spent to get into the conference.

Another example is spending money on office furnishings and surroundings. With Prestigious Properties®, we still maintain an office in Canmore, even though I don't live there anymore. It's a small office with only a few employees, but that didn't stop me from spending $40,000 of my own money on renovations to the office a couple of years back. As a result, we have probably one of the nicest offices in Canmore. Some of the individual offices have balconies with mountain views, and the office has beautiful statues and paintings throughout. It's a very high-end environment.

Strictly speaking, this money wasn't well spent. It doesn't contribute directly to the bottom line of the company, but I believe it contributes in a less measurable way. For example, we have an amazing accountant who has been with us for years. She occupies a nice office with a view in our building. I can't say for certain that the nice office has been the reason that she's stayed with us, but I have my suspicions that this is part of it.

We want excellent people, so we spend a little bit more money to attract them. Along with the nicely decorated and renovated office, we spend probably more than most companies on bonuses and benefits. We send our staff on vacations from time to time and we give them sizable bonuses from time to time as well.

We casually disregard money in a sense, but our record indicates that we have an excellent history of retaining quality employees. Of course, I can never know how the money spent will pay off, but in good faith, I spend it anyway. I believe this strategy has paid off well for Prestigious Properties®.

It's always an act of faith to spend money in business. Yes, you must do as much research and diligence as is necessary to reduce the risk of wasting money (we'll discuss that shortly). However, for every statistical probability there is always an anomaly. There's no guarantee that spending money on conferences or staff comfort will pay back in any meaningful way, but we do it anyway and on balance it does pay off.

The same rule applies to all investments in business whether a direct investment or a "soft" investment such as conferences or sprucing up the office. That's why you must develop a casual disregard for money. It may not come back to you immediately or on all occasions, but if it makes sense based upon your best research and best assumptions, then you must act in good faith and spend money.

LESSON 49:
GREEN MONEY VS. RED & BLUE MONEY

What is green, red and blue money? Green money is traditional money; it's what you think of when you hear the word "money." It's dollars, cents (in the United States, at least), bills, coins and digits on a bank statement. It is printed in green—or, more recently, a greenish color.

Red money is a mortgage or credit or a line of credit. It puts you in debt, in the red.

Blue money is time and expertise. The question you must always ask yourself when you undertake a project in business is: What is my time & expertise worth? How many blue dollars am I investing here? What is the risk beyond time and real dollars invested ? Can I lose more than I invest because I take on debt ?

In my opinion, most people do not value their time enough. Time is actually more valuable than money. Don't believe me? Think of it this way: money can be replenished at a later date. Sure, you don't like to lose money, but if you lose money, you can get more money later.

If you lose time, you cannot get more time later. Once time has been burned, you cannot get it back. (Perhaps this is why older people get up earlier than young people as they value the time left in their life far more than young ones.) If you lose your reputation that hurts, too.

Beginning real estate investors and business owners often act as though their time is worthless. If you decide that you want to purchase a property that you think will earn you $10,000 over the course of a year, but you have to spend 15 hours per week on that property, you're actually working for slightly under $14 per hour. Is that worth it? Well, it might be if you make $14 per hour in your regular job and want the long-term equity.

The above example is a little bit extreme, but new business owners and real estate investors make decisions like this all the time. When I purchased my first property (a rental-pool condo in Calgary) I knew that I didn't want to trade my time for the minimal profit that one property could provide. That's why I didn't buy a single-family home in Crossfield (an hour away) instead. I knew the Crossfield property would represent a significant number of blue dollars, which I didn't want to invest.

At the time, I was investing all my blue dollars into my software management company, a business that supplied an ample number of green dollars for my blue dollars invested.

What was the problem with the Crossfield property? I just didn't see how the significant blue dollars that I'd need to invest would produce a significant enough return in green dollars to justify the investment. This is because I could not produce an economy of scale. It was a single property and I couldn't systematize it in such a way that I would invest little time and reap large reward.

So I continued to invest my blue dollars primarily into my software company and my green dollars primarily into real estate. Eventually, I invested my blue dollars into real estate as well, and in those early years, I had to invest a lot of blue dollars. Real estate is up-front intensive. I did a lot of work in the early years and now, with the system that I have in place, I don't have to invest too many of my blue dollars to reap a significant return (in the good years!). When a large portfolio grows by 1 percent to 3 percent per year, the return for an investor, and myself and my partners, is significant.

In real estate you take on substantial debt, usually secured as a mortgage. You need a return on that. I have on occasion helped others co-sign debt. You must get a return on it.

So, as an example, if you can make 8% a year or 40% in 5 by just investing money, you must get a higher return by also co-signing a mortgage in a JV, for example. Let's say it ought to be 12%/year or 60% in 5 years. If you also invest your own time and expertise into the venture, i.e. you do all of it yourself, you must get an even higher return, aiming for 20%/year or 100% in 5 as shown in the figure below. The lines below 0 show potential losses if the market goes completely sideways; a possible albeit unlikely scenario with proper due diligence. Many real estate investors in 2008-2009 did not see this market correction coming and many a friend (incl. those in the REIN group) lost a pretty penny when highly levered assets did not go up in value but down, in markets such as Grand Prairie, Detroit, Las Vegas, Florida or California.

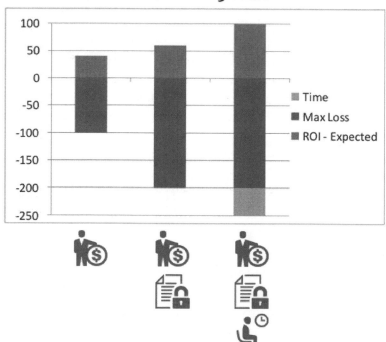

Two people I know at least went bankrupt due to personal guarantees on mortgages, i.e. red money. The risk of taking on debt shall not be underestimated, and as such it has to be rewarded if you co-sign a mortgage.

In addition, you may say that my time is now more valuable than it's ever been before. This is a benefit of building any business properly. There is an understanding that with an increased investment of your green, red and blue dollars in the early years, you will ultimately need to invest fewer blue and/or red dollars in later years and reap more green dollars.

A business that does the opposite is a business worth questioning seriously.

Take my Stony Plain houses, for example. It's been approximately one year since I learned that these properties were not operating as I'd originally intended when I went into partnership on these houses.

The biggest problem was that I didn't have a backup plan if the original partnership plan was to fall through. Fall through it did, and I ended up having to take care of the properties myself—that is, find a new property manager and new metrics for repairing a house vs. smaller but more numerous apartment units. If they were apartment buildings, I would simply have put them under the management of my normal team and treated them with the minimal blue dollar investment that I normally do with any other buildings.

But these two houses were outside the system (so to speak). I have no useful system for dealing with two problem single-family homes. It's been a year of getting renovations done, spending money and finding tenants. Finally, I am clear of the problem and as unbelievable as it is, I've probably spent almost as many blue dollars in the past 12 months on these two properties as on the other 1,000 units combined.

Which do you think has produced a greater number of green dollars for me, the Stony Plain houses or the 1,000 units?

Obviously the 1,000 units have been vastly superior at returning green dollars to me than the Stony Plain houses have been. When I started the project, I had the best intentions of earning some green dollars with very little of my own blue dollars invested, but it did not work out like that, and you may make a case that I did not value my blue dollars enough.

Blue dollars are in many ways more valuable than green dollars. Think and act carefully before you invest your blue dollars. Do your best to never throw away green or blue dollars, but if you must throw away one of the two, make it the green dollars since they can be replenished. Value your time like the precious commodity that it is and use your blue dollars wisely.

LESSON 50:
SPEND MONEY WISELY

I know that I already spoke about having a casual disregard for money, and I stand by that statement. However, I did not say that you should spend money recklessly. There is a big difference between having a casual disregard for money and spending recklessly. Having a casual disregard for money means spending money and having faith that it will ultimately be worth it. This does not mean that you're guaranteed that it will work. It means you expect that spending the money will be worth it. Spending recklessly means spending money without a plan.

So why would you expect the money to return when you spend it with a casual disregard? It comes down to a matter of research and diligence. When I spent good money investing in making a nice office space, I did not do it recklessly. There was a purpose to that expense.

First, at the time I was working there, and I knew that anywhere I was going to spend a great deal of time was a place I wanted to look nice. Second, I correctly believed, based on experience and evidence-based literature, that employees who have a comfortable, pleasant and classy work environment are far more likely to be happy with their jobs.

I wanted myself to be happy in my work space, and I wanted my employees to be happy in their jobs, so I reasonably believed, based on my knowledge, research, experience and diligence, that spending the money on making the office classy would pay off. This was not reckless spending but it wasn't guaranteed to be worth it either. Doing research is a key step in spending money wisely.

To this day I insist that the onsite manager's offices be spotless, functionally furnished, with pictures on the wall, comfortable and inviting to prospective tenants and the onsite manager, not some hole in the wall such as we find in many properties we buy (and then renovate). It pays back in spades. It does not mean we spend money on granite counter tops or stainless steel fridges in a suite where we can get only $700 in rent.

The question of how to spend money in any business is probably as old as business itself. It gets somewhat easier with experience, but one is never totally certain that the way he or she spends money in a business will be the best use of that money.

We deal with this question all the time when making capital investments in our apartment buildings. If we have $50,000 to spend, what is the best way to spend that $50,000? Spending the money in the right places (also known as "getting the most bang for your buck") is a skill that the real estate investor must become excellent at—and the sooner, the better.

How best to spend the $50,000? Should we outfit a building with new fridges in each suite? Should we replace the boiler? Should we re-pave the parking lot? Should we paint the building? Install a new canopy? Put in new hallway carpets? Add a new manager's office?

While we could do any number of those things, we generally prefer not to do those upgrades as they will not usually give us the greatest effect (bang) for our buck. We prefer to spend the small money to make the big changes.

For example, I love buying buildings with old, ugly, worn-out signs. A sign in the front of a building is often the first impression that a prospective tenant will have. They will get a feel for the building just from seeing that sign. Whenever I see an ugly, decrepit sign I'm flabbergasted that an owner could let the sign get so worn out. It costs probably $200 to replace it with a nice shiny new sign, if that, as often a coat of paint, a few hours of labour, and new letters from Rona for $7 will suffice.

A nicely painted door with brand new numbers on it looks great, as does a suite with new flooring. We often joke that paint is a structural element, if lathered on thick enough. We also like to install canopies over the front doors of our buildings. These touches are not the large, expensive items on a property, but they will generally create a more classy, clean and livable impression.

We know from experience and research that this is the case, so we focus our capital expenditures on the kinds of items that make an impression.

However, it's simply a fact that sometimes you have to spend real money on real items that won't create a stronger impression. There isn't a tenant in the world who cares what the boiler in the building is like—until it breaks down, that is. Nothing can make a landlord look worse than a major component such as a boiler going down.

With any business, there will be a version of carpets, paint and number plates, and there will also be a version of the boiler.

If you're a salesperson, think of your personal grooming, presentation skills and habits as the small impressionable items. Think of your car as the boiler. Not a single client is going to care about your car, until it breaks down and you miss an appointment.

Perhaps this is why in Germany to this day 75 percent or more of all taxis are Mercedes, since lost hours cost real money to any cab owner. Mercedes vehicles cost more, but they are also far more reliable. Thus, I tend to spend a lot of money on shoes, since broken shoes cost you a lot of "money" in a poor back or discomfort or missed appointments.

The point is that you will always have to spend money in a business and to spend it wisely depends upon a couple of things. The first is to research that what you're spending it on will produce the desired result. The second is to choose wisely between items that will help improve the salability of your business and the infrastructural items when necessary.

In a perfect world, you would have unlimited funds at all times to spend money on both, but in the real world, there are very few businesses that have this luxury. Therefore almost all business-es need to make these difficult decisions all the time. You're not alone in the bind of juggling cash flow concerns with the need to make capital expenditures. Most, if not all, businesses out there experience the same issue.

What the successful businesses don't do, however, is spend recklessly. At a certain point in your business, your number one priority has to be to focus all your energy on creating revenue. Some entrepreneurs throw good money after bad on useless and unnecessary items that they believe to be important. I've seen more than a few startups with large budgets for promotional pens and paper when they should just be out pounding the pavement.

Knowing the difference between recklessly spending money and having a casual disregard for money is an excellent start-ing point to spending money wisely. After that, the fine art of spending money wisely depends heavily on your research and balancing what will improve the salability of your product and the infrastructural needs.

LESSON 51:
CREATING MOMENTUM –
"THE FIRST MILLION IS THE HARDEST"

M y mother said this to me when I was very young, and for some reason it stuck with me through all the years. Keep in mind that my mother is not, and never was, a wealthy woman, but this expression has such uni-versal appeal that she latched onto it. As it turns out, she was correct.

My mom had a close friend whose husband had built a rather large and successful trucking company, and it was through this friend that my mother had heard the expression. I didn't realize until many years later that the same expression my mother told me in German when I was a child was also used in North America.

The actual number $1,000,000 is not the important thing, and in my own case it was significantly less than a million dollars that helped launch me into the next phase of business. In my case, you could say my proverbial "million" (that is, significant money) was made in the software consulting business in which I hustled for well over seven years after leaving IBM. There is no doubt that it was the major launching pad for me to go onto bigger and better things in business.

The reason that things get easier after the first "million" mirror "The Five Ways to Make Money," which we will discuss later in the book. Usually that first million is earned through your own work. You have to hustle your butt, pound the pavement, and just generally work harder than most others in order to get those first significant dollars.

You might even have to sacrifice something to make the first million, but whatever the case you won't get it without a lot of hard work. For me it was a matter of making sales call after sales call, presentation after presentation, and sending email after email. But I persevered, and the result was a small nest egg with which to start making other moves. Once I had that first significant dollar amount I learned first-hand what successful entrepreneurs have been saying for decades (this is where the saying came from). I learned that, in a sense, things get easier after the first million.

Things get easier for a few reasons. First, that significant amount gives you the ability to utilize the second way to make money (investing) and actually make a dent. Anyone can and should invest their own money. But if you're investing $10,000 the dent you're going to be able to make is a pittance compared to if you're investing $1,000,000. Invested at 8 percent yearly, a million dollars will return you $80,000, which is a decent salary on its own (especially if it is dividend income or tax-deferred and tax-preferred capital gains). When you get to the wealth station known as the first million, you can conceivably earn a good year's salary just off the interest from your investments. That alone makes it drastically easier to make much more money a lot faster.

The second reason why it gets easier after the first million relates to the entrepreneur's mindset. Once you have a track record of success along with a cushion of cash, it's far easier to be bold. Being bold is important because it allows you to take a few risks that might end up paying off in a big way.

For me, being bold came in the form of purchasing larger apartment buildings after I'd only done small individual condominium deals prior to that. Later I considered purchasing some franchises, which would have been strong cash producing businesses, but I decided in the end that the businesses (courier franchise, or restaurant-in-a-box or fast-food) were far too labor intensive and that I didn't want to commit that much of my own time, i.e., too many blue dollars required.

However, the lesson stands: the first million allows you to make decisions that are a little bit bold. It's different investing $200,000 when you have $1,000,000 than it is investing $200,000 when that's your life savings. It's incredibly difficult to be bold with every penny that you have.

The third reason that things become easier after the first million is that the first million acts as your track record. For me, it was far easier to attract investment money after I'd been successful in the software consulting business and then had a couple of successful apartment deals on top of that.

Anyone I'd asked to invest with me was starting to believe that I'd be successful by the time I started asking for money. If you ask for money and you've had a string of three successive failures, then you might have a little harder time getting investors to say yes than if you've already made your first million.

And the fourth major reason why it becomes easier after the first million is that when you have a little bit of money, you can actually start hiring people to take care of tasks that you used to have to do by yourself.

I initially hired an assistant to take care of many of the administrative tasks that I hated doing. This lifted an enormous burden from my shoulders and allowed me to spend far more of my time on high value added activities.

In a business, there are high value added activities and there are the more mundane activities, which must be done but don't add a large boost to the bottom line. Filing, answering phones, booking appointments, accounting, rent collection, securities filing, tax preparation and cleaning the floors are all examples of activities that are very necessary but that don't positively affect your top line. Having earned your first million, you have a lot more leeway to start hiring people to take care of tasks that are not suited to you and which don't help financially. Once you're spending more of your productive time on high value added activities, you really begin to fly higher.

Even my German mother knew that the first million was the hardest. For all the reasons stated above, this statement rings true.

LESSON 52:
DECATHLETE VS. SPRINTER
(GENERALIST VS. SPECIALIST)

We live in a highly specialized world. You see children in Canada playing hockey 12 months of the year while never playing another sport. Academics study for their advanced degrees for years, often immersed in the specialized minutiae of their particular track.

To be a successful piano player you have to study for years, practicing some four to eight hours a day. That can be done only if you love it. I play the piano too, and I like it, but I do not love playing chords or note sequences for hours on end. That's why I am a lousy piano player.

In professional life, we're implored from an early age to "learn a skill" and stick with it. Learning a skill or a trade is valuable in landing a good job, and it's the path that most people take and follow for many years.

It's the path that I followed for many years as well. I came from a specialized background, studying to become a software developer in my early post-secondary days, and taking technical jobs in the software field out of university.

The world needs specialists. Wherever you see a great product or service being delivered at large, you will see a large team of specialists all working together. Apple is famous for its great generalist, Steve Jobs, but the company would be nowhere without the original specialist, Steve Wozniak. The "second Steve" was the original creator of the first Apple computer. It was his partner, Steve Jobs, who took the computer and subsequently the company in many different directions, but from the first specialist Wozniak, Apple has always needed, and will always need, specialists to continue building great products.

Many people choose a specialty and work within that field for the rest of their days without stopping. This is a good thing, and the world owes these people a debt of gratitude. They impact our lives every day. Look around you at all the things in your world. Aren't you glad that the plumbing in your home was done by a genuine specialist? A specialist wrote that novel you like to read at night.

However, there's a place for generalists too. In business, especially small business, being a generalist can be a great advantage. In reality, though, many successful businesses are often started by the specialist who is also a generalist. This is the person who first plied the trade as a specialist before branching out into more general pursuits within the same business.

In my IBM days, I first specialized in UNIX database software. I eventually found my target niche within that mega-corporation as a kind of liaison between the customer and the development teams. I was a specialist who could speak the language of the generalist and at the same time was a generalist who could speak the language of the specialist. My unique skill set was valuable to

IBM and its customers.

But personally, I was still very much a specialist at that point. I still had no sense of sales, and since I was in a very compartmentalized company, I had never been exposed to any of the other aspects of the business. Marketing, sales and human resources were all taken care of in different departments. I was a product development guy at that point.

Ultimately I wanted to branch out, and that's why I took the sales position for Western Canada. I was still selling the database software, so the fit was perfect because it allowed me to leverage my specialized knowledge of IBM's database software while expanding my horizons into sales.

This was a critical step for me on my path to becoming an entrepreneur, but it wasn't until I left IBM to run my own business (along with my then-partner Howard) that I started deepening my general knowledge of running a business. Lightyear Consulting was a small entrepreneurial venture, and as such I had to start wearing more hats than in my previous incarnation with IBM.

When I started Prestigious Properties®, I really had to lean into the generalist within me.

Essentially, I am a B player in a few aspects of our business: market selection, asset acquisition, asset management and investor relations/sales. I also am not a D or F player (that is, a complete moron) in any of these important aspects of the business. One F can get you disqualified as an entrepreneur if you don't recognize it. If you are not good at sales, your business will likely fail. If you are a poor market research guy, you will fail too. However, you don't have to be an A player everywhere—like a decathlete in the Olympics.

Over time I replaced the B player (myself) with A players in every aspect of the business to get to greater heights.

If you watch the Olympics and watch the men's decathlon or the women's heptathlon you will realize that the winner is usually fairly good at all disciplines, a B player, with very few A's here and there. But most decathletes would not be able to compete in any of the 10 individual events in the Olympics and expect to be on the podium. The winner of a decathlon is also not an F in, say, high jump, as one very low score in any one discipline will not get you on the podium! Similar in a small business.

I've seen many starting business owners over the years who were wizards with the specialist aspects of their business, but who were terrible at some of the other aspects of their business. For example, at all of our buildings owned by Prestigious Properties® we have painters come in and paint suites for us. When they were done the job, we noticed that they really did a nice job, and we were very happy with their work, but then they didn't bill us for two months, and when they showed up with the bill, they demanded immediate payment.

We have a net 30-days payment policy, so it's difficult for us to process a payment before 30 days. The thing to do for the painters in question would have been to finish the job and then on the way out the door hand us the bill. These people were great at their trade but terrible at accounts receivable, which in a small business is very important.

As a beginning entrepreneur, I had no illusions that I was excellent at all facets of business, but certainly I was aware of the importance of being proficient, i.e. a B player at least. I worked on my presentation skills, my sales skill, my marketing skill and all the skills necessary to run a business (that is, move my B's to B+ or my C's or B-s to solid B's). I also had a certain awareness of the things that I didn't know. That's why I spent considerable effort finding and creating relationships with a property manager and a realtor when I first made the leap from small condominiums to apartment buildings.

Later, I was able to hire excellent specialists, and I became more of a switchboard, directing problems and opportunities to the right channel. Each of my in-house specialists now takes care of specialized issues, and my generalist streak has been given full rein.

Becoming a specialist has great value and I'd never urge anyone not to gain a specialist's knowledge. There are many advantages to having such knowledge. However, when starting a small entrepreneurial venture, there is every chance that you will need strong general skills and the ability to jump back and forth between different skillsets within the business, often in the same day. That's why I was not well suited for a large organization like IBM, as you will only be a generalist once you reach the very top, and for the first 25 years you'll be a specialist only.

LESSON 53:
EVEN STEVE JOBS WAS REPLACED

Steve Jobs is one of the most iconic businesspeople in history. He's right up there in the pantheon alongside Henry Ford, Dale Carnegie and Bill Gates. Yet, even after building a multibillion dollar company, he was still replaced. How is this possible?

Well, it's technically possible because he took Apple public and didn't retain more than 50 percent of the control. Perhaps there is a lesson to be learned from that alone, but this is not the big lesson, and even Steve Jobs said (in his famous Stanford commencement speech) that being replaced at the helm of Apple was the best thing that ever happened to him.

In the interim between when he was replaced and when he returned to Apple, he revolutionized another industry (the film industry, with Pixar), but Jobs also grew up after he was replaced at Apple.

At the time that he was replaced, his leadership had become delusional. He simply wasn't up to the task of leading such a megalithic enterprise as Apple had become. He was known for creating a divisive corporate culture within the organization and he was bordering on megalomania in his belief that his vision alone was valuable at Apple. During this delusional period, he was responsible for creating some of Apple's worst products and biggest flops.

Being ousted brought him back to himself, and by the time he returned he was a more stable and responsible adult, listening to the input of others and leading the charge with his trademark vision and focus, but also exhibiting a more balanced approach. When Steve Jobs returned, he was ready to be CEO of a massive, cutting edge corporation.

There are many lessons to be learned from this dramatic episode (Jobs's replacement). One is the fact that anyone can be replaced. One must have beliefs to be successful and to exhibit vision, but to be fully immersed in your own ego and maintain a belief of infallibility will certainly bring about self-ruin. Luckily for the world, Jobs was able to bounce back from that mini self-ruin. (Some argue, however, that he brought about a greater self-ruin because his death from cancer could have been avoided had he not delayed (for almost a full year) an operation on a tumor until the tumor had metastasized in his liver too.)

The bigger lesson to be learned is that different kinds of companies require different kinds of leadership at different stages of their growth. Jobs was the hard-charging visionary who pushed all the right startup buttons in getting Apple products to market and making a big dent in his industry and the world's vision of what computer technology could be.

He was a rebel with a background in art, psychedelic drugs and Buddhism, and while these diverse aspects of his background may have helped him throw off the shackles of societal norms (including the norms about what is possible in technology startups), it no longer served him as well once Apple was a full-fledged corporate behemoth.

When he was replaced, Jobs's rebel leadership was no longer the answer to Apple's needs, and the man who ultimately led Apple as CEO, John Scully, was a former Pepsi executive, a conservative leader with experience in mega-corporations.

I'm going through a similar circumstance at the moment with Prestigious Properties®. I was great at the early startup phases of the business, and I became very proficient at the medium-sized business stages. From $80,000 to $80,000,000 has been an incredible journey. So what is the next step? Do I lean in and try to take the business from $80,000,000 to $800,000,000?

This is a topic I think about regularly. Part of me is interested in such a pursuit, but then I remember that I want to enjoy the rest of my life without having too much stress and that I do not like larger organizations with too much structure. The long work hours and pavement pounding I once put into my business pursuits do not appeal to me as much as they once did. So perhaps the road to $800,000,000 is through partnerships, and perhaps I cede control to others, join with others and maintain a more advisory role—or it may not happen at all, or only very gradually. Perhaps there is a follow-on book here. We shall see.

Changing the leadership roles of the CEO in such different companies (an $80-million vs. an $800-million company) is a big stretch. Steve Jobs was unique in that he was the startup CEO, then he couldn't maintain that role when the company was massive, but even more remarkable was that he was able to come back and lead the charges and take a company that was (by the time he returned) failing and turn it into not just a massive corporation, but the world's most valuable company.

The final lesson of Steve Jobs's replacement was in his renaissance as a businessman. He was always a visionary and creative type; being ousted at Apple allowed him to get back to his roots at the same time as he grew up. In his own words:

> *"The heaviness of being successful was replaced by the lightness of being a beginner again, less sure about everything. It freed me to enter one of the most creative periods of my life."* He added, *"I'm pretty sure none of this would have happened if I hadn't been fired from Apple. It was awful-tasting medicine, but I guess the patient needed it."*

Being replaced, being rejected, even experiencing a powerful failure are all opportunities to re-evaluate and come back to the core of who you are, grow, and plan for your comeback. Comebacks are not inevitable, and many people allow a failure or an ouster to ruin them for life. Steve Jobs is a wonderful example for us about the power of the down-cycle in a professional life.

When business throws you such a curveball, whether it's atmospheric, such as a market collapse, or brought on by your own extravagant ego (as was the case with Jobs), you can take it as an opportunity to grow, just as Steve Jobs did.

LESSON 54:
RISK – HOW CONSERVATIVE DO YOU WANT TO BE?

FEAR = FALSE EVIDENCE APPEARING REAL

There is a perception about risk that is common but false: many believe that risk can be eliminated. In spite of what the big marketing of some of the financial services companies would have you believe, there is always risk when it comes to business and investing. Even beyond business and into the normal pursuits of life, there is always a degree of risk. You may fail.

Are you married or do you have a girlfriend/boyfriend? If so, it means that you made a choice, and by saying yes to one partner, you've said no to all other possible partners. That means you've risked choosing the wrong partner. You've risked the chance to find another, perhaps better, partner. All of those nights when you sat at home reading books or watching TV were nights when you could have been playing the field, potentially finding a better partner.

That's a risk that many million people take all the time, and it's a risk whose potential for a negative outcome is realized for many million. With divorce rates around 50 percent, the proof is in the pudding. Choosing a spouse is risky business. Yet would you rather take that risk and possibly find the right partner, or remain "risk free" and never partner up?

The answer to that question will be different for everyone, but the evidence of how many people give marriage a chance is found in the numbers who try. Nothing ventured, nothing gained, is as much a reality in the realm of love as it is in the realm of business.

In business, this maxim is especially true. We tend to think of choosing a partner as more of a life mission, and therefore as less of a risk. A mission requires risking it all, whereas a business venture is often viewed as an undertaking that could sink you financially and therefore in the eyes of others be a failure. Not surprisingly, people often recoil at the thought of risk.

In addition to that, some people are simply less inclined to risk than others. If I were to be placed in the trenches of a war, I've always thought of myself as a more of a machine gun artilleryman than a sniper: I may hit on the first shot, but if I miss, I have no problem taking more shots until I hit it my target.

Some people are snipers: they spend more time and effort doing research, and as a result they don't assume as much risk. But when they shoot, they hit their target almost every time. Still, they're taking fewer shots, and therefore they sometimes miss by doing nothing.

There is nothing wrong with this approach, but it can lead to missed opportunities.

In Prestigious Properties®, we have bought only a very small number (not even a handful, two actually as of 2013) of properties that lost money. In Detroit, we purchased a building for cash. Even with no mortgage on the property, we could not make the building cash flow (this means that property expenses, such as taxes, repairs, property management fees, insurance and utilities were more than our rental income). In addition, one of our buildings in Powell River, British Columbia, lost us money, primarily because the envisioned pre-Olympic boom coincided with the financial crisis of 2008–09.

But we also purchased multiple buildings in other, smaller markets, like Wetaskiwin and Fox Creek in Alberta, Sudbury (Ontario) and Yorkton (Saskatchewan). Each of these purchases, in addition to the ones in Powell River, which eventually did earn a significant return, was considered risky by our previous standard.

Previously, we'd purchased buildings mainly in Edmonton, Alberta, so when we diversified to some different markets, it was inherently risky. However, we weren't reckless, we learned a great deal from the Detroit experience, and as a result we did more diligence on the markets and buildings that we purchased in Fox Creek, Sudbury and Yorkton. Therefore we were reasonably certain that we would earn a profit in spite of the fact that the properties were more risky than our traditional purchases.

The fact was that, at the time, our traditional markets had peaked, and buying in those markets, while less risky, also carried the risk of almost no reward. History has borne this out and as we sit here at the end of 2012, values have only now climbed back to the values of 2007–08.

So taking the risk of buying in Yorkton, Sudbury or Fox Creek was actually a very important step along the way. There is no reward without risk.

I know a fellow investor who purchased 160 units in Fort McMurray, Alberta, in the late 1990s. For anyone not familiar with Fort McMurray, it's the epitome of a boomtown. It's the center of the great Canadian oil sands boom. Real estate values there today are outrageous, and people happily spend the money to live there for the opportunity that exists within the city. Fort McMurray is a force to be reckoned with. In all of Canada, only Vancouver's housing prices rival Fort McMurray's!

But in the late 1990s, there was a great deal of skepticism about the future economic potential of the region, and when my friend bought the property, he was met with more than a few sideways glances from his colleagues. He took a massive risk.

Luckily, he was a savvy investor and bought for the right price, $10,000 per door, which meant he paid a total of $1,600,000 for a big building of 160 units.

Today, that building is worth $300,000 per door, which means in appreciation alone, he earned $46,400,000 over a period of approximately 15 years. The cash flow in the building has been pretty good too (grotesque understatement).

This is an extreme example of profit, but the lesson stands: no risk = no reward. Sometimes risk does lead to big reward, though, as my fellow investor friend found out—but he still had to scrap and fight and work to hold that building during the difficult time before the market started quantum jumping. Even timing risky business maneuvers is not enough for success. You still have to take care of all the other elements of a business, each of which on its own can be very risky.

Enjoy your pristine ship. Shine it, admire it, but above all, get out there on the open seas and sail it. Yes, some ships will sink, but most do not, especially if one studies the weather carefully and has skill as a captain. The pain of never risking anything is greater than the pain of risking, failing and trying again. And if you go sailing, ask for an experienced captain who has seen a few storms. As the old saying goes: "We have old pilots, and we have bold pilots, but we have no old, bold pilots."

LESSON 55:
RISK – FAIL YOUR WAY TO SUCCESS

"Ever tried. Ever failed. No matter. Try again. Fail again. Fail better." – Samuel Beckett

S uccess in my life has come through a series of attempts. You have to try in order to succeed. As I mentioned briefly in the last lesson, I'm more of a machine gun shooter than a sniper. I've always believed that it's better to have a good product complete than a perfect product in the pipeline.

There will always be an opportunity to perform kaizen on the imperfect product, and there are numerous advantages to having the thing done. Let's imagine you're building a website for your startup business. You could spend months and months and months building the perfect website. Or you could complete it quickly and then go live with it. You will attract a certain amount of business to it, and when it's a functioning website, you will see what works and what doesn't. In addition, you will get feedback about what aspects of the website people like. In short, putting your website out will lead to valuable lessons that you otherwise could never get.

In one sense, going live with a bad website could be considered a failure. Anything that doesn't lead to perfect success could be labeled a failure if you choose to label it as such. But this does not mean that you just recklessly do whatever passing fancy crosses your mind. You must decide on only a very few opportunities. There are many thousands of opportunities and you will most definitely not be able to follow up on all of them, nor should you.

Research and due diligence still rule the day, but ultimately, you have to go for it, in spite of the risk. The reward will be either a) that you succeed, or b) that you fail and you learn. Often a failure will launch you into a higher degree of success than you'd even been aiming for with the original failure. For this reason, it's a good idea to think of failure as a blessing while still doing everything you can to succeed.

In my business life, I've experienced this several times. One of my greatest attempts that ended up looking like a failure was the restaurant that I started with a partner. The business opened its doors in 2003 and we eventually closed shop in 2005 (although I was ready to shut it down six weeks after we opened it).

I was not able to close the business because of a personal guarantee I'd made on the building lease for the first three years of the 10-year lease. My partner had no cash of his own invested, and as a result, he didn't mind losing a bit of money. He stood to earn a salary from the business, so being profitless wasn't a big problem for him.

This in itself is a lesson learned. From this experience, I learned that I always like to have my partners invested with at least some of their cash so that if the business loses, they lose. An active partner is great, but even they should invest some money.

The failure of the restaurant attempt ended up launching me into Fireside Property Group, our property management division. There were many reasons for starting that business.

First of all, it made sense because we'd just acquired a large building in Edmonton and Prestigious Properties® was reaching critical mass (we had enough units that it made sense to keep property management in-house).

Second, by then I knew how to build the business, and I had the connections of true professionals. I had built-in income, and I had the knowledge to do it. Even with those items in place, it still took a couple of years to become profitable as we added clients from other building owners.

But the greatest success carried forward from the restaurant failure was that I always made a point of having my partners invested in the business, and focused solely on the business. The timing was such that it also coincided during the breakup period with Dave, my overly aggressive partner in Prestigious Properties®.

This is significant, because the first active partner I had in Fireside Property Group (then Prestigious Properties® Canada Ltd.) was another man named Rick. He decided about three years in that he was not willing to invest the time and energy required to grow the business, despite having a 33 percent stake in it, so I bought him out. We managed to part company on very good terms and I retain a friendship with this former partner to this day.

With Fireside, I took the two biggest failures that I'd recently experienced and learned my lesson from them. Looking back now, as Fireside Property Group is a successful property management firm, managing more than 1,500 units primarily in Alberta, I can say that both of those "failures" were productive and were good examples of failing my way to success.

To this day, I still maintain that I will not let an overly aggressive partner dictate the trajectory of one of my businesses, nor will I go into partnership with someone who doesn't have a financial stake in the deal.

I still have some lessons to learn, but there is no doubt that failing has provided me with some of the greatest lessons I've ever received. Failure is a guaranteed outcome in business (at times). The important thing is how you respond to the failure. Do you continue to make the same mistakes, or do you learn, grow and use the failure as a launching point into your next major success? I know which one I prefer.

LESSON 56:
RISK – TOLERANCE TO
RISK FLUCTUATES

I remember a moment when I was working with IBM when I went to the water cooler for a drink of water and over-heard two men having a discussion. One of the gentlemen posed the following question: "If two people have similar educa-tion, similar drive, similar experience, and similar intelligence, what makes one of those two more successful than the other?" The second speaker responded, "The more successful one will be the one who is more willing to take on risk."

I'm not sure that the equation is as simple as greater risk = greater success, but I certainly agree that greater risk brings greater possibility for substantial reward. However, the possi-bility of greater reward does not mean that the reward will be realized. The only thing that taking on greater risk means for certain is that one is taking on greater risk. The result is always unknown, and there is no doubt that while some reap reward from risk, there are those who reap significant failure from the risks they take.

One thing certain is that to be successful in life, you will have to take some risk along the way. There is no escaping risk al-together, especially someone who is looking to grow their life, business, wealth and even happiness. You can live a super safe life, but it means never changing, and there's risk enough in that.

How much tolerance to risk do you have? However you an-swer that question right now is not necessarily how you will answer that question in the future. There's every possibility that you didn't answer the question the same way in the past either.

I was far more willing to take big risks when I was younger. When I purchased my first apartment building, I was willing to put a personal guarantee as well as $100,000 on the line. At that time, it represented a very large portion of my net worth. As a percentage of net worth, I would not risk that much today, although I'd risk more than that in absolute dollar terms, but this is because my net worth is far greater today than it was when I purchased that first building.

Risk is relative to your financial station in life as well. This is why things get easier after the first million. When you make what would be a relatively small risk in proportion to your net worth, it's a bigger actual risk than what you would have been capable of making when your net worth was lower.

Certainly I would not risk as large a percentage of my net worth now as when I was a younger man in my thirties. I'm in more of a wealth preservation mode now that I've been working most of my adult life toward building wealth. This wealth preservation mode is brought on by the fact that a) I've earned the money, and b) I'm in my fifties. For both of these reasons, I don't want to go completely back to the drawing board.

I've been an entrepreneur for so long now that I'm unemployable in most traditional firms, except perhaps as a CEO. I'm outdated in my original skillset as a programmer. And through my entrepreneurial years I've developed an income expectation that would not be achievable for me in a job.

I have no desire to start from scratch in any job or in any entrepreneurial venture, so I choose to preserve my wealth. This does not mean I don't try to grow it. However, I do not try to grow it as aggressively as I once did. I do not risk as much as I once did. I diversify my investments more now. I take all the steps necessary to preserve wealth, and this means minimizing risk to a greater degree than I did earlier in my trajectory.

When you're a young and driven entrepreneur, you're far more likely to take big risks and seek the big reward. Why not? When you're young, you have a lot more time and inclination to start from scratch if need be. You feel you have unlimited time, energy and opportunity. And while I would agree with the opportunity, you're always constrained by time.

Energy wanes over the years too. Today, I like to sleep in, rest well, exercise regularly, eat well, read the newspaper in the morning, and have a relaxed breakfast on my deck. I have no inclination to pound the pavement to the same degree I once did. Don Campbell, the head of REIN, calls this living your "Personal Belize."

To this day, I'm certain I could attract more investment capital to Prestigious Properties® by making more phone calls, having more meetings, and flying more often to New York or Toronto, where much capital is controlled. The problem is that I want to live the life I've already worked hard to create. This means that I must preserve my wealth, so I'm not willing to risk what I have for an unrealized promise of what might be.

Luckily for me, this station in life allows me to partner with others who are younger, more willing to hustle, and more willing to risk their time. This means that even though my risk tolerance is lower, I'm still able to accelerate my wealth and complete great projects by leveraging the efforts of others. In a sense, I'm paid for my knowledge now and for my prudent use of resources, namely my money, in the employment of others' effort.

My risk is limited, but my ability to grow wealth and get things done are still strong. This is actually one of the best positions to be in, and perhaps a good reason for you to continue working hard on the path that you've chosen. Your risk tolerance will fluctuate throughout your life. This is normal. Whatever station of life you currently reside in, you can maximize your results based on the risk that you're willing to take. Take stock of your risk tolerance and give it careful consideration when making an investment or a business decision. Then do your best based on what kind of risk you're willing to take.

LESSON 57:
KNOW YOUR WORTH

C an you imagine Warren Buffett cleaning toilets after hours? Does Richard Branson do his own tax filings? Can you imagine Elton John moving the piano before his show?

These questions are absurd. These business tycoons' time is worth too much for them to consider doing such tasks.

So why do businesspeople all over the world spend time doing tasks that they should not be doing? The topic of delegation is a big one, but I believe the root of these wrongheaded actions is that many businesspeople don't know their worth, or more frequently, they do not trust other people enough even for small tasks.

If you're a plumber operating a one-man business earning $60 per hour, and if it costs you $60 per hour to pay someone else to do your bookkeeping, then perhaps there's an argument for you do to the bookkeeping yourself. A bookkeeper is likely less than $30, so it makes sense to outsource that.

If you're that same plumber five years later, and now you have a team of five plumbers, each of whom earns $40 per hour, now it obviously does not make sense for you to do your own bookkeeping. Perhaps by that time, you, as the manager of the enterprise, are busy full time with keeping your plumbers working and charging customers for their work.

If this is the case, your job now pays you $100 per hour ($60 invoiced per hour to customers, minus $40 paid per plumber, i.e., $20/hour net per plumber times five). Therefore, it does not make economic sense for you to do a task yourself that you could pay someone else $60 per hour to do, nor may it make sense even for you to be a plumber at $60 per hour.

But, not knowing their worth, many entrepreneurs will continue to do the general tasks of the business that are not high value added tasks. This will stifle forward growth at some point. There is only so much you can do by yourself, and then at a certain point, you must start to leverage the efforts of others in order to grow further.

Knowing your worth implies that you are good at something, but not everyone is worth the same. Many entrepreneurs underestimate their worth, but there are others who overestimate their own worth. Becoming valuable is important no matter what business you're in. It's key that you figure out what your abilities are and then spend the time and effort developing a skillset to match your abilities.

At Prestigious Properties®, I'm lucky enough to have a partner (in Scotty) who is a very skilled sales professional. Scotty came from a skiing and car mechanic background, and although he loved skiing, it was apparent that he didn't have what it would take to be a professional skier.

So, he did what came naturally to him and he started working for a ski company. Scotty quickly started selling skis, and within the first year of his reign as ski salesman, his company's sales in his assigned territory had skyrocketed 600 percent.

Scotty's a natural salesman, and he took his natural ability and developed it further, to the point that he became a full-fledged expert. This was how he showed up at our doorstep, as a full-blown expert in sales. Just as in his previous incarnations, Scotty also boosted sales at Prestigious Properties®. Our conversion rates skyrocketed as well, and we raised 200 percent more money in the first year with Scotty on board.

Salesmanship is a skill with high worth. Scotty achieves such remarkable results in sales that it only makes sense that he should be worth a lot. You might say that Scotty has learned his worth along the way.

Many entrepreneurs, especially those not trained in sales, underpay their sales people. A good sales person might make more than the CEO or VP Finance!

Eventually, the goal for every entrepreneur should be to spend most of his or her time on high value added activities. There are a couple of reasons for this. First of all, the high value added activities are probably what got you into the business in the first place. If you got into the business of owning a flower shop, it was probably not so you could keep books, sweep sidewalks, or scrub toilets. Hopefully, you got into the flower business because you have a special love for flowers and a talent for knowing how they should be arranged and where they should be placed.

If you love flowers, you can probably speak about flowers in such a way that captivates and inspires others. Therefore, if you are a passionate flower entrepreneur, you should be sharing your love of flowers with anyone you meet. You should be doing large and small presentations about flowers to everyone you meet.

In real estate, there are two, maybe three high value added activities that each investor needs to focus on:

1.   Raising money
2.   Buying buildings, houses or condos with good terms
3.   Managing property impeccably

Doing all of these at the same time, along with all the other tasks of running a business, is very time consuming. Naturally, the real estate entrepreneur has to delegate any tasks they can. The less essential, lower value added activities such as bookkeeping and making appointments are common tasks to delegate, but these three value added activities are more difficult to delegate.

Of the three big activities listed above, the easiest to delegate is property management, and even it is not so easy, especially if you own single-family homes and especially if your properties are in small towns with few property managers (or, even worse, ineffectual, unprofessional managers).

Still, it's the easiest of the bunch, and when I started in real estate, I knew that I did not have the time or inclination to be a property manager. That's why I chose the rental-pooled condominium over the single-family home (in the small town of Crossfield) for my first investment. (Who knows, perhaps if I had chosen a good property manager for the house in Crossfield I might own 100 houses today, like some folks I know. More on this decision in lesson one.)

My next move of delegation was accounting and annual tax filings, in addition to legal and mortgage financing. The next, knowing my worth, was to hire an assistant, but that did not come until a few years into my real estate career. I was busy enough that I realized how much work it really was to raise money and purchase buildings, so I got an assistant and delegated many of the non-value added tasks. This freed me up to spend the bulk of my time raising money and buying buildings, which proved to be a very valuable decision.

It wasn't until years later that I was able to make the even more advanced step of delegating the two bigger value added tasks of raising money (Scotty) and building acquisition (Mike). To achieve that, I had to give up a portion of equity and fees. In essence, I took a smaller piece of a bigger pie. It again was a great move as my worth is now greater as an enabler than it is doing even the core activities that I once had to focus on.

Knowing your worth and then focusing your efforts on that core area are absolutely essential to business growth.

LESSON 58:
INVESTING – WEALTH PLANNING IS
ABOUT THE WEALTH OF THE PLANNER

One of the five ways to make money (which we'll discuss later) is to invest your own money. I also believe that learning the ropes by investing your own money must come before investing other people's money.

Investing your own money forms part of your education in the real world of investments. It's often quite an ugly picture in the investment world. On top of the outright scammers out there (of which there are many), there are also a slew of underperformers not living up to their promises.

However, the most common way that investors lose money is not by being scammed or misled, it's through the harmful effect of paying too much in fees. The investment business, or financial planning business is a business. Don't get me wrong, there are some awesome money managers or investment planners out there, earning their keep. However, the big investment industry players often charge so much in fees that over the course of 10 years, it is not uncommon for an investor to come out with exactly what they put in, or only slightly more, in spite of decent market performance. When you add the eroding effects of inflation, many investors actually end up with less in their investment accounts than they originally put in.

Like a restaurant, you must gauge if what you pay is worth what you get. Some planners are awesome and charge you 1% or 1.25% of assets under management – no problem. But there are many firms, especially mutual fund firms, that will charge a fee of 1.5 percent to 2 percent of assets under management, regardless of the performance of your investments. This was quite a good deal for the average investor back when they were consistently earning 8 percent on their money invested, but it's not such a good deal now when the investment firm might only earn about three or four percent – before their fees. It effectively means that once they remove their 2 percent fee and you take into account a likely (minimum) 2 percent rate of inflation, you have at best broke even or often, lost money by "investing" with that big bank or investment firm, while the bank or investment firm of course kept their 1.5 to two percent regardless of asset performance.

By investing like this, you'd have been in the same position if you had kept your money in a sock.

Who is the main beneficiary of all these fees? Well it is the banks who own them directly or indirectly, or their employed or self-employed so called "wealth managers" or "financial advisors". It is a multi-billion dollar industry, well oiled and well marketed. Why? Using a large Canadian top 5 bank as an example, let's do some math. It is a publicly traded firm with an earnings multiple of around 12. This means that for each $1 million under their investment, the bank collects 2 percent in fees, or about $20,000. When they deduct costs of about 50 percent for office space, a "wealth manager" and marketing, this is $10,000. Multiply it by the P/E ratio of 12 and this $1 million under management is worth $120,000 to the bank. Therefore, it makes sense that the bank would want to get your $1 million under their management. The more money they manage, the higher their value, so what do you think they focus their efforts on: growing their asset base or getting great returns to their clients?

To add $120,000 to their value, they simply have to manage another $1 million. And in an attempt to acquire that $120,000 in additional enterprise value, the bank will likely spend about $30,000, maybe even $50,000. That $30,000 or $50,000 is called advertising, dinner meetings and expenses. In essence, the bank will take the money that they're getting from you in the form of fees and then turn around and spend it to acquire more investment capital into their pool. Hence the fancy TV ads, the sponsored events like the Gran Fondo, the billboards or whole newspaper sections.

In many ways it's a broken system. Having the knowledge of how the fee structures work is an advantage to you when looking to raise money for your own real estate or other business projects. It's impressive to anyone who's been through the wringer a few times when you tell them that you will be paid mainly on performance rather than just fees.

The investment industry is a business. Its profits come from the fees you pay them, not from the performance of the investments they make with your money. It's their business to get your money away from you and into their coffers. Of course, they have to deliver some returns, or you would leave. Their main goal is not your asset performance, but an asset performance good enough you will not leave, and then growing assets under management. Does it really make sense to pay them 2% just to hold cash, as often a significant portion of a mutual fund is cash? Have you ever heard a wealth advisor suggest to not invest with them as you are rich enough, and rather donate some money, spend it or give to your children? Have you ever heard them recommend more income producing real estate or a franchise or a small business where a lot of money can be made for you personally ?

Spend time and effort investing your own money and see how much you are charged in fees. The learning experience of this alone is valuable. If you can navigate the landmines of investing your own money, you will be a wiser investor and will be more attractive to potential investors to your own business when you're ready to ask others to invest with you.

Lesson 59:
Investing – Choosing an Advisor for Your Investment Portfolio – Or Should You Do It Yourself?

Many people wonder: how do I manage my money? Do I do it myself? Or do I hire an advisor (or two or three)? Every person has a bias (that includes me, of course), so there are many ways to look at this question. Before you decide how you would like to proceed, the first thing to get clear about is: what is a financial advisor anyway? It turns out it's not such a simple question!

Remember, everyone has a bias. To understand the different types of advisors, you first have to understand their bias (or biases). To understand their bias, you have to understand how they get paid. Once you know how each type of advisor gets paid, you will have a better picture of how and why they advise you.

There are three types of advisors:

1. The first (and probably most common) type of advisors are those that sell only certain products and make a commission and/or trailer fee for each investment product they sell. Most of these advisors are salespeo-

ple and the fees can be very high, and their interests not necessarily aligned with your goals!

2. The second type are those that sell expertise for dollars. For example, it might be $1,000 for an initial consultation, and then $200 to $500 per hour after that. This setup gets you a better chance at impartiality.

3. The third type are those that take a percentage fee of assets under management. This percentage fee is independent of the product. It's often about 1.5 percent to 2 percent for the first million and then less as the asset base grows.

How do you decide which one is best? Why not try all three types? In fact, why not try two people per category and see where it goes?

However, the best investment you can make is in the 15 centimeters of real estate between your ears. This investment has the highest yield. The way to do that is to read books (such as this one, so thank you for that), read blogs, go to conferences and spend time networking (at both formal events and informally).

One rule of thumb that you can follow and is a very effective way to teach yourself how to invest is this: allocate money into 10 different buckets that are not too closely correlated.

For example:

1. 10% real estate

2. 10% gold/silver/platinum or other precious metals, in real form, stocks or ETFs

3. 10% oil/energy/gas/uranium stocks or exchange traded funds (ETFs)

4. 10% transportation (oil, gas, buses, trucks, shipping, cars) stocks or ETFs

5. 10% retail firm stocks or ETFs

6. 10% bonds or bond ETFs

7. 10% banks/financial institutions stocks or ETFs
8. 10% high tech stocks or ETFs
9. 10% pharmaceuticals/health care stocks or ETFs
10. 10% specialty/exotic (e.g., international currencies, penny stocks, colored diamonds)

Leave your money invested in each of those 10 categories for a year, then sell those that have outperformed and bring the quantities back to 10 percent each. If gold has gone down 20 percent and now is 8 percent of your total portfolio, then buy some gold or gold ETFs so that gold totals 10 percent again (see chart on the next page). Then go through each of the remaining nine categories and sell what is over the 10% average allocation, buy more of the underperforming ones. If oil has slumped, buy more oil stocks or energy ETFs, etc.

This is a proven and Nobel Prize winning strategy! Specifically, professors Markowitz, Miller and Sharpe won the 1990 Nobel Prize in the Economics category for this portfolio management approach. It's easy to execute from your computer with ETFs and some specialty private equity (so called Exempt Market securities) products. It's a low cost and low time investment. It's cheap and almost no advisor is required!

The end result will be that you will have a fairly balanced portfolio. If a balanced portfolio is your goal, then this strategy is outstanding.

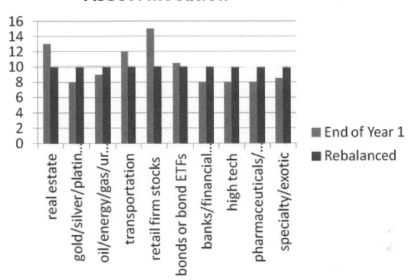

Leave your money invested in each of those 10 categories for a year, then sell those that have outperformed and bring the quantities back to 10 percent each. If gold has gone down 20 percent and now is 8 percent of your total portfolio, then buy some gold or gold ETFs so that gold totals 10 percent again (see chart on the next page). Then go through each of the remaining nine categories and sell what is over the 10% average allocation, buy more of the underperforming ones. If oil has slumped, buy more oil stocks or energy ETFs, etc.

This is a proven and Nobel Prize winning strategy! Specifically, professors Markowitz, Miller and Sharpe won the 1990 Nobel Prize in the Economics category for this portfolio management approach. It's easy to execute from your computer with ETFs and some specialty private equity (so called Exempt Market securities) products. It's a low cost and low time investment. It's cheap and almost no advisor is required!

The end result will be that you will have a fairly balanced portfolio. If a balanced portfolio is your goal, then this strategy is outstanding.

Other folks specialize because they know a market well or have certain beliefs. For example, some investors are gold bugs, some are oil guys, and some are real estate guys. Others love physical gold coins or gold bars (but not gold paper assets like stocks or ETFs) or colored diamonds.

When you're just starting to invest your own money, it's often wise to try multiple types of investments. It's also wise to ask yourself numerous questions such as: How active do I want to be with my investments?

Some types of investments are labor intensive (in fact they are often more accurately described as a business). Real estate can fit this description as it frequently takes a large amount of effort. The "10 buckets" strategy will be far less labor intensive, and you might find "hands off" investing to suit your investment personality.

If you've read this far into the book, you already know I'm primarily a real estate guy, although 10 to 20 percent or so of my net worth is in stocks. Specializing in real estate has worked well for me for many reasons. One of them is that I'm not patient enough to do well in stocks. Real estate forces patience on an investor because it is not so liquid. Once you're invested, you can't liquidate with the click of a mouse!

Since I'm primarily a real estate guy, I won't give you advice on what gold stocks to buy or whether silver at $20 per ounce is a good buy, or which ETF is best (although I do have opinions on this subject). Real estate has served me well, but you have to decide what is right for you. I've done very well in real estate and continue to believe in it in the right markets, with the right asset types, with proper leverage and impeccable management. In other words, I believe that a substantial portion (say 30 percent to 50 percent, perhaps even higher) of your investable assets should be in income producing real estate!

Another asset class is private equity. This means shares of private, non-public firms (as with real estate, it assumes some specialized knowledge on your part).

Co-owning a restaurant franchise, a UPS store, an M&M meat shop outlet, a Mr. Lube, a garbage removal firm, an Internet startup, a software development firm, or any profitable small or medium-sized business is usually far more profitable than co-owning a publicly traded firm. Private firms trade at a three to five multiple of earnings, but most public firms trade at 10 to 12 or more! Many REITs trade at 12-18 times earnings due to the low risk. The same profit in a private firm will cost you maybe half to a third of what it would cost in a public entity.

These two investment classes (real estate and private equity) are very poorly served by traditional advisors. This is primarily because they do not get paid for it. However, real estate and private equity are a substantial form of wealth for entrepreneurs or any successful business person, often 70 percent or more. I fit into this category, since real estate (through Prestigious Properties®) and private equity (through Fireside and a few other software related investments) have served me very well.

Of course I also have some ETFs and stock investments. For my more liquid investments and RRSP (i.e., non real estate and private equity related holdings), I try to follow the 10 bucket allocation model. This is largely because outside of my real estate and private equities, I'm not a specialist, and therefore I want a balanced portfolio. In addition, my wife and I use an advisor whom I pay with a percentage fee on assets under his management (although that is being revisited right now due to the excessive fees relative to asset performance) and follow a stock newsletter religiously now (after many years of trying it myself and failing).

What kind of returns can you achieve realistically in the low interest years of 2011 to 2016 ? With a well balanced portfolio of stocks, you can achieve approximately a 5-6 percent return per year. With bonds, mainly quality corporate bonds, you can perhaps achieve 3-5 percent. With real estate you can achieve 12-15 percent or more if you do it yourself, or two-thirds of that amount if you invest with syndication firms such as ours, as we have to do all the work and get the mortgage, and must be rewarded for it (see previous chapter on green, red and blue dollars). You must make more money if you do it yourself as you put your expertise and time on the line (see chapter on blue money), but also your limited credit (aka red dollars) via a mortgage. Taking out a mortgage in your own name carries a degree of risk, and you can (and people have on occasion) lose more than you invest. Since we put all the work in, have deep expertise, take this mortgage risk and sign personal guarantees on them usually, we have to get rewarded for it, with low fees and a win-win oriented equity/performance feature (see chapter later on win/win investing with others and JVs)

Some folks love stock picking and have done better than the average, but if you look at the stock market over the last 10 or 20 years and factor in a 2 percent mutual fund fee, 6 percent is actually a high estimate. It's likely that you won't achieve 6 percent unless you buy ETFs and have a low fee, or better, no advisor.

Many advisors should be called salespeople. There is nothing wrong with selling, it is vital to any business in fact, but it's important to know that the notion of neutrality in your advisor might be ridiculous if he or she is really a salesperson. You do not go to a BMW dealer to get advice on what car to buy or even whether to buy a car at all; you go there to pick a BMW. The same goes with financial products. You don't go into your bank or financial planner to get investment advice; you go in to pick investment products.

Today, we too use advisors as the real estate securitization space has changed in Canada. By Canadian securities law, enacted around 2010, any person selling securities has to be registered with an Exempt Market Dealer (EMD). An "exempt" market product is one that is exempt from the requirement of issuing a prospectus, a lengthy and expensive document required to be tradable on a securities exchange. This EMD has overhead and the selling process is now more involved but also more in-depth due to KYC (know your client) forms, more filing requirements and lengthier offering memoranda (almost approaching the sheer volume of a prospectus). The result: far higher sales commissions, and lower investor returns, but you will be provided with a choice of investment products. Since this industry is still very young it is too early to tell if products in this exempt market space perform better than expensive mutual funds or if they fall into the same trap of benefitting mainly the product operators and sales people.

In order to be educated about what kind of advisor you're choosing, make sure you ask your advisor the following questions:

1.   How do you get paid?

2.   What do you invest in?

3.   Show me a sample client's (name removed, of course) portfolio and its return over 3, 5, 10 or 15-plus years.

Very few will be able to answer and show results!

LESSON 60:
INVESTING – REAL ESTATE IN YOUR RRSP OR TFSA?

An RRSP or TFSA should be viewed as a basket of investments. In the basket you can place various eligible investments or financial instruments. Some of these RRSP- or TFSA-eligible investments can include stocks, bonds, GICs, mortgages, call-options, cash or mutual funds, but not real estate directly.

So how can you participate in real estate with your RRSP or TFSA?

For most Canadians, investing in or participating in real estate can be done inside their RRSP or TFSA; however, there are some restrictions. Either way, inside or outside an RRSP or TFSA, investing in the right real estate can pay excellent long-term dividends if done well. Of course, it's a great idea to max out your contributions to both of these tax free/deferred vehicles (see the lesson on maxing out RRSP), and at the same time, it's wise to have some of your investment money in real estate. Why not learn how to participate in real estate through your TFSA/RRSP?

Three broad options exist to participate in real estate within your RRSP or TFSA.

OPTION 1:
MORTGAGES.

Most real estate is encumbered by a mortgage. A mortgage is a loan, secured by real estate. It's not directly real estate. However, a mortgage is a safe way to invest in real estate. Since it's debt and not equity, you do not participate in the overall performance of the real estate. If you invest in a mortgage, your TFSA or RRSP becomes the lender. You are the bank! You can hold:

A. A single mortgage

B. A share of a mortgage (called a syndicated mortgage)

C. Shares in a MIC (Mortgage Investment Corporation). A MIC pools many mortgages and allows the individual investor to co-own a share of multiple mortgages in their RRSP or TFSA.

The risk of this investment (payment default by the borrower) has to be compared to the fixed return of this investment. The return may be as low as perhaps 4 percent to the high single digits. On the more risky assets, you could earn as much as the low double digits (example: 10-14 percent).

A second consideration is whether or not the mortgage is on a to-be-constructed property or an existing property. As a broad rule of thumb, a to-be-constructed property carries a much higher risk of non-payment, as the property does not yet exist. As such, the interest rate on this mortgage should be much higher than a mortgage on an existing property (to compensate for this additional risk).

Consider return of your capital before you consider return on your capital when evaluating this first type of RRSP-eligible investment option.

A tertiary consideration is the position of your mortgage on the property title. If you are in first position, and the mortgage is unpaid, you are first in line to get paid from a foreclosure action (should an undesirable foreclosure happen). Even then, loss of capital is possible, especially in a construction mortgage.

If you're in second or third position, other lenders get paid first. Thus, the risk of non-payment increases with the increase in position on title. Some trustees or MICs don't allow second or higher position mortgages, but some do. Therefore, before you invest, do your homework on the risk of the loan and then gauge if the offered interest rate compensates for this risk.

OPTION 2:
PUBLICLY TRADED STOCKS THAT INVEST IN REAL ESTATE

On both the U.S. and Canadian stock exchanges there are a number of firms that invest in real estate. Some invest in apartment buildings, some in commercial properties such as industrial parks, and some in office buildings or retail malls. Others invest in hotels, campgrounds, trailer parks or recreational properties. Some invest internationally in numerous cities and nations, and some only in certain cities. Some hold existing properties and others invest in land projects or construction.

A common sub-class of these publicly traded firms is a REIT (Real Estate Income Trust). A REIT pays out the majority of its income monthly, and as such can be an excellent vehicle for retirees or those folks seeking monthly income. A couple of the options are the expensive brother of the real estate stock (or REIT), a mutual fund, and its less expensive diversified sister, the index fund or ETF.

All these publicly traded vehicles provide the benefit of instant liquidity, quarterly reporting and regulatory oversight, but also the severe drawback of stock investing in general. Specifically, a publicly traded stock is at the whim of market sentiment. At times you will experience wild, unexpected swings because some politician said something or a report came out that was less positive than expected, buy/sell manipulation by insiders, or panic selling due to rumors or opinions by market analysts or newspaper articles (which may or may not be accurate).

OPTION 3:
PRIVATE FIRMS THAT INVEST IN REAL ESTATE.

Many people seek an investment vehicle outside the often irrational stock market. People have to live somewhere if the market is rising or falling. People still go shopping (albeit less frequently) if the market is down. Trucks need repair facilities owned by someone. Office workers need space.

Real estate has been around for thousands of years and will be around for thousands more. Have you been to Rome? Some buildings were built over 2000 years ago and still exist, but I digress.

To buy or build real estate, much expertise and much money is required. Therefore, the idea of coupling expertise with money partners is a perfect marriage. A corporation or partnership is formed. Partnerships are not a new concept. England, Holland and a number of nations explored the world several hundred years ago by ship. To finance those fairly expensive shipping expeditions, partnerships were created.

The captain and his crew got a share, as high as 50 percent of the profits (spices, gold, slaves, land) and the ships' financiers got the rest. Write a check for 4,000 pounds, and you will get a mountain named after you in the New World and one percent of the profits; if you write a check for 10,000 pounds your name will be on a new city and you get 2 percent of the wares or something along these lines. Thus the idea of limited partnerships was born.

The idea of a limited partnership is that one party has the expertise. In a real estate context this might mean prospecting, analyzing, buying, getting financing and managing apartment buildings. The other party has money to invest, seeking a fair return, but lack the expertise, the time or the desire to prospect, analyze, buy and manage assets.

One party invests, the other party does the work, and profits are split according to a pre-determined, and annually inspected, formula. Since this corporation or limited partnership owns real assets, in the real world, with real money changing hands for real assets, the values can be established readily, without the often irrational stock market value swings. It can provide a better alternative to investing in the publicly traded market, if fees are low and equity splits win/win profit oriented at the end.

My company Prestigious Properties® has helped hundreds of people utilize their TFSA and/or RRSP to invest in real estate with excellent results, although of course the years 2008 and 2009 were not too sexy, but that is now behind us.

Once you max out your RRSP and/or TFSA, your next step is to find a suitable investment that will offer you a substantial return. An excellent part of your tax free/tax deferred portfolio should be real estate. These three options are good ways to participate in real estate through your TFSA/RRSP.

LESSON 61:
INVESTING – MAXIMIZE YOUR RRSP:
MAKE 50-66 PERCENT "ON THE HOUSE"

D o you pay income taxes? What is your marginal tax rate? For most Canadians it's well over 30 percent and for many it's over 40 percent! Therefore, if you put money in an RRSP the government sends you a refund of slightly over 40 percent if you are in the highest marginal tax bracket!

If you put $25,000 in an RRSP by March 1, then you get a check for over $10,000 back! This means that your net investment is only $15,000. In essence, you invest $15,000 and it's worth $25,000. That's a 66 percent return in a few weeks. Not bad.

If you're in the 33 percent tax bracket, and you put $15,000 in an RRSP by March 1, then you get a check for about $5,000 back. Thus, your net investment is only $10,000, and it's worth $15,000. That's a 50 percent return in a few weeks! Not bad, either !

It's free money, "on the house," care of the Canadian government. No other investment gives you such a high, immediate and risk-free return. None!

That's why it is prudent to maximize your RRSP contributions, as you get significant free money today, and delay the repayment of it, via taxes on taking it out of your RRSP eventually, for years or even decades.

Once the money is in the RRSP account, you can then decide how to invest it. Of course, I believe that a real hard asset, outside the stock market, such as a high demand and recession-proof apartment building, is one of the best options, and that's why Prestigious Properties® offers investors the option of investing from within their RRSP.

80 Lessons Learned:
From $80,000 to $80,000,000

PART 3 :
REAL ESTATE LESSONS

LESSON 62:
HOW TO START OUT IN
REAL ESTATE INVESTING

S ome of you have come from humble beginnings. We all have humble beginnings in some sense. We're thrown into the world, and we have to make it on our own. As a child we had our parents' help, but eventually we have to make it on our own.

My parents helped me with many things, but figuring out how to build a portfolio of real estate investments was not one of them. In fact, when I arrived in Canada, I was shocked and amazed to see young adults my own age (mid to late twenties) who were attending classes with me at the University of Alberta and who owned their own home! I had never owned a home; I had always been a tenant (either with my parents or by myself), and never once imagined owning one. In fact, it had never even occurred to me that someone must have owned all the real estate in Germany where I grew up, or in Canada where I lived after 1986.

My dad was a manager at a construction company, managing HVAC installations for large buildings. He had a good job, and he taught me many things, but we weren't home owners! Unlike North America, home ownership is not a rite of passage or a cornerstone of financial success in Germany, so when I saw those young men and women owning a home when all I had was a bike and some kitchen utensils, I started to wonder if they were onto something.

But I had other things on my mind, and there were many steps between then and now. Today, my company Prestigious Properties® Inc. controls approximately $100 million worth of real estate, mostly in Western Canada.

I did not inherit the knowledge to become a real estate investor. There's a common belief in society that says to do anything great you must come from greatness. This is not true. Not only did I not inherit business or real estate knowledge, I also didn't inherit any money. I came to Canada with less than $1,000 in my jeans. I had zero savings. My family was a humble one. They grew up in postwar Germany. Money was sparse, and on top of that I had siblings. This meant that the money my parents did have wasn't going to spread far enough to see us all through university. I worked every summer through university and I took officer training in the German Luftwaffe because there I could receive funding for my education.

I most definitely didn't have a large pool of funds to draw upon to kickstart my real estate investment career.

So, am I a great wizard seeing the future in my crystal ball? Or am I a super individual, smashing through barriers with a single flick of my finger? The answer might surprise you. I'm just like you. I started off like anyone else, with baby steps, but wanting something better. Getting from where I was to where I am now was a series of incremental steps. That's the path I recommend to anyone reading this book.

You might be thinking that real estate investing will provide you with a lot of money. Well, it can probably do that (over a long period of time), but for you to be able to pull it off, you're going to need a few things, such as:

1.   A solid money foundation. (See the section below about the five ways to make money.)

2.   Knowledge about the basics of getting started. Any real estate investment is only going to work with certain other fundamentals in place. (See the section below about getting started.)

3.   Other people's money. (See the section below about structuring joint ventures.)

Real estate investment is not a "get rich quick" scheme, it's a "get rich for sure" scheme on the road of incremental progress. After two decades of hard work, I too became an "overnight" success.

LESSON 63:
THE FIVE WAYS TO MAKE MONEY

I've thought long and hard about this, and I believe that there are only five ways to make money. Of course there are thousands of sub-categories to the five I've identified here, but in essence each kind of money-making boils down to one of the five ways discussed here. In addition, many of the ways to make money require us to utilize more than just one of the methods discussed here.

Money is integral for all of life. We trade it for all manner of goods and services, and no matter what, you'll need some way to generate money in your life. But beyond just making a living, there's a good chance that you want to make a life, build an empire, create a continual source of income, or all of the above. Making money is endlessly fascinating and endlessly important, even for those who do not have any or state that it doesn't matter to them.

Even for people who've found their perfect job and their joy in life through their work, it's valuable to think at least a little bit about making money. For such people, they've likely perfected the art of number 1 (working), but they should still strive to do well at number 2 (investing your own money).

There's a good chance that if you're reading this book, you are probably wondering how to generate cash for your real estate transactions. Perhaps you're looking for ways to start leveraging other people's money.

If you're new to real estate investing, you may want to focus on mastering number 1 (working). This will be your foundation for a successful life as an investor. I'm not one who suggests, recommends, teaches or thinks it's a good idea to invest other people's money on the first, or even the second, attempt at investing. To be successful in life, business and real estate, I believe in the power of experience. You need it, and you should seek it while risking your own money.

Number 2 (investing your own money) is a wonderful step to take before you ask others for their cash. Focus on the fundamentals of work and investing, and one day you will be able to ask others for their money. Building a foundation of your own money from your own work and your own investing gives you the right to try number 3 (investing other people's money), and it often necessitates number 4 (employing others).

Throughout it all, you will likely become knowledgeable. You've earned the right to sell your knowledge at that point, and that's when number 5 (earning money from intellectual property) comes into play.

Many people only earn money from number 1. Fewer people earn money from number 2, and fewer still from numbers 3 and 4. The number of people who earn money from number 5 is very small in comparison to the total population. You can earn money from all five—in time—but you have to take each one of them seriously in order to earn money from them.

So, let's look at them a bit closer.

1. WORKING – EARNING AN INCOME

Working. This is the most common way to start. Working is exchanging your time for money. The more time you give, the more money you get. It's a pretty linear relationship that has been proven successful through the centuries.

Work has a bad reputation in some circles; there are people who believe it's beneath them to trade time for money. But work is where it all starts, and you should never feel belittled by working for your money. Most successful people work very hard, even long after they have to.

In addition, some people believe work is the only way that they can make money. Obviously, this is not true, and everyone should develop at least one additional way to make money beyond working.

What's important in working is to figure out how to save a (hopefully large) portion of your income. Saving also has a bad reputation in many circles. This is partially for good reason, as saving alone is insufficient for creating wealth. This is due to the fact that dollars are depreciating every year through inflation. But saving does have its place.

If you save money, you're on your way with your own nest egg and you can begin to invest your own money, which is the next logical step for many.

2. INVESTING YOUR OWN MONEY

Investing your own money is an essential step toward creating wealth. It's the powerful step of using money to grow money. This concept alone is enormously powerful, and just like you usually learn to ride a bicycle before you're allowed to drive a car, you should also learn to invest your own money before you invest others' money.

However, if you build a strong foundation of knowledge as well as a track record with your own money, and if you've become an expert at one kind of investing, then you've earned the right to ask others to participate.

3. INVESTING OTHER PEOPLE'S MONEY (OPM)

Once you've mastered investing your own money, then you have the right to ask for other people's money. The source of the investment money could be people who know you well or people who initially do not know you at all, such as joint venture partners. It could be money partners or people who control your access to mortgages or lines-of-credit (such as banks).

Whatever the source, investing other people's money always requires an additional commitment of due diligence and care on your part. Losing your own money is a terrible shame. Losing other people's money is potentially lifestyle threatening for your investors. People invest their money with the best of beliefs and intentions, and you as the expert need to exercise a deep level of care and skill when you invest others' money.

4. EMPLOYING OTHER PEOPLE

This is like number 1, except now rather than trading your own time for money, you're now trading others' time for money (for you). Obviously this involves a degree of risk because the people whose time you're trying to leverage will need to be paid regardless of whether or not you're making money. To do this, you'll have to be well capitalized, have a plan, a strong market and a good product/service to sell.

Employing others also works far better when you've earned the right to employ others by building your own expertise. Like investing other people's money, there are now others depending upon you, so it requires a deep level of commitment, knowledge, planning, care and skill.

5. EARNING MONEY FROM INTELLECTUAL PROPERTY (IP)

Have you ever written a poem? Have you ever written music? Have you ever made a painting? Have you ever made a movie? Have you ever invented something? Each of these is an example of intellectual property (IP)!

Vast businesses are built around this: think Bono, think The Beatles, think Microsoft, think Oracle, think Apple, think Nike, think Pfizer. In other words, think the drug industry, the music industry, the movie business or a book publishing company. Of course, to deliver the intellectual property, there has to be an infrastructure around distributing and marketing the product. But if there is demand for your intellectual property, then you'll find the infrastructure.

So there you have it in a nutshell: five ways to make money.

Are you aiming to fire on five cylinders? Are you currently firing on half a cylinder? Try harder, or try different ways, to fire on all cylinders. Depending on where you are in life, and which of the five you've mastered, move cautiously but consistently toward another.

LESSON 64:
WORKING – EARNING AN INCOME
(INVESTING YOUR OWN TIME)

"It is amazing what you can accomplish if you always do."
Thomas Jefferson (Third President of the United States)

It might seem painfully obvious that work is a way to make money. But if your goal is to get ahead in life (financially and in terms of happiness), then you must master the art of working. We currently living in an unparalleled era of work avoidance. There are millions of people who don't want to work and don't know how to work.

You may scrape by in life with an anti-work attitude, but it will certainly make your life more difficult. I believe government handouts (through pensions, tuition subsidies or free healthcare, for example) play a big part in people of all walks of life having an attitude of entitlement about how much they should earn and how grand their benefits should be. Perhaps that partly explains the rise of Asia, or Asians in North-America, since many of these benefits do not exist in Asian countries, or if they exist they are very small.

People working behind the counter of massive government-funded edifices are shielded from the cold, hard facts about how hard it is to make money. If you want to get a clear picture of how much work, training, knowledge and understanding are needed in order to make money, you must get out from behind the edifice and attempt to make it on your own. Knowing the truth about making money will serve you well in your working life, and it is there, your working life, where you will build your entire foundation for a lifetime of wealth building success.

But many people already fail at this. They don't take work seriously. They show up late for work. They chat with friends online. They do personal business on the side. They don't understand the business they're in. They don't give a 100 percent effort to their employer.

Yes, you can hide for a few days or a few weeks, but most employers realize who is an excellent worker and who isn't after a while. If you work hard at your job, you get ahead. To succeed at your job, give the extra 10 percent, or the extra four to five hours every week. Read up on your industry. Go to industry conferences. Seek a mentor. Read, read, read! Learn, learn, learn! Doing well at working takes effort, but it's effort well worth it, as every hour of effort strengthens your financial and moral foundation.

Eventually, through enough hard work, you will get promoted. You will get more money per hour for your work. If you have more skill, you will get more money. Formal and informal education helps. If you work hard, and get more money than you spend, you can save some money. Don't ever underestimate the value of your work. You might be sitting in a career right now thinking you just can't wait to get out and become a full-time real estate investor.

That sounds sexy, but the reality is that your job will provide you with the financial foundation to actually begin investing. People often dream of the result before they even begin. How are you going to begin? Build a foundation through your hard work. This formula worked for me, and it has worked for every successful investor I know.

Take your job seriously, work hard at it, be wise with your money, and live below your means. I didn't buy my first brand new car until 2003. Why? Lynda and I lived within our means. We never had any debt, except when we eventually bought our first house in Toronto five years after we got married. Lynda and I lived in a small (rented) townhouse when our children were young.

I worked hard at my job, I saved money, we lived within our

means, Lynda worked full-time or part-time and we were able to save some money. Yes, we did go on vacations to Europe or Hawaii with the kids eventually, and yes, we did eventually buy a second car (a basic necessity in Alberta), but that was way later. In the early days, we lived within our means, with an ugly used car and cheap furniture. We carried no debt and I spent considerable energy on my work. It was the early foundation from which everything else followed.

Yes, you will hear the odd grandiose story of the investor who never really had to excel at work first, or the investor who used other people's money on his or her very first deal. I never said these scenarios were impossible, but they are very rare and are not something most should strive for.

It's like an average NHL hockey player comparing himself to Sidney Crosby. Sure, Crosby played professional hockey at a very young age, but the fact is that only a very few NHLers can and should play in the NHL at age 18. The vast majority need to play extra years of junior hockey before they get promoted to the NHL. At the end of the day, they're still playing in the NHL, so what do they have to complain about? Think of it the same way when you want to leapfrog the working step on your way to becoming a full-time investor.

LESSON 65:
INVESTING YOUR OWN MONEY

If working is the equivalent of playing junior hockey, then investing your own money is the equivalent of playing hockey in the minor leagues. When investing your own money, there's truly something on the line, and it really is a training ground for you, especially if you have designs on investing others' money in the future.

When you buy real estate, mutual funds, stocks, ETFs, GICs, bonds or whatever fits your risk tolerance, skills and timeline, then you're investing your own money. It takes time to find out what a good investment looks like. Take it seriously. This investment could be more passive (a stock, let's say, or a mutual fund, or an ETF) or more active (say real estate or active stock trading or a franchise). What's important isn't the amount you invest, it's the process of understanding your investments and seeing the power of money at work.

If you invest well, then you're not trading time for money. Now you're into the world of using money to create more money. If you invest well, then your investments will churn cash for your next investment; and if your goal is to leverage other people's money, then you'd better create a solid track record. Investing your own money first is the best way to build that track record.

Investing your own money gives you a chance to develop a specialty. Nobody who isn't a specialist should have the right to ask for someone else's money to invest. When I say that you should specialize before you can ask others for investment money, I mean that you should specialize down to the smallest degree possible to begin with.

This means that instead of being a commodities specialist, you should be a wheat specialist, or better yet a mid-west durum wheat specialist. Rather than be a precious metals specialist, you should be a gold specialist, or better yet a gold prospecting firm specialist in South America. And rather than being a real estate specialist, you should be a specialist of one property type (say single-family bungalows), in one area (say, a five- by six-block radius). After you gain more experience, then you have the right to expand your expertise because then you can apply the rules you've learned from your initial specialization to a broader context.

Investing your own money will help you become a specialist. Many people, after floundering around with the extreme fees of the institutional investment world, end up realizing that their own home has added more to their net worth than their other investments. This is often the impetus to begin investing in real estate for real.

For me, I actually didn't make money on my first home, but I saw the potential of it, and I'd spent some time studying how to invest in real estate. Eventually (10 years after first thinking about it) I started investing in real estate and it wasn't long before I started to realize some gains.

I decided to specialize, and just as I'm recommending you do, I did it with my own money first. I gained momentum with my own money, and rather than spending it on fancy luxuries, I plugged it back into my own investments. I can't stress enough how important this process was to me in becoming a professional real estate investor. It is amazing how many people attract a lot of capital because of their slick marketing rather than their expertise. Don't fall for it. Look for expertise, proven over a lengthy period of time, built with their own money first.

LESSON 66: INVESTING OTHER PEOPLE'S MONEY (OPM)

Even if you're only investing other people's money in a small way (say, your parents' or friends' money on single-family homes), it's still the big time when it comes to the average person. You're earning income on other people's money! Don't ever forget how special that is, and don't ever forget how much responsibility it carries with it.

Don't ever believe that investing other people's money means that you're earning a passive income. Yes, there is a sense in which it is passive, especially when it comes to appreciation. But to earn income from other people's money you must work a lot. There's research, writing offers, re-writing offers, seeking legal advice, more research, interviewing potential property managers or tenants, accounting, property management oversight, property acquisition, getting bank financing, and raising money. Then there's banking, writing up reports, and doing ongoing research.

The good news if you're investing other people's money in real estate is that the job is heavily front loaded and it does get easier the longer you hold the real estate, especially if you have impeccable property management in place. If you don't have impeccable property management in place, why are you asking other people to invest their money?

Part of the reason they would invest with you is because you have a system for every aspect of the business, especially management. They can buy their own properties and manage them poorly themselves! Passive investors don't want or need that, and that's why they're giving you money to invest.

Investing OPM always assumes a degree of risk. Don't believe anyone who tells you that it's not risky to invest money, especially other people's money. Even the best predictions are less than 100 percent accurate. When you buy a property to hold or to flip, you will never know exactly what the outcome will be.

Perhaps a war will break out and the entire market will correct as it did in 2008–09 in the so-called Great Recession. Perhaps your three-month renovation project becomes a nine-month project. Perhaps your inspector missed the fact that the property has major foundation issues. Things like this happen. It's called risk. But that doesn't mean we do nothing. Assess the risk involved and go ahead: present the deal and ask for OPM.

If you're investing with private money and you borrow at, say, six percent, then you invest it (based on well-researched assumptions) expecting a 12-150 percent return. This is what you expect based on your research. Regardless of what actually happens you must pay the rate you agreed to pay when you borrowed other people's money. Still, you invest at a more uncertain yet frequently much higher rate. This is called risk taking. For any risk, there will be reward, and it's your job to assess them both and take the risk when the reward seems right.

If you're involved in a joint venture, then both the investor's return and your return are dependent upon you putting together a successful deal. It's not unheard of for both parties to lose money or just barely squeak by. If you're barely squeaking by, what's the point? Investments are for making money, not working hard to break even.

For most people, investing other people's money is a step to take only if they've already succeeded at 1) working and 2) investing their own money. Most investors aren't fools (although there are some) and they look at your previous career and track record to gauge the likelihood that you will make them money. A lot of people only dream of using OPM. Don't be a dreamer—be an action taker based on a history of (small) successes. Then charge small fees and performance based equity stake or bonus. No one minds paying for your performance if you indeed perform. Don't be like a mutual fund that charges big fees regardless of performance, and OPM will flow your way after some considerable groundwork based on hard work, expertise and ability to invest your own money in the chose endeavour.

LESSON 67:
EMPLOYING OTHER PEOPLE
(INVESTING OTHER PEOPLE'S TIME)

This is using other people's efforts to produce money for yourself (and them, through salary or commission). This assumes that there will be enough income produced from the efforts of the people you're employing that every employee can be paid and all other expenses and taxes can be paid. As the employer, you're paid last. You have a duty to make sure all your bills are paid on time; this includes employees' salaries.

Employing people is no easy business. As soon as you employ others, you may run into such issues as staff productivity, improper training and unhappy workers. These are not trivial matters, and they can have a seriously negative impact on your business.

It's often a good idea to employ the efforts of others as a means of augmenting your own efforts first (this means contracting certain tasks to free up your own time). So, for example, you might decide that your time is too valuable to do bookkeeping anymore and therefore hire an outside bookkeeping firm. This also releases you from the trickiness of having full-time staff. Now you just have to pay a bill to the bookkeeping company rather than keep a payroll. It's easier, but it will have the same effect: it's a form of using other people to help you make money.

However, for as much effort and difficulty as managing and maintaining a staff can be, it is also a way to truly gain momentum. If you're a plumber who can make a maximum of $60 per hour, then hiring other plumbers and keeping them busy with work at that same rate (while keeping half for your business), means you will earn far more money by keeping a staff than you could by working in the field.

It is very hard, unhealthy actually, to work more than 2,000 hours a year; it's isn't sustainable. Thus, at $60 per hour you can make at most $80,000 to $100,000 per year. And you always have to market, sell and account for your time, which may take about a quarter of your time. The only way to make far more than $100,000 a year as a small entrepreneur is to have additional staff who assist you in marketing, organizing events, promotion, accounting, cleaning, billing, etc.

The more each individual tradesperson makes, the more the owner of the business makes off each employee. A law office earns hundreds of dollars per hour from each lawyer who works there. It takes a lot more effort to keep the staff trained and happy than just having a one-man or one-woman business, but the upside is enormous.

Employing others likely assumes that you are an expert at something. You can try to maintain a staff of workers in a particular field without being an expert, but it's not recommended.

I have a small staff with Prestigious Properties® along with a couple of partners. I can't imagine being the big cheese of that office without being a real estate expert. Some of my people are more specialist than I am at specific aspects of the business, but

I am an overall real estate expert. This makes it much more powerful when we have meetings or work on projects. I understand them, and I can communicate with them in a way that they understand.

You might have a small or large business where you pay people a wage or salary and then use their time to make money for yourself. Usually you have to work hard to lead by example. You will likely need to risk some of your own or other folks' money.

LESSON 68:
INTELLECTUAL PROPERTY

Intellectual property is probably the least common way to make money. But it's through the ownership of intellectual property that some of the greatest fortunes have been built. Think of Bill Gates and his Microsoft set of software products, or the John Deere Corporation and the machines they build and patent, or think of the Beatles, Elton John or Michael Jackson, or think of Harry Potter or James Bond movies. Elton John makes money today in his sleep, as does the Jackson clan (after Michael Jackson's untimely death), and so could you!

It's almost always the case that intellectual property alone is not enough to earn money. Both Microsoft and John Deere, or the various book, movie or song writers mentioned, have massive businesses surrounding them to generate the profit. What good would the patents be if nobody was developing the product and bringing it to market?

There is, however, a value to the intellectual property, since it can be licensed—say, 99 cents per song, or $2 per ring tone, or $200 for a new Microsoft product, or $20,000 a month for a DB2 (or IMS, CICS, MQseries or Websphere) license that I used to sell at IBM or Lightyear Consulting. In addition, intellectual property is bought and sold all the time to others, perhaps to Disney or from a small software firm to a big one, or to Sony Records.

Developing intellectual property is time-consuming business, however, and the payoff is not certain. For every Bill Gates, Steve Jobs or Stephen King, there are probably 100 (or 1,000) people who are equally driven, talented and intelligent, but perhaps who didn't have the right timing, or who just barely missed the boat. For example, my former partner Howard and I launched a software firm to develop what today would be called an app for the emerging PalmPilot wireless market in the late 1990s. After spending about $250,000 on it we realized a further $1 million was required to bring it to market and we abandoned this venture. There are thousands of similar stories of "almost" Apple or Microsoft stories, one being the PalmPilot which was touted as the "next best thing" around the time of the early 2000s.

The good news about intellectual property is that with the rise of the Internet and all the various means of reaching an audience (websites, blogs, Facebook, Twitter, live streaming, YouTube, etc.) it is easier than ever to develop your intellectual property and bring it to market.

Of course, there is a downside to that, for as easy as it is to develop the product and bring it to market, it's equally easy for people to pirate that product and spread it around the Internet for free. Whole industries in certain countries, such as China, live off the cloning of original products.

Do you have some special knowledge? What do you do that not everyone else can do? What do you know how to do that others would want to learn? That knowledge can be the basis for developing intellectual property.

But not all intellectual property is created equal. Intellectual property can take years and years, along with thousands of experts, to develop (think Boeing jumbo jets) or it can be as simple as creating a training program about your favorite activity (knitting, perhaps).

Just as with your skillset, not every piece of intellectual property will be equally valuable. Your intellectual property might only be worth a few hundred or thousand dollars, or if it's like the iPhone, Star Wars movies, or Harry Potter books it could be worth billions.

It doesn't matter where you are in your business or real estate trajectory; it is a very interesting process to consider what intellectual property you could develop. What do you do that's rare? What do you do that is different? What do you do that's valuable? Consider a book, online course, blog, or website and monetize it!

LESSON 69: THE FIRST STEPS TO BECOMING A REAL ESTATE INVESTOR

F requently, the question on any new investor's mind is, "How do I start?"

While it's possible that you may be able to use other people's money on your first transaction, it is not likely. Investors who should be using other people's money on their first deal are few and far between. Most likely they brought some other form of experience to their first deal that allowed them to raise joint venture money immediately. With that disclaimer out of the way, let's talk about the steps to take when getting started.

First of all, you should assess your cash situation. Cash is a combination of real cash (in your bank account, or a sock, or under a mattress), or the cash of a committed friend or family member. If you don't have enough real cash, then the next source might be a Home Equity Line of Credit (HELOC) or (for short) Line of Credit (LOC). On a LOC you have to pay interest only on the portion you use, which is good.

So don't use it all immediately to buy a yacht or a fancy condo in Hawaii. These luxury items can wait. The likely result of spending cash or lines of credit on superfluous luxury items is a lifetime of being behind the financial eight ball. On the other hand, if you invest your LOC into a cash-producing asset, you will begin the process of getting ahead. But if you're reading this book, I suspect you've already figured that out.

The next step is to research the market. Decide what area of the country you wish to invest in and then what type of property you wish to invest in. This is a big country, so will it be the Lower Mainland of British Columbia? Edmonton and area? Southern Alberta? Rural Saskatchewan east of Saskatoon? Toronto and the GTA? Kitchener-Waterloo? Ottawa? Montreal? You get the picture.

The key point is that you are not looking for a "deal"—you're looking for a very specific deal in a very specific place, based on a very specific type of property. Only once you know your market extremely well will you even know what a deal looks like.

Is there a secret knack for finding deals? The secret knack isn't so secret—it comes from first knowing what a non-deal looks like in a certain area, by knowing both an area and a property type really well, or by having a team that brings you those deals based on their very intimate knowledge of this very specific area.

Once you've chosen the area and the property type, spend a ton of time becoming an expert on that property type in that area. Then and only then should you start writing offers and buying. When you're starting out, it's better to have several smaller properties than one huge one. Many properties allow you to sell one if you have to.

For example, if you focus on townhouses, you must know after your research (also referred to as due diligence or DD) if a 1,200–square-foot townhouse facing north is worth more than a similar one facing south, how much more a 1,400–square-foot townhouse is vs. a comparable 1,200–square-foot one, how much a finished basement is worth, what the rent would be for the 1,200–square-foot-one facing north vs. the 1,400–square-foot one facing south, etc.

You have to be an expert, because you must be able to discern within minutes if a "deal" is actually a sound business investment. Thus, you must know if $138,000 for that 1,200–square-foot south-facing townhouse is market price, overpriced or a screaming bargain. You must assume you are not the only person looking for a townhouse, and if you know it is a bargain, $20,000 below market, so will others.

It takes time to research any area. It also takes a little bit of money for driving time, flying there (if it's out of your hometown), donuts, lunches and materials to research. The bigger an area is, the more time you will have to commit to researching it. The entire province of British Columbia takes more time to research than the Lower Mainland which takes more time than Greater Vancouver which takes more time than North Shore which takes more time than North Vancouver east of Hwy 1 which takes more time than Deep Cove. More time researching could lead to good things, or it could lead to a paralysis of analysis, a condition in which you are "handcuffed" from taking action.

I suggest you start with a very small area, for example, one suburb of one of the Top 10 REIN (Real Estate Investment Network) towns in B.C., Alberta or Ontario. Perhaps the best town to research is the one you live in. It will certainly reduce your management headache when you eventually buy.

Then, once you've decided on a very specific area of a city or an entire small town, you must decide on a type of property. A representative list is as follows:

1. townhouses
2. condos with an ocean view
3. single-family homes older than 50 years
4. new subdivisions
5. pre-sales
6. acreages
7. horse farms
8. trailer parks
9. office buildings in crappy parts of town
10. high-end luxury condos with high-end finishing
11. land with subdivision potential
12. strip malls

13. defunct shopping centers

14. warehouses

15. storage facilities

16. fixer-upper homes.

Any of these property types allow you to make money once you know what you're doing.

In my opinion the best one to start with (as there is plenty of supply and plenty of seller motivation) is a small house or a townhouse. Another option to start with is a condo, but only one in a well managed complex, as you can't control costs of the condo association to the degree you can control costs and management in a single unit, like a townhouse or small house. It's probably not best to start with a big house either, as this type of property is usually more expensive and consequently harder to cash flow, although in a fix-and-flip deal that might be okay—if and only if the numbers work very well for a successful resale.

You often make the most money with properties that lack curb appeal and need repairs. Many prospective homeowners look for a pristine property that requires no work. (I happen to be married to such a buyer—maybe you are too?) Therefore, you can often negotiate a substantial discount for a property that needs TLC. Be careful, though! You must be able to accurately gauge how much it will cost to fix the visible, and frequently less obvious, invisible problems. This is where the four (of five) ways to make money come in, as you use your own cash, and that of others to fix an asset, investing your own time and that of others for your often substantial gain.

You have to decide how much time you want to spend working in this asset—it may be several weeks of full-time work in a rundown property. Do you have the time? Early in my real estate career I was running a busy software-consulting firm with frequent travel and I did not have that kind of time to devote to turning around such a property. That's why I eventually bought an entire apartment building where others would do most of the work.

If you make one mistake on a big project, it could be the end of your tenure as successful owner of that property—you may lose the property (and possibly the property that is securing the HELOC you used to buy it).

When you're starting out, you might be tempted to rush into a deal. But it's better to pass on a bad deal than to realize six months into your ownership that you paid too much for a property and it is a drain on both money and time.

For each piece of real estate you have to hang in financially and emotionally.

This means that you must make a very realistic assessment of your cash situation (including closing costs, vacancies and upgrades required, in addition to "normal" expenses such as mortgage payment, taxes, utilities, condo fees, insurance, management fees, etc.). It also means that you must make a realistic assessment of your mental toughness or time commitment. Vacancies will arise. Basements will flood. Tenants occasionally have to be evicted. Perhaps the police will get involved. Furnaces break down (sometimes at midnight). Get used to it, or anticipate it. Be prepared to handle those things yourself, or preferably hire a property manager that does it for you, but then be prepared to pay this person or company well. This obviously implies that you've purchased a property that cash flows well enough to afford management.

You also need a team around you: a realtor (or two), a lawyer knowledgeable in real estate and licensed in the province you buy in (not where you live!), an accountant or bookkeeper, a mortgage broker and most likely, a property manager.

Ask yourself: who will manage this property impeccably? If the answer is, "I don't know," then by default it is you. If doing it yourself requires you to neglect your family or health, then spend some time reconsidering, and hopefully you'll find a property manager, as without one your team needs to also include plumbers, painters, gardeners, electricians, roofers, cleaning crews and eviction experts—an overwhelming amount of coordination and supervision work for a part-time investor in most cases.

Cash-to-close on a property comes in two forms: real cash and a mortgage. To get a mortgage, you need various documents, including property documents and personal documents showing the bank that you are credit-worthy. Prepare a binder with all of this information in advance so that when you show up at the bank you're ready. Today I have all my tax information online going back four or five years, since banks always ask for it. I also have a summary and detailed property information on every property we own, as banks always ask for this as well when you apply for the next mortgage.

Spend a lot of time preparing this set of documents, then find a mortgage broker to get you a mortgage or at least tell you what kind of mortgage you can get, given the type of property you've targeted. Horse farms are treated differently than trailer parks, which are treated differently than condos.

Before closing, ensure you have someone in that market to manage the property impeccably. That could be you, although a professional with in-depth market insight, knowledge of legalities and local knowledge is likely better. Spend some significant time finding that special someone, as good property managers are very hard to come by.

Once the deal makes sense—that is, you've got the money (cash plus mortgage), and you've got the property manager—ask yourself if you will be able to hang in emotionally and financially. If so, close on the property!

Happy hunting!

Oh, and by the way, many hours are wasted when hunting and walking through the mud or underbrush. Many more hours are spent just waiting in the right spot. Then one day: BAM! Hopefully you are awake then as sometimes that moment is short, and perhaps the opportunity passed or a better prepared hunter got to the target first. So be prepared and ready when you need to be ready!

LESSON 70:
IS A 50/50 JOINT VENTURE FAIR?

When you first begin to consider the notion of a joint venture (JV) with a money partner, some questions you might ask yourself are these: How much am I worth? How much ownership should I have, and how much ownership should my money partner have? There is a fine line between self-confidence, arrogance and self-deception. Be aware of this line. Confidence is important to negotiate a good deal for yourself—but please be realistic.

Fifty/fifty seems to be the norm for a JV on a single-family home, but is it the right split? Why not 70/30 or 25/75? Why not charge a fee upfront when all the work is done? Why not charge a fee as you go along? Why not own more than 50 percent over a certain sales price target or investor ROI?

Some of my investors have made more than 300 percent ROI! In cases such as those, 50/50 seems like expensive money. But those investors referred others, so in hindsight that was the entry price to mutual success.

The first deal is always the hardest, the second is a bit easier, and the third deal is a bit easier. The 15th is easier still ...

Usually you have to do your own deals with your own money to prove a point or to prove that you have expertise in a certain area. That's why it might be a good idea to sell too early on your first joint venture. It helps you show a track record. With the success of the first deal, you can do a second and a third deal. Then you can show off your track record some more. Then you have the right to ask for other people's money. People with money today, in a volatile stock market or with low bond rates, are always looking to invest their money wisely. Don't be afraid to tell your story.

Treat every "no" as a "not yet."

The JV money trail always looks like this: no, no, no, no, no, no, no, yes.

Like a stone cutter at work, it takes many hits on a single stone for the stone to crack. Seven times is a proven sales rule-of-thumb. It takes seven times of asking, on average, to get a deal. Ask again and again.

Even though it may be hard for your ego, it might not be a bad idea to give away a little too much on the first deal, take a little more in the second deal, a little more in the third deal, until the formula fits these criteria:

1. IT HAS TO BE WIN/WIN.

This means that both you and the investor win. If one of you wins and the other loses, then the whole deal is a failure. Both you and the investor have to feel it is a fair deal and no one gets ripped off.

As I have shown in the earlier chapter on green vs. red/blue money you must get a higher return if you take on additional risk, such as being on the mortgage in a classic JV situation. Doing work and using someone's expertise often acquired over a decade or two (blue $s) has to be rewarded, but so has to be the willingness to provide credit, and green $s of course. As a rule of thumb, the expert gets 30% of the profit, the mortgage provider 20%, and the cheque writer 50%. As such, if both the expert and the money provider co-sign for a mortgage, they split that 20%, for a 40/60 suggested split between expert and investor. Again, a rule of thumb, to be modified taking into account risk, loan-to-value, cheque size, city, expertise required and actual work performed.

2. IT HAS TO BE REPEATABLE.

This means you have to make money while you hold the property, or shortly after you purchase it.

Build your portfolio slowly, holding some properties and selling others. The ones you hold have to pay you too. As the active partner you'll be doing a lot of work. For example, you'll be getting the mortgage, finding the trades, doing the upgrades, managing the property manager or filling vacancies.

It's a lot of work, and to produce an income for you, 50/50 often works poorly, especially when the cash flow is low. You'll need additional income to wait for the big equity pop at the end, which is often years away.

So, why not charge a fee upfront (perhaps one that's credited against your future earning, or perhaps you call it a sales commission or an asset acquisition fee)? Or perhaps you charge a fee as you go along (perhaps it's charged against your future earnings—usually it's called an asset management fee). You can negotiate whatever is a win/win because no one minds that you make lots of money as long as they make a decent ROI for the risk involved.

3. IT HAS TO ADEQUATELY REWARD THE RISK.

This means that some deals need to show a higher ROI than others. Building brand-new homes in brand-new markets with no expertise, subdividing land, condo conversions, and flipping pre-sale condos (especially if they wouldn't cash flow if you have to hold them) are all high risk, and you might have to offer a higher ROI if you do any of those.

Buying lower-priced townhouses or small multi-family buildings or apartment buildings with rental and equity up-side in growth markets is fairly low risk; it's my bread-and-butter money-making technique today and how I got to well over $80 million in assets in less than a decade. I call it "the milk cow business." I still occasionally like to fix-and-flip small multi-family buildings to make some quick cash once in a while, since man can't live on milk alone; some beef is required from time to time (I call this the "beef cow business")! If I can't sell them, I can always refinance them and rent them out with good cash flow.

On a standard buy-and-hold, there's perhaps less equity upside, but you can use a lot of the bank's money and thus create high cash-on-cash ROI. The potential to lose capital is very low, so you don't have to offer too high a return on investment. In other words, you can take 50 percent or more of the profits.

If your property will be a strong rental, then you're minimizing risk for your partners, so you have the right to ask for more of the deal. That's why you should always have multiple exit strategies. Always have an option B, so you can escape without loss of capital. Once you mitigate that risk for your partner, then you can ask for more of the deal.

4. IT HAS TO BE SELLABLE.

A great property, or a great deal, or even a great asset manager, aren't any good if you can't present it to your investor in such a way that they'll understand it and buy into it. You must have a properly packaged proposition with appropriate legal and marketing material (perhaps a website). You must have some degree of salesmanship and team members that execute with you or on your behalf.

The investor wants a track record and assurance that they won't lose any money. They want a return of their money and then a return on their money. The track record, you the person, the risk, the likely or potential reward and the packaging have to be aligned for the deal to be sellable. Talk about yourself and the specific deal, since an investor always looks at both. Include numbers and pictures or graphs. Some investors are very analytical and like lots of numbers; some like pictures of the property, and some like a particular estimate such as 48 percent (if that's your target return over 5 years.) You'll probably never know which type your investor is. That's why you always use a variety of approaches.

Happy JVing!

LESSON 71:
BUYING VS. OWNING – YOU MAKE
MONEY WHEN YOU BUY

There are those real estate investors who absolutely love the acquisition phase of real estate investment. Purchasing, negotiating, haggling, landing investors and closing deals is exciting and fun. It's the thrill of the chase and the satisfaction of the catch that hooks many into real estate. But acquisitions are just one phase of the real estate game, and many don't know the difference between buying and owning real estate.

Owning an asset requires a series of tasks that are much more prosaic than buying the asset. Unplugging toilets, painting walls, advertising for tenants in various media (such as kijiji, rentfaster. ca, local papers, signs and flyers), collecting rent, and sometimes evicting tenants are all included in the job of owning real estate.

You may delegate those tasks, but you will still be involved in them to some degree regardless of whether you delegate them. It might be boring, but this owning phase is key to real estate profitability. It's especially important if you lack the patience to continue owning the property and end up selling too soon. I decided early on to delegate this task to others, although I get involved with marketing, writing ads, training onsite managers and property upgrades to a large degree; but you may be different and it may appeal to you.

Buying is important to real estate profitability too; in fact, many say you make the most money on the day that you buy. I think the truth of that statement is debatable, as it's equally plausible that you make the most money on the day that you sell. What I mean is that you have to eventually realize the profit, even if you bought an undervalued asset to begin with.

If you purchased a home that should be valued at $300,000 for the price of $260,000, but the property required repairs in order to raise the value, but you don't do the repairs during the holding period, then you won't realize the gain on the day you buy. The truth is that all phases are important to making an eventual profit. Regardless of how you buy the property and how you hold the property, you still have to monetize it eventually, so selling is probably as important as any other phase.

Buying is absolutely crucial as it sets the bar for how much cash flow, mortgage paydown, and appreciation will be required to earn a profit. If you buy right, it matters a lot less what the market does. Think back to the great real estate boom of Alberta. Let's take 2007 as the reference point. At that time, prices peaked, and I recall writing a post on an online forum predicting that market values would reach the 2007 highs again by 2012. Sure enough, by 2012, prices had indeed approximately reached the 2007 peaks.

Let's imagine that you purchased a single-family home in Edmonton in 2007 when the average price for your property type (let's say a 1950s bungalow with a basement suite) was about $315,000. At some point during the trough of the real estate downswing, the value of that property likely dropped to approximately $285,000, or even lower.

Now let's imagine that you were a savvy investor, and you were well aware that prices were at or near the peak, so instead of paying $315,000 for that property you instead searched long and hard, doing a great deal of property and market diligence, and you purchased the property for $285,000. I'm not saying it would have been easy, but through an exhaustive search, imagine you found a good deal on a property that needed a bit of work.

Then imagine that you slowly chipped away at the repairs that the property needed, spending $15,000 of the cash flow money to improve the property over the five-year holding period. By 2012, you own a $315,000 property that you paid $285,000 for and added $15,000 worth of renovations (money that came not from your pocket but from the cash flow). This is the essence of sound real estate investing. It's essential that you pay the right price. Without paying the right price, it will be very difficult to make a profit, or at the very least, it will force you to extend the time it takes you to make a profit.

Paying too much for a property affects the owning phase of real estate investment in a negative way too. Take the same example we just gave above, but now imagine that you did spend the $315,000 that the average property was worth at the time. First of all, your cash flow would be diminished by higher mortgage payments.

This would make it more difficult to pay for the needed repairs out of the cash flow proceeds, and would increase the likelihood that you'd have to pay for the upgrades out of pocket. This effectively raises the purchase cost of the property, and is never desirable.

Purchasing real estate at the right price is a true art form and I could honestly write a whole other book on the topic. But I believe that the most important factor in paying the right price is patience. You simply can't rush into a deal because you feel like you need a property.

Good deals do not come along every day, but they do come along regularly enough that there is plenty of money to be made from finding them, buying them, managing them well, and then monetizing them. With more than 10,000 properties trading every year in Edmonton, for example, surely 5 to 10 percent of them are good deals.

To buy well, you need to focus your attention on buying well. You need to shake the tree to a degree, and this means effort. You may write five offers before you actually close on one deal, and depending on where you are as a real estate investor, you might be expending a lot of your effort raising money as well. It's not easy to delegate the tasks of money raising and acquiring properties at the beginning, so it's intensive work for the owner of a small investment firm (as I was from 2002 to 2005). But buying those first few properties at the right price, with the right financing in place at the beginning, is what sets you up for a lifetime of wealth creation. It's worth the effort to learn how to buy right and spend the time and energy doing it.

LESSON 72:
BUYING VS. OWNING – THE THREE R'S
OF PROPERTY MANAGEMENT

The owning phase is often not as exciting as the buying phase, but it's every bit as important. Without taking the correct actions during the holding period, it will be a lot harder to make a profit at the end when you're ready to exit.

It may not be as exciting, but the good news is that it's often a lot less work than the beginning phase of acquisition. Real estate is front loaded in terms of work and very rear loaded in terms of profit. But the in-between time of owning the property is not usually too demanding in terms of work or too rewarding in terms of profit. Of course, there are times when you have to do more work during the holding period, notably when there is a vacancy.

During vacancy periods, you will likely have to not only find a tenant, but you will also likely have to do repairs. It's a fact of life as a real estate investor. Without doing those repairs, you're seriously risking the erosion of your property value. Retention of value through proper asset management is the major component of the owning period. How you manage the property during the holding period is of utmost importance for your future profitability.

I always say that making money in real estate is achieved by holding the property, preferably for five years or more. But holding the property for five years or more is only possible if you can hang in there for five years. This means hanging in there both financially and emotionally.

Hanging in there financially is largely a function of purchasing the property at the right price with the right financing—in other words, a deal that makes sense, with at least break even cash flow and a buffer of cash for the odd vacancy and repair.

Hanging in there emotionally is largely a matter of valuing

your time. When you set out to own a property for a minimum of five years, the first question you need to ask yourself is "Who is going to manage this property impeccably?" If you don't know the answer to that question, the answer by default is you. But the problem with you doing it yourself is often that the job of managing the property might not even pay you minimum wage.

This is especially true about managing single-family properties. In multi-family, the return might be better than a minimum wage job, but then why would you want to manage a multi-family property? It's usually easier to find a competent property manager for a multi-family than it is for a single-family. Usually new investors look at the cost of property management and say something along these lines: "What! That's half my cash flow!"

When people say this to me, I often ask them, "Do you make your own bread?" With a puzzled look they often say, "No." You can make your own bread if you want for a cost of probably $0.80 worth of ingredients. But it also takes three hours to make bread. Buying bread may cost you $5.00, but the task is completed instantly when shopping at the supermarket. Is your time worth more than $1.67 per hour ($5.00/3)? If so, it might be a more prudent investment to buy your bread than to make it yourself. Property management is the same. Just like a baker, it can become profitable to make bread for a living, but then it becomes a volume game, a business and not just an exercise to fill your stomach. I learned that in 2005–06 and founded a property management firm that today manages around 1,500 units with my partner, Keith. (Perhaps I'll get into those details of growing to 1,500 units under management in the next book.)

Just remember that to profit in real estate you need to hang in there emotionally. What do you think it does to your emotions when you're working a full-time job, and then you spend all your evenings working for minimum wage or less? Paying a property manager is often the price of hanging in there and therefore profiting from real estate.

THE THREE R'S OF PROPERTY MANAGEMENT

Renting – Whenever we hire a new onsite manager for one of our buildings with Prestigious Properties®, I always ask them what they think their job is. Typically, they list a bunch of tasks—often things like keeping the hallways clean and collecting rent. While both of those tasks are very important, I always tell them that their job is to protect our top and bottom line, which means keeping the suites rented. I want a low vacancy rate in all of my buildings, regardless of the economy. Their main job is sales, namely selling vacant units to prospective clients.

There are many important aspects to keeping suites rented, some of which are continually improving the units, pricing correctly, marketing the asset, curb appeal, telephone manners, and salesmanship among the onsite managers.

When it comes to filling a vacancy in your property, the management firm really earns its keep because this is another time-consuming job of the property manager. In a way it's like a mini acquisition, but instead of acquiring a property, you're acquiring a human who is looking for a home. I find if you treat humans with respect, regardless of their life circumstances (and believe me, many of their circumstances are outright miserable), with friendliness and with personal relationships, it is not too difficult to rent a well managed asset.

Repairs – Continually repairing a property is the cost of doing business in real estate. There is a common belief in this notion called cash flow. Yes, it's true that it exists in theory. For me, I never expect to get any cash flow out of a property unless the mortgage is perhaps sub 60 percent loan-to-value. But when you're in the position that most real estate investors are in for the bulk of their investment careers, you must forget about the elusive cash flow, and just consider it a fund for future repairs, which will inevitably come.

As mentioned earlier, the cash flow makes only a brief stopover in your bank account, for a few months perhaps, before it is used to pay for something to be repaired, whether something minor such as a fridge or a new door handle, or something major like a new roof or a new boiler.

Not only are constant and ongoing repairs necessary for retaining the long-term value of the property, but without them you will also have a hard time renting the property when the next vacancy occurs. At the very least, it will cause you to lower your rental rates, which again negatively affects your bottom line.

Whether you manage the property yourself or hire a property manager, repairs must be done. A good property manager will coordinate any renovations or repairs you might have and suggest competent professionals to complete the work. In addition, they may be able to advise you on the value of doing any additional renovations that might lead to a stronger rental income. Perhaps they see a way to add a room or build an entire suite in a property for relatively low input costs. This kind of advice is invaluable.

Whoever coordinates the repairs, you're going to be the one who writes the check. Save up that cash flow for the inevitable rainy day known as repair time.

Reporting – The main jobs of renting and repairing are supplemented by the third major task of the property manager: reporting. With all that money flying around, it stands to reason that keeping track of it is quite an important task. Whether you hire professional management or not, it is vital to keep detailed and correctly categorized reports of everything that happens with your properties.

If you're working on only your first few real estate investments, then you will want to keep detailed records so you can more easily sell yourself to future money partners. It's fantastic for your professionalism to show income and expenses in detail. It's also a benefit to show how you manage your asset's value by continually improving. If you can show proof that all repairs, bills and mortgage payments came out of cash flow proceeds, then you will look very good to your prospective investors.

One of the biggest benefits of property management for multi-family buildings is that management firms take reporting to a much higher degree, such as bar charts or trend lines or red/yellow/green signals. They will even pay all your expenses out of the account they keep on your behalf.

Property management for Prestigious Properties® even pays our mortgages for us. After all the expenses are paid, they then write us a check for what's left over, and to top it off, they send us a detailed report showing every expense and every bit of income. In essence, property management does much of our accounting for us.

Reporting is the final major function of property management, which is the major task of the owning phase, not just to stay sane, especially if you own multiple assets, with perhaps multiple partners, but also to gauge cash availability, requirements to sell or abilities to refinance.

LESSON 73:
REAL ESTATE IS NOT A
GET RICH QUICK SCHEME,
IT'S A GET RICH FOR SURE SCHEME

I always say that real estate is not about getting rich quick. It's about getting rich for sure. This means something very specific, and it means something general as well.

In general terms, it means that while there may be fancier ways to make millions of dollars, they are not always so certain. Time has proven that investing in fundamentally sound cash-producing real estate assets is a certain way to grow wealth, whereas other business and investment ventures are more hit and miss.

Building a technology company is one such example where the difference between winning big and losing everything is a razor-thin line. For every Steve Jobs or Bill Gates there are a hundred unknown men and women who didn't end up as the heads of billion-dollar enterprises and are now mid-level bank managers, accountants and salespeople. I owned a wireless software company with two partners in the late 90s that built mainframe screen emulators for the Palm Pilot. I also dreamed of stock options and Ferraris driven through the San Francisco Bay Area. Since this book is not about wireless software ventures you can imagine how that story ended.

The story told of the conquering billionaires of the world is one of pure talent and overcoming obstacles. Yes, skill, drive, capital needs and determination all play a big role in this kind of other-worldly success, but luck and timing play a role too.

Real estate, on the other hand, is fairly predictable, boring even. Okay, it might not feel boring when you're signing that first personal guarantee for $1 million or more, and it might not feel boring when you're on the hunt for a deal that will make you hundreds of thousands (or millions) of dollars.

However, in terms of the growth of real estate and the mechanism it employs to make you wealthy, it is indeed fairly predictable. This does not mean there aren't once-in-a-generation market corrections that wipe out many real estate investors, as we saw in 2008–09. What it does mean is that generally, if you follow the rules and the well-worn path to real estate wealth, you will most likely achieve the result that so many others have, which is moderate to outstanding wealth creation.

Of course, nothing can be predicted with 100 percent accuracy, but generally we know how the mechanism of real estate works and generally how it reacts to economic cues. Everyone needs a place to live. This fact will never change. Therefore, being in the business of owning what people need to live in will always be a good business—to varying degrees. Just as the food industry is a sure thing because people will always need to eat, there will always be a need for rental real estate. If it's impeccably managed, well maintained, sensibly levered and in a desirable location, you have a perpetual, inflation-protected money machine.

Contrast this with technology. What if you were the last person to have a great innovation in the world of cassette tapes? What if your innovation happened the day before the CD player was released into the world? Suddenly your product would not be necessary. This will never happen in real estate to the same degree. It happens on a smaller scale when you own real estate in locations where population is diminishing rather than growing, but again, it is easier to minimize this risk by understanding the economy.

Generally speaking, real estate is a get rich for sure scheme.

LESSON 74: REAL ESTATE IS LIKE A THREE-COURSE MEAL™

The more specific reason why real estate is a get rich for sure scheme is the fact that real estate is like a three-course meal.™ (Yes, that is my intellectual property—still un-monetized.) It's a three-course meal that lays out like this:

1.   Appetizer = Cash Flow

2.   Main Course = Mortgage Pay-down

3.   Dessert: Appreciation

You don't need to eat an appetizer or dessert, but you do need the main meal. If you stop eating, you stop existing. Real estate is the same.

PROFIT CENTERS IN REAL ESTATE: A THREE COURSE MEAL

1.   Appetizer: Positive Cash Flow

2. Main Course: Mortgage Pay-down

3. Dessert: Value Growth
    - Improvements
    - Re-positioning
    - Reduced expenses/higher rents
    - Time

In real estate, one can rely on the constancy of the mortgage paydown. When you sign those mortgage documents, you're committing yourself by law to make those pesky monthly payments, and with every payment you pay not only the interest the bank charges but also a portion of the principle.

However, you're not paying down the principle, your tenant is, and that's the beauty of real estate. Someone else pays you to get wealthy. This fact is as simple to understand as it is difficult to execute.

The mortgage payment is the main course, and the longer you hold the property, the more wealth the mortgage payment produces for you. The mixed blessing is that wealth created through mortgage paydown is not liquid. The only way to unlock the accumulated cash from the mortgage paydown is to either refinance the property, thereby pulling out excess equity, or to sell the property and take home the remaining cash after the rest of the mortgage is paid out from sale proceeds.

The benefit to impatient people like myself is that you cannot spend the equity immediately nor can you sell an asset as fast as, say, a stock. It will make you a more patient person, a more patient investor and a purveyor of more assets with similar characteristics.

On one hand, it might be seen as a drawback that can't access the locked-up equity quickly, but on the other hand, if you can't access it quickly, it's more likely to accumulate slowly and surely. You almost forget the equity is there, but when it comes time to realize the gain, you're pleasantly surprised.

To this day, I credit this lack of liquidity with helping me build wealth. I'm quite an impulsive person, and tend to make decisions quickly. Often I've had the urge to sell a property for one reason or another, but didn't act on that urge because of the lengthy process involved in selling a property.

Then, lo and behold, a couple of weeks later, I've realized that it's better to keep the property. Months or years later, holding the property for longer proved to be wise. Much wealth has been created by just waiting in real estate. That's why I believe the noble art of getting things done is great, but the even nobler art of leaving things undone is better. Hence, I also trademarked this simple nugget of wisdom:

"Don't wait to invest in real estate—Invest in real estate and wait!"

Time favors the real estate investor because mortgage paydown ensures that money will be made from owning real estate, regardless of the economy—so long as the property is impeccably managed.

It's pleasant to have the cash flow, but you can live without it. When I say cash flow here, I mean the kind of cash flow that you actually keep. New investors often have the misunderstanding that cash flow only flows into their jeans, when in reality, it flows in and it also flows out.

Cash flow (especially in the early days of ownership) has this purpose: reinvesting into the asset, or building a buffer for a rainy day. As mentioned elsewhere, maintaining the asset is necessary, so much of the cash that the property produces must be allocated back to the property for maintenance and upgrades. I never assume that cash flow will be removed from a property during the hold, at least not in the first five years of a 70-80 percent levered asset.

Appreciation is a delectable dessert. We do everything we can to make sure that we get to eat dessert in real estate. We study the markets, we buy at the right price, and we hold for the right amount of time. Appreciation doesn't always arrive in the time horizon we hope (and of course the 2008–09 correction taught us that lesson), but generally speaking, if we stay in the game long enough, it does come. Prices in 2013, in most markets in Canada, are well above 2007 levels again, so holding through this three- to five-trough was necessary to actually get some dessert. Prices in 2023 will be higher than today, and even higher in 2033.

While the main course (mortgage paydown) produces moderate wealth, the dessert (appreciation) often produces immense wealth. When a market's values start to rise, it is best to be levered as highly as possible in as much real estate as possible, since this is when you start making money on borrowed money, not just the money you initially invested.

Owning $80 million worth of real estate (with $40 million in equity), when a market appreciates 5 percent, equals a $4-million growth in net worth, whereas owning $40 million worth of real estate at the same 5 percent pace results in a $2-million growth in net worth—not bad, but not as stunning as a $4-million growth.

Thus, lever as high as the cash flow allows, then dial it up or down a notch depending on your comfort level, risk tolerance and market outlook.

Real estate, as exciting as it seems during the chase of a hot deal, and as frustrating as it seems when a tenant decides to stop paying, is basically predictable, boring even. You learn to systematize everything, even the non-paying tenant, and you find that even the unexpected is expected. The end result is that real estate is a boring get rich for sure scheme.

Learn to follow the sure steps and use it as a steady way to increase your wealth over the years, and you will be sure to create immense wealth. Always remember that a) to create wealth for sure you need to be able to hang in there and b) the longer you're in it, the more wealth you create.

Always eat your main course, and whenever possible have an appetizer and dessert. Following the dinner rules, get out there and create wealth for sure.

LESSON 75:
MAKING THE JUMP FROM
SINGLE FAMILY TO MULTI-FAMILY

Many single-family investors have the idea that at some point they'd like to switch from investing in single-family dwellings into multi-family buildings. There are some great reasons to do this, and there are also a couple of reasons on the flip side why single-family investments remain a better option.

The truth is that there is no one "right" way. Instead there are only ways that work for individuals based on their own lifestyles and reasons for investing.

In my own case, multi-family was the right way, and it was the right way fairly quickly in my real estate career. Since I was involved in a busy and profitable partnership in the software consulting industry when I started investing in real estate, I had the good fortune to understand the value of blue dollars well. I knew that I wanted grand results for the smallest blue dollar investment possible.

After buying and owning my first three rental-pooled condos for a few years, I knew I wanted to invest in the same type of property, in bulk. I'd also been on the boards of two of the three condos that I purchased and was able to see the inner workings of multi-family building management. It made sense for me to lever my time by buying a whole building rather than buy one small property at a time.

I had no intention of giving up my business immediately, so I wanted to get the biggest bang for my buck in terms of blue dollars invested. I also had a sense that it actually didn't take that much more time to invest in one multi-family building than one single-family building, but the return was much higher. Finally, I realized through my experience on the condo board that property management could be delegated far easier in a multi-family building than in a single-family property.

ADVANTAGES OF MULTI-FAMILY

A major advantage of multi-family is that financing is completely dependent upon the building itself. When the bank finances a multi-family building, they assess whether the building itself is a strong business, they do not assess whether or not the buyer can carry the financing. Therefore, in theory, you can buy an unlimited number of multi-family buildings but can only purchase a very limited number of single-family properties.

Many single-family investors come up against this problem. In effect, they're stifled by their own success because they purchase three, or five, or eight, or 10 properties, and by then they're true experts and ready to invest more, but at that point, it suddenly becomes much more difficult for them to attain financing for their next purchase because the bank weighs a borrower's ability to service debt rather than the building's ability to service the debt. This never happens with multi-family because each building is weighed on its own merits, independently of the investor.

The second major benefit is that multi-family property management is actually easier! The reason is that something we call an economy of scale. Whenever you can put many of the same thing in one place, it becomes easier to manage. When cars are assembled, you don't see the steering wheel being installed in Georgia, the carburetor installed in Michigan, and the headlights installed in Kentucky. Car component parts may be manufactured in different places, but when the car is assembled, it's done so in one assembly line. It just makes more sense to do it all in one place.

If you're managing six different single-family homes—even if they're all in the same city—you have to deal with six different utility bills (even if tenants pay them as you may still be on the hook if they default or move), six different roofs, six different furnaces, six different tax bills, six mortgages, six different hot water tanks, and at least that many keys. The list does not end there. There is six of everything. In addition, there's more travel involved to take care of the properties, even when the properties are relatively close to each other.

Compare that to owning one 12-plex, which you might be able to purchase for a similar price as six separate singles. When you own the 12-plex, you only have one boiler, one utility bill, one mortgage, one tax bill and one location. Property management is also much easier to find, and cheaper as a percentage of revenue, to as low as 3 percent on an asset over 100 units. From a management perspective, it is far easier to invest in multi-family than single family. If you respect your blue dollars like I do, this aspect of multi-family buildings is too good to pass up.

The third major advantage of multi-family investing is that it's far easier to invest at a distance than with single-family. Again, this is due to management. The company you hire to manage a multi-family building will be professional and will have a system in place to take care of everything. Therefore, you can manage the managers from a distance more easily than with single family. The other reason it's far easier to invest in one city and live in another with multi-family is the fact that the upfront work of acquisition can more easily be done when looking for big buildings than small. Of course, it's still inconvenient to travel to a new city for building tours and due diligence, but at least once the process is complete, you will own multiple units. With a single-family home, you still have to undertake the same process, only at the end of it, you're left with only one unit. It's another result of the economy of scale that a multi-family building provides.

Buying a multi-family building does take more due diligence and up-front work, but the leverage on that time is also far greater than with a single-family home. It might take twice the time, but the reward is often 10 times or greater than that of a single-family property.

The fourth major advantage of multi-family investing over single-family investing is that the property is priced according to the income of the property. When you purchase a multi-family building, you're doing so at a multiple of the total income of the property (known as a CAP rate or yield, which is the net operating income divided over the price). The multiple that buildings are bought and sold at varies from city to city and province to province, but determining the actual value of a building is a function of the income, which is excellent news for investors.

When trying to determine the value of a single-family home, there are a bunch of soft factors at play that make it not only difficult to determine the value, but also less profitable as a rental property. There is often little or no monetary value as a rental for an expensive kitchen, a large yard or a well-decorated bathroom. Yet, when trying to purchase a single-family home as a rental property, you're competing against buyers who value those factors along with a whole host of others. This generally means that it's much harder to purchase single-family homes at the same CAP rate as multi-family buildings. When you buy a multi-family building, you're buying based on its money-making capability, which is comforting to an investor.

On the flip side, multi-family buildings usually require a far bigger commitment of money. This alone is quite daunting to an investor, especially one who has not yet gotten used to biting off their investments in $1,000,000 (or frequently much larger) chunks.

When I purchased my first multi-family building I put in $100,000 of my own cash, which was a very large portion of my net worth at the time. In addition, I had to sign a personal guarantee for approximately $500,000. I had a lot of fear about signing the document, and actually lost sleep over it for several days. It's not easy to take such a risk, and your permanent 50/50 JV partner has to be on board too.

In contrast, Prestigious Properties® just bought a building in Calgary; I had to sign a personal guarantee for $10,000,000, yet I barely blinked an eye as I knew it was a good deal (in fact it has already gone up in value from $14.6 million to close to $20 million in about two and a half years). Once you get accustomed to the large figures and become confident in the acquisition and management systems, the big numbers become less daunting.

The other major downside of multi-family instead of single family is that it's much more difficult to liquidate a portion of your inventory. It's always difficult to liquidate real estate compared to other forms of investment, but when all your holdings are tied up in one or two buildings, it becomes even more difficult. If you own 10 single-family homes, and you need to write a big check for something, it's far easier to just sell off a portion of your holdings (one or two properties) if need be.

Selling off assets to generate cash becomes common when people have children going off to university, or when they want to retire. When invested in several smaller properties, investors simply liquidate one or two properties to fund whatever is needed.

This is one major advantage of single-family investing over multi-family investing. One way to mitigate this risk as a multi-family investor is to keep a few single-family properties in your portfolio even as you move into the multi-family arena.

There are some great reasons to make the leap to multi-family investing, and there are a couple of very strong reasons to stay in single family. As I said earlier, there is no one better way; there's just the right method for different individuals.

LESSON 76:
HOW I GOT STARTED: AWARENESS, KNOWLEDGE, ACTION!

"Give me six hours to chop down a tree and I will spend the first four sharpening the axe." – Abraham Lincoln

LoLooking in on my real estate trajectory from afar, some might give the opinion that I started in the game a little bit late (late thirties). It might be reasonable to consider whether I would have had much greater success had I started younger and perhaps been more aggressive.

I don't question my own path in real estate because I know the value of knowledge, and I understand how I came to acquire knowledge. When I think back to the early days of university when I lived in Munich, Germany or even in Edmonton, Alberta, it literally never occurred to me that someone owned all the buildings surrounding me. As a result, it never occurred to me that since someone owned them, they must make money doing so. The thought never crossed my mind. To get from that lack of knowledge to the point where I was even ready to purchase a single investment property was a huge leap.

It was when Lynda and I were living in Burnaby, British Columbia, with our very young family, and I was working at a job I didn't really love that the light bulb went on in my head that I should purchase real estate as an investment. That epiphany happened sometime between 1988 and 1990, and it was 10 years from then until I actually purchased my first rental-pooled condo. Clearly the intention alone wasn't enough, although it did continue to push me in the right direction.

Then I went back to Munich for my first position with IBM, and the contrast from my previous stint in Munich was drastic. This time, I noticed that there were buildings, which people undoubtedly owned, and I started to wonder how much they earned in terms of rent and how much expenses were.

I consider all of this time as valuable education time, for a couple of reasons. First, I was becoming a pro in the software industry, which ultimately formed my management style of compartmentalizing a project (and later buildings) in clear and distinct modules. Second, I was laying the groundwork to earn the initial capital for those first investments.

My first formal real estate education was a weekend course in Toronto after I moved there from Munich. Lynda was in Alberta with her family and our two kids at the time, while I was searching out a suitable place for us to live. With my family away, I spent one weekend at a real estate seminar that I'd seen advertised for $99.

Raymond Aaron was the teacher, and it promised to teach one

everything needed to know to become a real estate millionaire in one weekend. I was skeptical, of course, but went anyway. I eventually bought a book or two and did join Raymond Aaron's quite useful mentoring program, but through that experience, I realized that real estate was not too difficult and that the best way to take my education further was to buy some property.

When we moved to Calgary a couple of years later and I started to work in software sales for IBM, purchasing a rental property was my intention, but from then it still took nearly three more years until I actually pulled the trigger on that first rental-pooled condo with $20,000 in cash (I ended up selling this $80,000 condo for more than $160,000 around 2004, a 400%+ cash-on-cash ROI).

It was five years between the light-bulb moment in Burnaby and my first course in real estate. Then it was another five years from my first course until I bought my first property! It was still another six or seven years before I monetized the gain!

So first was the awareness of real estate, then I started to educate myself theoretically and got my ducks in a row (ever so slowly). It wasn't until owning that first property that the education started in earnest. I learned more from being on the condo board of the rental-pooled condo than from anything else.

The education of the first couple of condos enabled many good real estate decisions that followed. Specifically, I learned the value of blue dollars in real estate.

My realtor and my property manager in Edmonton provided the final big pieces of my preliminary education when I bought my first multi-family buildings. I knew that I didn't know everything, but thanks to my experience on the condo board, I did know what I didn't know. This meant that I was cautious about finding the right realtor and property manager to enable me to learn some additional pieces before being thrown into the fire of multi-family ownership.

I don't want you to get the impression that my education as a real estate investor stopped at that point. It didn't, and I still learn lessons regularly, but what you just read is a fairly accurate account of my preliminary education. It was what I needed to get started. The rest, I was able to learn along the way.

I don't know if I'd have been able to hang in there for all these years if I hadn't learned so much in advance. In particular, the understanding of the value of blue dollars was pivotal, and is one of the biggest shortcomings I see with most real estate investors starting out.

Knowledge is its own acquisition. I don't regret the leisurely pace that I took to get into real estate. It's true that that the longer you're in the real estate game, the more wealth can be built, but there's no sense in rushing in when you're not ready.

More fortunes have been lost (often before they're even made) by the rushing mentality. I recommend first acquiring the knowledge; joining REIN or other real estate education groups is a wonderful way to gain such knowledge. (I did join REIN in about 2002 after I had purchased my third building, and have been a member ever since, as continuous skill upgrade, new techniques, market insights and camaraderie are all part of this continuing journey we call life, success and happiness.)

In my case and in many other cases (I suspect), knowledge does not necessarily have to come as formal education. I honed my personal communication, presentation and management skills when little was at risk.

I'm a firm believer in educating oneself in all aspects of professional and personal life. The time and energy invested in oneself usually pays off in spades (also see Lesson 48, Have a Casual Disregard for Money).

LESSON 77:
THE CASH FLOW MYTH

So many real estate investors believe in cash flow. For all intents and purposes the dream of cash flow is a myth. It's possible to earn real cash flow, and after many suc-

cessful years in real estate, my company Prestigious Properties®
is putting some effort toward creating that plan, but for the vast
majority of real estate investors, it does not exist.

That's not entirely true. It does exist, just not in the way that
most envision it. The common vision looks something like this:

1.   I buy a property with $300 cash flow per month.

2.   Therefore, if I buy 20 properties with $300 cash flow, I
     will have a total of $6,000 cash flow per month.

3.   I can then quit my job and live off the cash flow.

This is not a good plan. The cash flow of $300 on each property
that flows into your jeans at the end of a perfect month will most
definitely flow out of your jeans in a less-than-perfect month
some time down the road. If you save the $300 monthly cash
flow for an entire year, you'll end up with $3,600 in the bank. I
strongly suggest you keep that money in the bank because there
will undoubtedly be a rainy day for each property you own.

I've created a cash flow plan for several years, and I suggest
you do the same if you're involved in real estate. The bigger and
more complex your real estate holdings are, the bigger and more
complex your cash flow planning must be.

However, the basic breakdown looks like this: maintenance is
ongoing, and a large chunk of the actual cash that the property
generates monthly will be plugged back into the property in the
form of maintenance (or perhaps paying holding costs such as a
mortgage, property taxes & utilities during a vacancy, or a combination of the two). On top of the basic maintenance there are
also larger capital expenditures (improvements).

Sometimes you can fund improvements from the cash gener-
ated through rents, but other times you will need another form
of cash to fund bigger expenses. A roof, a boiler or furnace, a hot
water tank and windows are all large expenses that real estate
investors must pay every now and again.

You might do one big item every two or three years, for example, on any given property. Often the cash flow doesn't fund

such improvements, but the building's rising value can. The only problem is how you unlock the building's excess value in order to pay for the larger improvements. Refinancing is often the only vehicle to raise the extra funds needed.

This is one of the best reasons to refinance, the others being a) to pull cash out, and b) to decrease the mortgage payments by securing a superior interest rate.

Timing the extraction of equity for large capital expenditures is part of the reason I came up with and trademarked the phrase: Cash is King, Cash Flow is Queen.™ To me the phrase signifies the fact that cash flow is very important in real estate, but having a firm understanding and handle on the actual cash situation is slightly more important.

Some investors focus too heavily on cash flow and as a result never consider the value of the buildings and its cash requirements. They therefore often leave their buildings in rough shape when they exit. With this kind of short-term thinking, investors are leaving much profit on the table.

I said above that cash flow is mostly a myth, and this is mostly true. If you buy real estate, or the publicly traded equivalent of it, a REIT, you will get some cash flow, say four to five percent per year on the money invested. But if your overall asset value, or the price of a REIT, declines by 10 percent per year due to property value decline, are you actually ahead? No, you are not. Cash flow, and equity value in the invested asset, are very closely related. Equity is not cash … yet! So, you must always look at both: the cash flow and the remaining equity in the asset. The total of both is your overall return, and it is not always greater than zero!

The time horizon of real estate investments means that most investors stay in debt for most of the duration of their holding period on any given property. Investors are often forced to remove equity through a refinance to pay for bigger capital expenditures, and frequently to pay for lifestyle needs (such as sending kids to university or buying retirement homes). This means that they often continue to own highly leveraged assets.

However, when a property has a small mortgage on it (and

sometimes no mortgage at all), real cash flow is possible (the kind you don't have to reinvest). This might seem like the ultimate achievement for an investor. However, in a fast-rising market, lower leverage means you have a lower return on equity (i.e., of dollars invested in the property).

When only 20 percent of the purchase price comes from cash and the other 80 percent comes from a mortgage, the cash-on-cash return is leveraged five times. If a building worth $1,000,000 appreciates 6 percent, then the return for the investor who is leveraged 80 percent is actually 30 percent ($60,000 divided over $200,000). A 30 percent return is incredible in a single year. This happens whenever a market is strong and investors are highly leveraged.

That same investor who does not have a mortgage on the same property would only earn 8 percent, so being highly leveraged has its place.

For some investors, the ultra-high cash flow of a mortgage-less building is more attractive. These days, I'm one of those investors. Luckily, through Prestigious Properties®, I do not have to do this with all of the buildings, but strategically, it makes sense that we do it with some of our buildings.

We've made the decision that some of our buildings will remain in our portfolio—in essence—forever. Of course, nothing is forever, but we have a few buildings where cash flow is so strong, and the potential to pay down the mortgage is so great, that it makes sense to keep them in our portfolio as low-mortgage properties forever.

While living off cash flow is not a total myth, it's a distant enough fantasy for most investors that it's best to think of it as a myth, even as you attempt to get there. As mentioned previously, real estate is a matter of hanging in there—both financially and emotionally. On the emotional side, it's a lot about protecting your time, and being comfortable with debt, but on the financial side, it's about having another plan for income other than cash flow.

LESSON 78:
GOOD DEBT VS. BAD DEBT

Robert Kiyosaki, author of the famous Rich Dad, Poor Dad book series, hit the financial education scene in the mid-1990s. Much of his legacy can be boiled down to one distinction he made between good debt and bad debt.

Kiyosaki taught a very broad and general audience, including me, a lesson that successful entrepreneurs, business owners and investors had known for years: for wealth creation, it's good to use debt to purchase assets that create an income, but it's not good to create debt for assets that do not create an income.

People do the latter all the time when they borrow money for cars, vacations, clothes, trips and even their personal residence. Although a personal residence is somewhat different, as it doesn't create an income, one has to think of it as an expense we need to pay anyway since we need somewhere to live. Since we're going to spend that money anyway it makes sense to spend it on a property we'll eventually own, and which will likely appreciate in value.

A personal residence sits in the gray area between good and bad debt. It has one aspect of good debt, and one aspect of bad debt.

The following are the two attributes for an asset purchased with "good" debt:

1. IT PRODUCES INCOME.

Good debt is debt that funds the purchase of an asset that produces income. Even if the cash flow isn't too strong on an income-producing asset, it still produces income, which at the very least should pay all of the expenses. Real estate comes to mind, but there are other examples, such as franchises.

Real estate is an excellent example. It's the only asset class I know where the average person can leverage an investment at

80 percent and the asset will still produce enough income to carry itself and often earn extra.

2. IT WILL APPRECIATE.

Appreciation is never guaranteed, but through a lengthy and thorough due diligence process, one should be able to surmise with relative certainty that the asset will appreciate. When investing in a McDonald's restaurant franchise, or in the stock of a company with a strong balance sheet, or in real estate, one should expect that the asset will appreciate over time, so long as one buys the right one of each.

The following are the two attributes for an asset purchased with "bad" debt:

1. IT DOESN'T PRODUCE INCOME.

A shiny new motorcycle doesn't produce income. Neither does a Jet Ski, a car or a boat. People take out loans all the time for these shiny objects, or "bling bling" as Tim Johnston, Don Campbell's former partner in REIN, called it. These are assets that only cost you money and never pay you back, unlike a cash-producing asset. Personal residences don't produce income either, unless

2. IT DEPRECIATES.

Some assets are worth far less than you pay for them in a very short period of time. Cars are the most notorious example of this, yet most people finance the purchase of their automobile. New cars cost a lot of money once you factor in the payments, maintenance, fuel, insurance and parking.

I didn't buy a new car until I was in my forties. To this day, I maintain that this prudence was beneficial to me through the early years when I was trying to build up a base of wealth. In terms of net worth, there's nothing worse than owning a big hunk of metal that loses value every day in addition to costing a substantial monthly payment. It might be hard on your ego to not own such fancy items like cars and boats, but over time chicks (or guys, if you're a woman reading this) will dig your net worth. Perhaps that fact will provide you with some solace as you run around town in your ugly, old (debt-free) car.

A personal residence has one attribute of good debt (it appreciates) and one attribute of bad debt (it doesn't produce income), but I still maintain that purchasing your own home is a good idea since you'll have to spend money on accommodation anyway.

The fact that a home will generally appreciate is an additional reason to purchase rather than rent. There are some good debt/bad debt sticklers out there who maintain that even a personal residence is a bad investment due to the fact that the asset doesn't produce income, but I don't agree with them. I say bite the bullet and buy a personal residence.

The simplicity of this lesson speaks volumes about why Robert Kiyosaki was such a runaway success in financial education. With this basic understanding of good debt vs. bad debt, people can learn to make decisions about their own wealth creation. People often borrow and spend indiscriminately. Knowing how powerful good debt (in a positive way) and bad debt (in a negative way) are will set you on a path to a stronger financial future.

Even when you are experienced in wealth creation and investments, it is wise to relearn this lesson. Bad debt can quickly sneak up on even savvy investors and businesspeople, so always keep this lesson top of mind.

LESSON 79:
INCOME THINKING VS.
NET WORTH THINKING

Wealth creation is largely a mental game. First one must think the result, then act on it, and then comes the result. Our process toward success comes first in thoughts, then in deeds. The result is just the outcome of the process.

Wealthy people often move some of their focus from income thinking and put it on net worth thinking. Don't get me wrong, everyone needs to have an income. It is vital to always maintain an active portion of income, even while developing a net worth.

Real estate on a smaller scale is a wonderful part-time business because it allows investors to increase net worth while still earning an active income by working a regular job.

The biggest problem with having all your earnings in the form of income is that you pay a much higher rate of tax on that income. But when you build your net worth, you're actually building up tax-deferred and tax-preferred income that can be realized in the future.

It is a balancing act to maintain both a regular monthly income to sustain your family and your lifestyle as well as build for the long term.

In my opinion, real estate is vastly preferable as a vehicle for building that long-term net worth than stocks or mutual-fund–based RRSPs or any other standard investment option. As mentioned previously, real estate creates wealth through mortgage paydown as well as appreciation, and when you combine that with the power of leverage, it becomes a proven recipe for substantial success.

I learned this lesson when I purchased my first rental-pooled condo. After owning for a few years, I took a step back to assess the situation. What I saw was that after five years, I'd paid my mortgage down about $10,000, and in addition, the property had appreciated 20 percent. Since I purchased the property for $80,000 with only $20,000 cash for down payment, I'd earned $30,000 on $20,000 invested, or 150 percent. That's not an insignificant amount to earn for almost no effort required.

I joined the condo board as a way to learn, but that alone wasn't too much work, and it wasn't even necessary. A 150 percent return over five years is excellent, and seeing the growth in my net worth made me realize that perhaps it was wise to try this on a larger scale.

What that first condo did not do for me was increase my monthly income. I did not take any cash flow out of that property. All the cash flow that I received was kept in the bank in the event that I should need it for the property, and surely enough I have needed it for various upgrades over the years. The investment was purely a net worth play.

Of the four original condos that I purchased, I still own two of them (one in Edmonton and one in Kelowna), and to this day I love those properties. The value of the Kelowna condo is now maybe $120,000 (also purchased for $80,000), and I refinanced them both a few years ago, thus essentially no cash is invested.

I'm left with a property that I have none of my own cash in, and which pays down a few thousand per year off the mortgage. I literally spend about one hour per year of my effort on that property. If for no other reason than the perspective of real estate's power, I love this property, and that's probably part of the reason I keep it. In terms of blue dollars invested, the property is worth thousands of dollars per hour to me.

Those thousands of dollars are realized through net worth, which means I can't remove the cash whenever I want, but at the same time it grows my wealth and it's tax-preferred income, so it has many benefits.

Growing a net worth does not allow you to purchase as many shiny objects or take as many fancy trips as income does, but chicks (and spouses) over time do dig your net worth. As a long-term coolness plan, it's wise to invest your energies into developing your net worth. Of course you can't forget to keep your income strong enough to sustain a happy and healthy lifestyle, but to become truly wealthy, you must switch some of your thinking from income thinking to net worth thinking. The result of time and sound investments is a growing net worth, so start now and let time do its job.

LESSON 80:
CHOOSE REAL ESTATE INVESTMENTS THAT MAKE SENSE TO YOU

New investors often forget that real estate is not supposed to be exciting and glamorous, but a boring investment is the best investment. As I've discussed numerous times in this book, this meant for me that my first few properties needed to be extremely low on blue dollar investment. I was not too concerned with earning big money immediately. I was concerned with creating long-term wealth and using real estate as the vehicle for that long-term wealth creation.

When I purchased that first rental-pooled condo, I was actually looking at another property in another town. But when I carefully considered that other property, I realized that the blue dollars invested would be too great for me. Luckily, through my experience managing projects in the software industry, I knew that the time invested in a project was as important to consider as the return on investment.

Choosing the rental-pooled condo was one of the best decisions I've ever made in real estate. This may seem incredible as I've had to make thousands of decisions, and many of them, especially in recent years, have been far bigger deals than that first condo. The title of this book is 80 Lessons Learned on the Road from $80K to $80M for a reason. That first $80,000 was the foundation for all the future success.

As any good builder knows, you build upon a strong foundation and go up from there.

There are so many other potential outcomes that could have happened in my career had I chosen the wrong investment first. The biggest risk if I had purchased that single-family home would have been the risk of getting frustrated with real estate. I did not have the time or inclination to take care of a property at the time, and it would have been easier to get rid of a problem property than continue in real estate.

If you've had some real estate frustrations up to this point, I'm not suggesting you give up, but what I am suggesting is that you consider that perhaps you're not in the right kind of real estate for you—at this time.

Let me give you an example. There is good money to be made by buying a property at an affordable price and then renovating it. Holding the property after the renovations and utilizing the normal real estate wealth-building rules makes this strategy even better.

However, if you're too short on cash to take care of those renovations, or worse yet, short on time to oversee them (or at least oversee the contractors), then your strategy is simply wrong for you.

Most people have to work full-time jobs (or run a full-time cash producing business). There is nothing wrong with this, and in fact it is the correct order of things, especially for a young person. The value-adding renovation strategy is great but only if you have the blue and green dollars to make it happen without destroying your life at the same time.

What many people do is work their full-time job during the day and then run over to their property to help complete the renovations. For the many people who know that they can't come up with the money to pay for all the renovations, this is an important money-saving measure.

Having the money and the renovation contacts can allow you to step away from a major time investment on renovations projects. If you don't have the money, and the time commitment means a major strain on your life (if you don't see your family for months, for example), then the strategy of adding value through renovations is not the right one for you.

I'm still a big proponent of rental-pooled condos for beginners because it's the one real estate investment that's hands off. It truly does not take much time to manage a rental-pooled condo.

Single-family homes that don't require large renovations as well as townhouses and condos might make sense for you if the numbers work. As mentioned elsewhere, the number-one question you need to ask yourself with any piece of real estate is, "Who is going to manage this property impeccably?"

It's essential that you purchase any property in such a way that you can pay for impeccable property management. In an effort to outsource as effectively as possible, this is perhaps your most important outsourcing. I even recommend lowering your leverage and (its corollary) raising your down payment in order to make the property work financially in such a way that you can pay for impeccable property management.

The right property for you will likely be a property that you're not managing yourself. There are exceptions to this rule, but generally the decision that allows you to hang in there emotionally and financially will be the best decision.

The upfront work of raising money (whether your own or others') can be taken on as a temporary project whenever you want to purchase a property. You decide how aggressive you want to be on that front. The job of property management is ongoing, it's inconvenient, and often it's demanding. Sometimes it's even heart wrenching—for example, when you have to evict a single mom with kids who can't afford her rent.

Hiring property management is the key factor in allowing you to hang in there emotionally as it puts a layer of protection between you and the property.

Choosing the right kind of real estate for you can mean many different things depending on where you are in your real estate trajectory. You may be ready to make the leap from smaller single-family or townhouse investments and move into multi-family or commercial investments. It will be a decision based on your own circumstance.

What's important though is that you make sure you're in the right kind of real estate for you. This will almost always be real estate that you don't manage yourself. If you're just beginning, it will likely be real estate where the stakes are not too high, and once you're a true blue expert, it might be larger projects with millions of other people's money invested. It's not important what type as long as it's the right type for you.

LESSON 81:
REAL ESTATE TRANSACTION COSTS
AND THE VIRTUAL LIFE OF A BUILDING
(NOT QUITE THE EXTRA 10 PERCENT,
BUT HEY, A BONUS LESSON IN ANY CASE!)

Much of what I've offered you in this book is about being informed. I am a strong analyzer, and I seek to break down any complex matter into its various parts as a means of understanding it better.

Part of being a better investor is about having better knowledge and applying that knowledge better. Some of the lessons learned aren't difficult to understand, but understanding them on their own merits, unwrapped from the other aspects of the business, leads to a better ability to think about real estate.

One of the double-edged swords of real estate lies in the fact that transactions in real estate are very expensive. Every time you sell, buy or refinance a property, the transaction costs are enormous.

When selling, you typically have to pay a large fee to a realtor, often in the range of 5 percent of the total selling price (especially on single-family homes) depending on the cost of the home and what commission you negotiate with the agent. This is not insignificant. In effect, it can wipe out a couple of years' worth of appreciation that the property has built up.

Or course, you can sell the property yourself, but depending on your situation at the time, this might be highly inconvenient. In addition to realtor fees, there are always lawyer fees, and if you live outside of Alberta there is also the land transfer tax. All of these extras add up to a significant cost.

But there is another cost as well to a transaction in real estate: the cost of time and effort. Selling a piece of real estate is not as simple as selling a stock or a car. It often takes many months to sell any piece of real estate, especially when the market is not hot.

In addition to the cost of selling, there is often a mortgage pay-out penalty when refinancing (if you refinance before the end of the mortgage term), so even if you don't want to sell to unlock some cash, you still pay a price for the transaction.

The illiquidity of real estate and the cost of transactions are downsides of real estate. It's another reason to lean toward the side of keeping properties for longer rather than shorter periods of time. Every time you transact, you pay.

On the flip side, it is one of the advantages of real estate as well. Because it's difficult to make snap decisions on real estate (due to illiquidity and transaction costs) many investors are almost forced to hold onto properties. It's an asset class that promotes holding properties longer rather than shorter, therefore investors more often profit over time—and time is your best friend in real estate.

It's a double-edged sword, and something to keep in mind. Keep a portion of your investments liquid, but also keep a portion of them illiquid, stuck in real estate investments that make sense, slowly accumulating net worth on your behalf. This is a strong recipe for success as an investor, waiting.

In stocks, the trend is your friend. In real estate, time is your friend. I do not know what real estate values will be two years from now, but I know that it will be two years later than today and that therefore the mortgage will be lower, which will mean I've made money, even in a flat (or even slightly declining) market!

Real estate always has two lives. There's the physical life, the side you think of when you think of your house. It has shingles on the roof, toilets in the bathroom, bedrooms, siding, a hedge, a front door and many more physical features. You have to take care of the physical aspects of a property when you own it, and you have to consider the expenses related to the physical part of the asset.

In addition to the physical life of the building, there is also a virtual life. The virtual life includes the mortgage, the title of the property, the encumbrances or caveats on title, the cash that the tenant pays you, and any insurance that you buy for the property. Taking care of the virtual aspects is every bit as important as the physical aspects, and if you don't care for them well, you will soon find yourself in as much hot water as if you hadn't taken care of the physical aspects.

Too many investors, in a rush to get into a property, will take any old mortgage. This is detrimental for obvious reasons. At the beginning of a real estate investing career, it is too easy to be excited by the possibilities inherent in real estate that a mortgage with a slightly too high interest rate or a slightly too low down payment doesn't seem like a big deal.

However, just as time is your best friend in terms of mortgage paydown and appreciation, it can be your worst enemy in terms of cash flow. People often tend to believe the future will get better very rapidly, but unfortunately this is not necessarily the case. While the future rents and values are most likely to go up over the long term, there is every possibility that they will go down or flat-line in the short and medium term. Paying "just a bit" too much for a mortgage can be detrimental over a five-year period in a flat market.

Similar problems are created by not paying close enough attention to any virtual aspect of a property. The wrong insurance can sink you if you don't have coverage for loss of rent in the case of a fire or flood (the bank will still want its mortgage payment, even when you're not receiving a rent check).

Real estate is simple, but it's not easy. Take care of both the physical and the virtual aspects of your aspects.

Don't wait to invest in real estate; invest in real estate and wait.™

80 Lessons Learned:
From $80,000 to $80,000,000

EPILOGUE

I hope you enjoyed this book. Several lessons will have been obvious to you, most perhaps. However, even if you took away only two or eight good ideas, it was money well spent, and it was worth my time writing this book. My goal is to leave this world a better place, with more people being smarter about their lifestyles and investing behavior. I hope this book helped to improve your life.

Feel free to drop me a line at thomasbeyer808080@gmail.com on what lesson you found most profound, or what specific action you decided to take.

Now, after reading this swimming instruction manual, go get wet—as this is the only way to learn to swim!

May God be kind to you and enhance your plans—and remember that behind every rain cloud, even a thick dark gray one, the sun is still shining!

Thomas

80 Lessons Learned:
From $80,000 to $80,000,000

AFTERTHOUGHTS

BY GREG HABSTRITT

Having known Thomas and watched his investing closely for more than 7 years, I've had the pleasure of seeing him emerge as one of the most pragmatic, thoughtful and strategic investors in Canada. He's never afraid of making a tough decision, admitting a mistake, or helping a new investor learn the ropes.

Not only is Thomas a role model for so many investors, he's both a mentor and a friend to me, and I'm thrilled to see him finally share his wisdom and insight with this book. It's a rare exception of a truly successful professional sharing the secrets of success not just in business and investing, but in life as well.

Greg Habstritt,
Best Selling Author, The RRSP Secret
Founder, SimpleWealth Inc.
www.simplewealth.com